Romantic Encounters

Romantic Encounters

WRITERS, READERS,

AND THE *LIBRARY FOR READING*

Melissa Frazier

Stanford University Press

Stanford, California 2007

Stanford University Press

Stanford, California

©2007 by the Board of Trustees of the Leland Stanford Junior University.

Printed in the United States of America on acid-free, archival-quality paper

Library of Congress Cataloging-in-Publication Data

Frazier, Melissa, 1965-

  Romantic encounters : writers, readers, and the Library for Reading / Melissa Frazier.

    p. cm.

  Includes bibliographical references and index.

  ISBN 978-0-8047-5517-7 (cloth : alk. paper)

  1. Russian literature--19th century--History and criticism. 2. Romanticism--Russia. 3. Senkovskii, Osip Ivanovich, 1800-1858--Criticism and interpretation. 4. Biblioteka dlia chteniia. 5. Russian periodicals--History--19th century. 6. Irony in literature. I. Title.

  PG3015.5.R6F73 2007

  891.709'145--dc22   2007003247

Typeset by Bruce Lundquist in 11/14 Adobe Garamond

For Lucy and Rose

Contents

Acknowledgments

I am grateful to a number of institutions for their generous support of my work. I would first like to thank Sarah Lawrence College and especially the Dean of the College, Barbara Kaplan. I would also like to express my appreciation to the University Seminars at Columbia University for their help in publication. Parts of Chapters Two and Three were also presented early on at the University Seminar on Slavic History and Culture, and my ideas have more recently benefited from discussions at the University Seminar on Romanticism and Its Aftermath. I would like to thank the Russian, East European, and Eurasian Center at the University of Illinois Urbana-Champaign for the support that enabled me to attend the Summer Research Lab in 2004 and 2005. I owe a special thanks to Stanford University Press and to Norris Pope, Director of Academic Publishing, above all for his tact and intellectual generosity; thanks go also to my production editor, Mariana Raykov, for her prompt and thorough responses to my many queries. I am finally grateful to the librarians at the Esther Raushenbush Library at Sarah Lawrence, especially the dauntless people at Interlibrary Loan over the last several years: Janet Alexander, Geoff Danisher, and Bobbi Smolow. Chapter Four is especially for them.

Essential support has also come from individuals. Among my fellow Slavists are many who offered thoughtful readings, insightful comments, and much good advice at often critical junctures, and I would like to thank above all Caryl Emerson, Boris Gasparov, George Gutsche, David Herman, Katya Hokanson, Hilde Hoogenboom, Anne Lounsbery, Irina Paperno, John Randolph, and Miranda Remnek. My interdisciplinary colleagues at

Sarah Lawrence have been deeply involved in this project from the start, and I am especially grateful to Neil Arditi, Bella Brodzki, Eileen Cheng, Elizabeth Johnston, Angela Moger, Ellen Neskar, Chi Ogunyemi, Mary Porter, Karen Rader, Sandra Robinson, Lyde Sizer, and Fred Smoler. Their sharp criticism and warm encouragement have made me a much better writer. Last but not least: Senkovskii's staunchest supporter, and my own, remains my husband, Joseph Hatem. I thank him for his fine cooking, his unwavering belief in my intellectual abilities, and his ever-ready sense of humor.

Note on Transliteration and Translation

Scholars of Russian literature writing in English often opt for the more familiar Anglicized versions of Russian names, so that the name more accurately rendered as Dostoevskii or Dostoevskij, for example, usually appears as Dostoevsky. In the shifting sands of Senkovskii's identity, however, consistent spelling becomes an essential landmark. I have adopted Anglicized names only in a very few instances: Dostoevsky, Gogol, Alexander Pushkin, and the names of Russian rulers from Peter the Great through Nicholas I. Otherwise, I have used a modified Library of Congress system of transliteration (omitting most diacriticals). Any changes in the spelling of Senkovskii's name accordingly reflect his own. All translations are mine unless otherwise noted.

Romantic Encounters

Introduction:
Romanticism and the *Library for Reading*

Gogol finishes the first volume of his *Dead Souls* (1841) with a question that he doesn't answer: "Whither art thou soaring away to, then, Russia?" He continues, "Give me thy answer! But Russia gives none. With a wondrous ring does the jingle bell trill; the air, rent to shreds, thunders and turns to wind; all things on earth fly past, and eyeing it askance, all the other peoples and nations stand aside and give it the right of way."[1]

Russia as a troika speeding off into unknown space, an empty form ever awaiting content, is a uniquely Gogolian image that captures both the eternal question of Russian identity and a Romantic vision of the sublime. It is also one last expression of the negativity that defines *Dead Souls*, beginning with the description of the hero on the very first page. Chichikov, we are told, "was not handsome, but he wasn't bad to look at either," "he was neither too stout nor too thin," and while "you couldn't say that he was old . . . still he wasn't what you might call any too young either." As the narrator concludes the nondescription that opens the book: "His arrival created no stir whatsoever in the town of N—and was not coupled with any remarkable event."[2]

My own exploration of Romantic readers and writers, like Gogol's, is framed with a series of "nots." While this book intends to make large statements about European Romanticism generally, my starting point is not located in a more central part of Europe—Germany or France, for example—but on its margins, in Russia. Even within this periphery I have not chosen to focus on a well-known writer like Gogol or Pushkin, nor have I organized my work around a genre well established in the Romantic canon such as the historical novel or lyric poetry. Instead I have taken for my hero the little-known Osip Ivanovich Senkovskii, and for my quintessentially Romantic form the literary periodical he edited, the *Library for Reading*.

Just like Gogol's fictional Chichikov, the real O. I. Senkovskii was a slippery character with a clear affinity for borders and border crossings. The future Russian writer was born in Poland in 1800 as Józef-Julian Sękowski, a scion of the minor nobility endowed with little money but a great deal of intellectual aptitude. Sękowski's prodigious intelligence and his mother's contacts were enough to bring him to the University of Wilno (Vilnius) at an early age, where he soon joined the Brotherhood of Scamps, a literary and philosophical society that included many of the leading Polish intellectuals of the day. There he showed something of his future journalistic prowess by contributing pieces to the Brotherhood's satirical journal, the *Sidewalk News*. Sękowski's actual course work, however, focused on Oriental languages, and upon his graduation in 1819 he went on to study and travel in the Middle East for another two years, financed in part by the Russian mission in Turkey. His return from the Middle East at the age of twenty-two brought Sękowski to St. Petersburg, where he promptly accepted two posts, the first as translator at the Ministry of Foreign Affairs and the second as professor of both Turkish and Arabic languages at St. Petersburg University, and he embarked on what promised to be a brilliant academic career.

But Sękowski's interest in literature never left him, and throughout the 1820s he published a number of popular translations and free adaptations "from the Arabic" followed by satirical pieces in the spirit of the *Sidewalk News*, as Józef-Julian Sękowski, Polish Orientalist, gradually transformed himself into Osip Ivanovich Senkovskii, Russian man of letters. In 1834 the widely respected publisher and bookseller A. F. Smirdin ensured Senkovskii's place in the history of Russian literature when he asked Senkovskii to serve as editor of the *Library for Reading* at the unprecedented salary of 15,000 rubles a year. Often under a variety of pseudonyms, Senkovskii was also a major contributor to the journal, publishing articles and reviews on an astonishing array of topics that ranged from science and military history to fiction and literary criticism. With Senkovskii at its helm, the *Library for Reading* was either a great success or an utter disgrace, depending on the criteria one adopts. While quickly achieving a subscription rate several times that of its nearest competitors, the journal was also widely accused of doing so only by appealing to the least sophisticated elements in the reading public. The heyday of the *Library for Reading*, and of Senkovskii, was the 1830s, as by the 1840s ill health had forced Senkovskii to withdraw partly and then, in 1848, entirely from the enterprise; Senkovskii also gave up his professorship in 1847. In poor health, he soon found himself living in obscurity and, due in part to some poor investments, in actual poverty, a situation only partly rectified in 1856 when the journal *Son of the Fatherland* invited Senkovskii to submit a series of feuilletons under his most famous byline, Baron Brambeus. Senkovskii's almost instant return to literary prominence was cut short, however, by his premature death in 1858.[3]

I have chosen to begin my work with this apparently unlikely figure and the journal he produced because the play of center and periphery on many different levels is fundamental to my conception of Romanticism. My broad aim in this book is to show European Romanticism generally to be a construction (or constructing) of fragments and ever-shifting borders, a sort of dance around the margins of an apparently empty center that can be either a sublime locus of potentiality or just that, empty. With their own complicated marginality, Senkovskii and his *Library for Reading* are wonderfully effective tools for explicating this Romanticism in all its possibilities and perils. The two together also serve more specific purposes. To restore Senkovskii to the Russian literary world he once ruled is to change the contours of that world both from within and from without. In Senkovskii's presence we will find that we have to change our understanding of what Russian Romantic literature in the 1830s looks like and why. Perhaps more important, as an insider who was also an outsider to his own literary tradition, Senkovskii also suggests a particular approach to the question of Russian identity and of Russia's relationship to the West.

This question found especially involved expression precisely in the Romantic period, when a rising Russian literature engaged in a highly self-conscious appropriation of a Western European literature, which was in turn marked by a valorization of national originality. While Pushkin could laughingly ask if the hero of his *Eugene Onegin* (1821–31; 1833) was not really just a Muscovite in Childe Harold's cloak, his sublime nonchalance was very much his own. Most of his compatriots were made far more anxious by the fact of their obvious and wholesale borrowing, and the possibility of the inclusion of Russia in the circle of Europe was an issue hotly debated throughout the 1820s and 1830s.

It is not my aim to present Russia as somehow more central to the European experience as the Russian Romantics themselves often did, either by recasting the borders of Europe or by adopting some sort of teleological stance whereby last shall be first. The example of Senkovskii instead lends itself to the argument that in the Romantic context there is no center, only margins.[4] Romantic nationalism is a privileging of difference, as various peoples across Europe—from the Germans and the British to the Russians and the Poles—took a leaf from Herder's book and argued for the value of their literature not because it was Greek or Roman or even neoclassical French, but simply because it was theirs, the expression of their own national identity. In one sense, then, each Romantic nation becomes central to itself. Yet when every nation is central to itself, it is also peripheral to all others, and a self-conscious play of self and other as native and foreign finds many different expressions in Romanticism. We might note, for example, the use of dialect in Scott's *Waverley* novels and Gogol's *Dikan'ka* tales, or the Orientalism that marks any number of Romantic writers, from Goethe, Byron, and Hugo to Pushkin and Lermontov.

In other words, if Russian Romantics are concerned with the apparently shifting outlines of their own identity, a certain self-conscious fluidity also marks Romantic conceptions of nationality in general, and our awareness of the latter necessarily complicates our understanding of the former. Certainly if we start with the assumption that the Romantic process of national identity formation was never actually intended to be completed, then notions of originality and authenticity and of a hierarchy of Romanticisms become considerably less useful. I would instead put all these Romantic literatures striving to find (or create) their own essence on an equal footing, and use the particularly Russian anxiety of influence only to argue that absolute presence not only eludes them all but also on a fundamental level was intended to do exactly that.

This idea of nationhood, or national tradition, as an unstable and ongoing process is a valuable tool in reevaluating Russia's place in European Romanticism; it is also an approach that is dictated by Romantic theory itself. As Monika Greenleaf argues in *Pushkin and Romantic Fashion: Fragment, Elegy, Orient, Irony* (1995), one of the threads that connects the disparate manifestations of Romanticism is Romantic irony, and while irony is a notoriously difficult word to define, still it clearly refers to a particular construction of the self. Peter Conrad in *Shandyism: The Character of Romantic Irony* (1978) describes the Romantic ironist variously as an intellectual libertine, a moralist in disguise, an improviser, a virtuoso, and an architect of "chimerical, collapsible palaces of thought held aloft briefly by an architecture of mental association."[5] Behind these various incarnations of ephemerality, intellectual promiscuity, and a sort of brilliant showmanship is what Gary Handwerk in *Irony and Ethics in Narrative* (1985) calls "a form of discourse that insists upon the provisional and fragmentary nature of the individual subject," "an intentional decentering of the subject that operates as an opening out to the other."[6]

The notion that Romantic narratives intentionally "use ironic structures to call into doubt the integrity and borders of the subject" is not a given in the scholarly literature on Romanticism.[7] A perhaps more traditional view would in fact argue the opposite, claiming that if Romanticism offers a fragmented or divided self, it is only because the movement more fundamentally yearns to restore wholeness. Handwerk, however, like Greenleaf, takes the example of Friedrich Schlegel and his friends in the German *Frühromantik* to present a very different sort of Romantic subjectivity. Here, Handwerk argues, subjectivity can only be understood as "intersubjectivity," as an ongoing and inherently unstable relationship between self and other that in its very fragmentariness offers the only means of (re)encountering the Absolute; in an apparent paradox, the fundamental duality of self and other is only overcome when the subject splits and recognizes both the other within and the self without.[8] It is the Schlegelian idea of the chameleon-like self (re)creating itself only through ever-changing interactions with other selves that underlies my understanding of how various European literatures, Russian among them, might relate one to another. This idea is also the topic of this book as represented in the ongoing interactions of Romantic writers and readers, above all in the pages of Senkovskii's *Library for Reading*.

Again, despite Romanticism's reputation for artlessness and sincerity, it is important that we recognize that these encounters of writer and reader are anything but. Just as Romanticism understands a national literature as the original and unique expression of its people, so does it see a given text as the original and unique expression of its creator. Along with a new concept of authorship, Romanticism also offers an emphasis on authenticity that seemingly grounds the text in the real experiences of a real person.

As suggested above, however, to take the Romantic concept of originality without a good dose of Romantic irony is to ignore the extent to which Romanticism is not about originality nor even imitation, but rather simulation.[9] Just as Conrad describes it as a kind of virtuoso effect, so Handwerk speaks of irony as "enactment," and we will see that Romantic writers from Scott and Constant to Pushkin, Gogol, and Lermontov are a paradoxical amalgam of real people and imaginary personae, just as the audience to whom they write is made up simultaneously of personal friends, real customers, and reader-constructs. The result is that "romantic art," as Maurice Blanchot defines it, that "concentrates creative truth in the freedom of the subject, also formulates the ambition of a total book, a sort of perpetually growing Bible that will not represent, but rather replace, the real."[10]

The later literary periodicals and especially Senkovskii's *Library for Reading* offer an ideal starting point for a discussion of this Romanticism, although not entirely expectedly so. Indeed, when Romanticism is associated with a periodical, it is never with the *Library for Reading* and rarely with any of its more immediate contemporaries, including in Russia the *Telescope* or *Moscow Observer* or in Great Britain *Blackwood's* and *Fraser's*.[11] The most obvious candidate for the part is instead the considerably earlier organ of the German *Frühromantik*, the *Athenaeum* (1798–1800). Philippe Lacoue-Labarthe and Jean-Luc Nancy, much like Blanchot, openly define Romanticism as "a place (Jena) and a journal (the *Athenaeum*)."[12] Schlegel and the writings in and around the *Athenaeum* also lie at the heart of Greenleaf's rich contextualization of Pushkin's work in *Pushkin and Romantic Fashion*. Handwerk, too, begins with the *Athenaeum*, and even a brief glance at one small part would suggest why. The sort of intersubjectivity that Handwerk describes is readily if very concisely evident in the well-known *Athenaeum Fragment* 116 alone, one of a series of fragments that Friedrich Schlegel published in 1798 in the second part of the *Athenaeum's* first volume.

Athenaeum Fragment 116 typically expresses the ironic interaction of writing and reading subjects on the level of form as well as content. Like the journal itself, the *Athenaeum Fragments* offer a prime example of what the *Frühromantik* called "sympoetry," as while the *Fragments* appeared anonymously and are usually associated with Friedrich, many were written by his brother August Wilhelm Schlegel and also his friends Novalis and Friedrich Schleiermacher, either singly or sometimes in combination. If these *Fragments* in particular are then literally the product of an ongoing conversation among reading and writing friends, it is also true that any fragment suggests something of the same. Again, like a single issue of the periodical itself, a fragment opens itself to a response and a completion that would arise from the give-and-take of the various and shifting reading and writing parties.[13] The form that *Athenaeum Fragment* 116 embodies is then also its topic.

In *Athenaeum Fragment* 116 Friedrich Schlegel sets out to describe the "Romantic kind of poetry" as an inherently fragmentary and heterogeneous genre. This fragmentariness and heterogeneity derives from what Schlegel himself terms the genre's "sociability." The aim of the ideal Romantic form, as Schlegel explains at the beginning of this long aphorism, "isn't merely to reunite all the separate species of poetry and put poetry in touch with philosophy and rhetoric." Instead its mission is to "mix and fuse poetry and prose, inspiration and criticism, the poetry of art and the poetry of nature; and make poetry lively and sociable, and life and society poetical; poeticize wit and fill and saturate the forms of art with every kind of good, solid matter for instruction, and animate them with pulsations of humor."[14]

What Schlegel offers us is literature not as the product of a single writer but as itself an ongoing social interaction. He adds, "Romantic poetry is in the arts what wit is in philosophy, and what society and sociability, friendship and love are in life."[15] Evidently the model for Schlegel's literary genre are the real encounters of the real friends and lovers at Jena that gave rise to the entire *Athenaeum* project in the first place. Yet a real gathering and its literary representation are not one and the same. When the members of the *Frühromantik* met at August Wilhelm Schlegel's house in Jena to read their works to one another, author and audience were present in the flesh and their exchanges took place in real time. In their literary and philosophical incarnations, however, the shifting parts of writer and reader are played by figures less real and more virtual, not by actual bodies but instead by elements of the text that they themselves then infinitely reproduce.

While Schlegel's prose is as always dense and allusive, *Athenaeum Fragment* 116 has nonetheless long been read as a kind of statement of purpose, an explanation of Schlegel's intent not just in the movement we now know as Romanticism, but also in the collaborative, generically inventive, and periodical endeavor of the *Athenaeum* itself. As Greenleaf describes the project as a whole:

> The Athenaeum considered itself an ongoing experiment. . . . Ignoring old generic prescriptions, just as socially they ignored class, racial, gender, and

conjugal borders, they envisioned forms that would do away with the old-fashioned idea of an author altogether, that would preserve the impromptu, witty, collective inspirations of the group as a whole: aphorisms and fragments whose authorship was attributed to the entire collective; philosophical dialogues that recorded the oral spontaneity and mutual fertilization of their thoughts; symposium-like novels through which the society's many voices would speak; fragments of lyrical poetry that would resemble Sappho's in their decontextualized, impersonal intimacy, like fossils involuntarily bearing the imprint of their historical time.[16]

I should acknowledge from the start that the *Library for Reading* does not quite reach these heights, nor does it ever offer the sort of abstract statement of Romantic interests and aims presented in *Athenaeum Fragment* 116. What the *Library for Reading* does offer are open expressions of intentions of a far more pragmatic kind, as it most strikingly represents the strange synergy that occurs when Romanticism meets an apparently rising marketplace.

It is of course largely because the later literary periodicals such as the *Library for Reading* deliberately present the exchanges between readers and writers in commercial as well as more purely social terms that they have often been considered less than entirely Romantic, perhaps above all by the Romantics themselves. Indeed, the average Romantic seems to have met the rise of the increasingly market-oriented literary periodicals with something more like revulsion. In 1831 the English Thomas Carlyle complained that "all Literature has become one boundless self-devouring review," while in 1840 the Russian V. G. Belinskii despaired that "the journal has now swallowed up our entire literature—the public doesn't want books—it wants journals—and in the journals they publish whole plays and novels, and the issues of the journals—each one weighs forty pounds."[17] Similarly Balzac in *Lost Illusions* (1837–43) famously showed a France of the early 1820s where all-consuming and entirely mercenary journals were indeed in the process of "swallowing up" all of literature.

It is in fact precisely because of their commercial leanings that I find the example of the later literary periodicals especially illuminating, as in direct contrast to Carlyle I would argue that this act of "self-devouring" represents not the end of "all Literature" but rather the extreme point of a certain kind: in the later literary periodicals we find that same "Romantic kind of poetry," only now with certain underlying tendencies made especially clear. It is first of all not true that Romantic writers of an earlier and more canonical type were immune to commercial considerations, and indeed, looking backward from the *Library for Reading* it becomes evident that Romanticism even in the apparent absence of a literary marketplace was quite fascinated with the possibilities of a professional writership and mass readership. It might be argued that the particular features that mark the later literary journals such as *Library for Reading* nonetheless derive not from any Romantic notions but rather from what is taken to be the real literary marketplace that provided their most immediate context. As I will argue in Chapter One, however, it is then also the case that any attempts to derive artistic effects from this particular socioeconomic cause prove to be at the very least problematic.

Unfortunately, what we might call the facts pertaining to an apparent rise of the literary marketplace are so colored by contemporary Romantic rhetoric as to render their later interpretation quite difficult. The standard argument would seem to be that the later literary periodicals, Senkovskii's among them, replace imaginary encounters between idealized reader- and writer-collaborators with more real (because more commercially viable) encounters between readers and writers of a more material, more numerous, and more democratically constituted sort, in the process producing an entirely new kind of literature, one stretched to fit the Procrustean bed of literary capitalism. As I hope to show, however, it is in the end not entirely clear that the later readers and writers really are of a more material, more numerous, and more democratically constituted sort—although neither is it clear that they are not—and this confusion in level or type of reality is not accidental. Instead, as I will argue in Chapters Two and Three, it is the deliberate blurring of writerly and readerly identities that marks Romantic intersubjectivity from the start.

Certainly there is a difference in the "Romantic kind of poetry" as produced by Senkovskii and his like, but the difference seems to lie less in the realities of a newly arisen literary marketplace than in the rise in cynicism that accompanies that marketplace's increasingly active simulation. Even allowing for a certain amount of polemical exaggeration, the anxiety expressed by Carlyle, Belinskii, and Balzac reflects a darkening of the atmosphere particularly evident in Senkovskii's case. Senkovskii vividly renders Conrad's image of the Romantic ironist on any number of levels, from his polyglossia and encyclopedic erudition to his endless play of masks and apparent lack of principle, as, in the crowded space of his mind, Senkovskii is exactly the antiquarian turned showman. But with his particularly slippery adoption in the *Library for Reading* of impersonations of all kinds, Senkovskii also offers a much more cynical version of Romantic subjectivity, one that has less to do with the Absolute than with his own desire for critical omnipotence. Still, as we will see, the difference between irony as a plenitude of meaning and as what Paul de Man defines as "the systematic undoing . . . of understanding" is crucial but almost impossibly small, and Senkovskii's darker brand of irony serves to cast its more idealistic renderings in high relief.[18] Perhaps more important, the difficulty at times in distinguishing his play of personalities from that practiced by Pushkin, say, or Friedrich Schlegel, serves also to emphasize the extent to which critical omnipotence was Romanticism's aim all along.

Handwerk argues that the Schlegelian construction of subjectivity as an ironic intersubjectivity is ultimately an ethical as well as an aesthetic act, a recognition of the other both without and within that posits the creation (or creating) of the self only in the context of an entirely nonhierarchical community. Without in any way contradicting Handwerk, I would nonetheless note a certain bent in Schlegel's work, as in Romanticism as a whole, that is somewhat at odds with this ethical stance. For the reader- and writer-friends, whose collaboration on the creation of the work so often figures the process of intersubjectivity, tend also to collapse into an all-encompassing critical consciousness. Indeed, Romanticism, Schlegelian and otherwise, never loses sight of the fact that the critic is that strange creature, a reader who is also a writer and so potentially contains intersubjectivity within him- or herself alone.

With its emphasis on the critic, Romanticism characteristically produces not a work but rather a work about the work or, in Blanchot's formulation, "the work of the absence of the work."[19] This sort of literature might not be quite "one boundless self-devouring review," but it is at the very least, as Lacoue-Labarthe and Nancy define it, "*theory itself as literature* or, in other words, literature producing itself as it produces its own theory."[20] It is finally this fundamental absence lying at the center of Romanticism that Senkovskii and his *Library for Reading* exemplify especially well. Senkovskii latched always onto those aspects of Romanticism that lent themselves to his own self-aggrandizement, and as the apparent commercial success of the *Library for Reading* stretched the tension between writers and readers, real and imaginary, almost impossibly thin, any actual literature seems to disappear. Instead, Senkovskii's brief period of dominance notoriously emptied much of his journal and even a significant part of Russian letters of any-thing other than his own critical content.[21]

Senkovskii's nonetheless entirely Romantic aspirations for critical omni-potence were clearly exaggerated by the possibility, if not necessarily the reality, of a literary marketplace. His critical tyranny also gained a particular force for being based not in a more traditionally Romantic locale such as Germany, Great Britain, or France but rather in Russia. Russian writers of Senkovskii's own day regularly bemoaned a literature that, unlike those more enlightened literatures further West, was made up almost entirely of criticism. Well before his 1840 protest that "the journal has now swallowed up our entire literature," Belinskii was busily excoriating what he saw as a uniquely Russian failing to criticize in the absence of any literature in the first place. In his 1834 essay "Literary Reveries" Belinskii famously cried, "We have no literature"; and while this plaint is indelibly associated with Belinskii's more radical stance, it also quite clearly echoes a line of criti-cism heard in Russian literature throughout the 1820s.[22] When Romanti-cism is defined as an essentially critical movement, however, this objection sounds more like praise, as it is then Russian literature that most strikingly expresses the literary tendency of its time in the very lack that marks the Russian nation as well.

For Romantic readers and writers can only encounter one another in some sort of space, and in Chapters Four and Five I attempt to delineate its possibilities. Chapter Four operates within the confines of the library in the *Library for Reading* to describe the virtual space where readers and writers neither entirely real nor entirely imaginary meet to create literature in terms of Schlegel's "Romantic kind of poetry," the literary marketplace, the antiquarian past, and the Orient. Chapter Five then moves outside the library to consider the broader expanse wherein the *Library for Reading* op-erated: the space of Senkovskii's own self-imposed exile and of Russia. At this point it becomes evident that the instability of Romantic identities that Senkovskii and his *Library for Reading* so effectively display is finally also the instability of the Romantic nation, as I return here to the issue of imitation and originality that I raised at the start of this introduction. Senkovskii's own uncertain Russianness, like his wildly vacillating reader- and writer-figures, is inevitably as always only his own extreme version of something else. That something else is first of all Russianness of a more indigenous or at least more mainstream kind, as the great anxiety that drives Russian

Romantics even when not of Polish extraction is the fear that there is nothing indigenously Russian at all. That something else is also Romanticism as a whole, not only as it develops in an allegedly second-tier nation like Russia, but even as it shapes itself in those purportedly more authentic and more original nations farther West.

When Romanticism is imagined as a library, hitherto submerged features gain special prominence, not only a creeping tendency toward commercialism but also a persistent sense of literature as a site of collection and display. Casting Romanticism in the larger terms of Senkovskii's Russia produces still more dramatic results, above all as it makes strikingly apparent the strange fact that the Romantic nation itself was almost entirely the invention of the multi-, or extranational, Senkovskiian type. Senkovskii's own manipulation of peripheral status in order to better ingratiate himself with his imperial center has long served as evidence of an utter lack of principle. But the comparison of his practice with that of the many other Romantics shaped by the related experiences of exile, expatriation, and empire suggests that Romanticism as a whole was also marked by an essential and ineradicable otherness in space, a kind of constant oscillation between center and periphery that played itself out both within and also across so-called national traditions.

In the end Senkovskii's marginality proves surprisingly central, or perhaps the concepts of "center" and "periphery" simply lose their meaning. Either way, as Senkovskii can only layer imitations one on top of the other, his critical practice points straight to a Romanticism that only posits a notion of originality without ever actually delivering on it. As readers and writers, libraries, and literary traditions multiply and overlap, we find instead that Romantic originality and authenticity only ever recede from us and were even largely intended to do so. To borrow again from Blanchot, the intent of Romanticism was not to represent but to replace the real, and if this absence of presence sounds thoroughly post-Modernist, I think that it is. Yet it is also quintessentially Romantic, as the unanswered question that ends Gogol's *Dead Souls* expresses an emptiness fundamental to the movement as a whole.

"Whither art thou soaring away to, then, Russia?" Gogol asks. "Give me thy answer! But Russia gives none." Nor does Romanticism provide an answer, as from the point of view of the *Library for Reading* the lack that Gogol casts in terms of both Russia's own anxiety of influence and its messianic aspirations functions also in more broadly European terms. Blanchot describes

Romanticism as the moment when "literature encounters its most dangerous meaning—which is to interrogate itself in a declarative mode."[23] Certainly Senkovskii and his *Library for Reading* will not serve to answer a question that we were never meant to answer in the first place. The two together can, however, help us to pose the question as dangerously as possible.

1.   Romanticism and the Literary Marketplace

Senkovskii's reputation rests not at all on his Romantic practices, but rather on his often crass commercialization of Russian literature. The *Library for Reading* is usually considered the first commercially profitable literary journal in Russia, its unprecedentedly large subscription base providing for a substantial salary for Senkovskii, generous honoraria for contributors, and at least in popular opinion, a general decline in literary quality. Such is his fame that any book with Senkovskii at its center necessarily starts with reference to his role in the workings of the Russian literary marketplace. If Senkovskii's efforts to put Russian literature on a commercial footing are well known, however, they are also deeply implicated in the discussion of Romanticism that I propose.

Any talk of Romantic readers and writers would seem inevitably bound up with the real changes in publishing and conditions of publicness that seem to have taken place in different ways and to differing degrees all over Europe in the early nineteenth century. With the apparent rise of the literary marketplace a faint clink of coins can be heard at every turn, tempting us to account for any peculiarities in the literary renderings of readers and writers in terms of the newly commercial interactions of their real-world counterparts. Certainly the possible effects of the real money paid to real writers by real readers insinuate themselves throughout Romanticism, and much has been written on that topic, particularly in the British context. Still, the intent of this chapter is to argue that the relationship is just as likely to work the other way. In the case of Senkovskii, his notoriety has perhaps obscured the fact that it is ultimately very difficult to decide whether his writing offers a direct reflection of an emerging Russian literary marketplace, an imaginary Russian version of a literary marketplace perhaps already in existence elsewhere, or something altogether imaginary. This ambiguity, I would argue, is in fact both entirely intentional and entirely Romantic.

Whether in Russia or elsewhere, any easy assumptions of direct socioeconomic cause and literary effect deflect attention from the fact that the realities of the literary marketplace are very difficult to determine. The term *literary marketplace* usually refers to a fairly recently arrived-at set of socioeconomic conditions governing the production and consumption of literature. Whereas at one time writers were either independently wealthy or supported by a wealthy patron, under the conditions of a literary marketplace both readership and the production and availability of books increase sufficiently so that writers are enabled to turn for financial support not to their own means nor to individual patrons but to the reading public at large, giving rise to what we might call a profession of letters. In our own time the notion of professional publishers mediating between professional writers and a more or less democratically constituted reading public is a familiar one. Actually pinpointing the particular time and place of its realization, however, poses a number of problems.

When scholars speak of the rise of the literary marketplace in Europe in the late eighteenth or early nineteenth centuries, for example, they are usually referring to changes in the production and distribution of only one branch of literature, the kind we most often call "high." After all, "low" literature in greater or lesser quantities has always marketed itself directly to readers, and in Russia the successes of the *lubok* literature and even early novels like Matvei Komarov's *The English Milord Georg* (1794) well predate the achievements of Senkovskii's *Library for Reading*. Unfortunately, while a distinction between "high" and "low" literatures is then fundamental to our discussion of the literary marketplace at this juncture, it is also one that the discussion itself will inevitably erode. For once "high" literature aspires to a mass readership it tends to look a little "low," and while scholars of Russian literature have no trouble, for example, in assigning Pushkin to the "high" category, they display a great deal more ambivalence about Senkovskii, who reached many of the same readers but seemed to care just a little too much about making money. But if we simply dismiss Senkovskii as a hack writer, it is no longer clear why the great financial success of the *Library for Reading* is relevant to the discussion of the rise of the literary marketplace in Russia at all.[1]

We might try to set aside the theoretical question of what we mean by "literary" and turn to the growth of the "marketplace" itself. This more pragmatic approach is equally problematic, however, simply because the literary marketplace even by the early nineteenth century is an immense and many-layered structure involving first readers and writers and then the whole complicated apparatus of book production and distribution that fills the gap between the two, a loose institution of sorts that includes everyone from book publishers, booksellers, and typesetters to librarians and censorship officials. When we talk about the real rise of a real literary marketplace, then, we are talking about the confluence of a whole host of factors including, for example, changes in the education and social status of readers, writers, and publishers; technological advances in the manufacture of books; economic vicissitudes; and changes in the political environment that in turn imply the greater presence or absence of government intervention. Any claims about the marketplace are then in some way incomplete, because there are too many possible facts to work with and too many assumptions that necessarily guide our choice of facts.

The assumptions themselves are historically significant, however, and among those prevalent in the Russian context, one is particularly striking because it is so widely shared: whatever their facts, historians of Russian literature hold to the belief that something important happened in the development of a Russian literary marketplace sometime in the first half of the nineteenth century. There is a strong sense of a turning point or points being reached during the 1820s and 1830s, although some, for example William Mills Todd III, question whether what was achieved was a real literary marketplace or only an approximation. Scholars like André Meynieux focus on Pushkin's role in the establishment of copyright, while others emphasize the role of the almanac *The Polar Star* (1823–25) in the professionalization of Russian letters. Nearly everyone claims the importance of the publisher A. F. Smirdin in what Grits, Trenin, and Nikitin in *Literature and Commerce* (1929) call the "canonization of the book trade," and in this judgment they only echo the opinion of Smirdin's actual contemporaries.[2] In other words, however much they must qualify their presentation of the facts or even our understanding of the very idea of a literary marketplace, observers of the Russian literary scene in the early nineteenth century nevertheless all interpret their material with reference to a rising literary marketplace, and we would do well to consider why.

Perhaps we hold to the notion of a literary marketplace, even to dispute it, above all because, in time-honored fashion, we measure Russian reality against that of Western Europe, so that the apparent fact of the rise of a literary marketplace in the early nineteenth century in Great Britain, France, or Germany leads us to look for one in Russia, and by "us" I mean not scholars of Russian literature alone. Nineteenth-century Russian readers and writers in their own day were also very aware of changes and trends in Western Europe, and they were quick to seek to identify these changes and trends in themselves, so that the question of the presence or absence of a Russian literary marketplace itself dates from the very same period. The same also holds true for Western Europe, however, a point that suggests other possibilities.

It certainly may be that early nineteenth-century Russian literature and its historians operate in terms of a concept that found its reality in the Western European context. It may also be that in Western Europe, too, the literary marketplace was first a concept and only then a reality, and a concept that derived not from someone else's real socioeconomic conditions (perhaps someone further West?), but from Romantic notions of writers and readers simultaneously both real and imaginary. Last, it may be not one or the other. The relationship between writer and reader that the *Athenaeum* first constructs may prefigure what we presume to be the later reality of the literary marketplace, but as that later reality is in any case colored by the earlier theory, it is nearly impossible to say where one stops and the other starts, and to attempt to do so might be to miss the point. For, as this book will argue as a whole, the real accomplishment of Romanticism in Russia as elsewhere is not its reflection of a particular reality nor its creation of an imaginary one, but its deliberate blurring of any distinction between the two.

The Real Literary Marketplace

The rise of a real literary marketplace is prompted by a complicated set of interrelationships involving, at the very least, readers and writers, publishers and booksellers, technological innovation, and government censorship. A review of all the aspects of a Russian literary marketplace in the early nineteenth century, even without reference to the situation at the same time in various parts of Western Europe, is well beyond the scope of a single chapter, and has perhaps not been accomplished in its entirety even by the many books written on the topic. Yet even a brief sketch of what we might call the "real" situation in Russia should suggest both why some scholars see the 1830s as the start of a literary marketplace in Russia and why others would qualify that claim.

READERS

Of all the various factors that play into the rise of a real literary marketplace, none has proven more attractive to scholars and yet more elusive than the reader. A great deal of interesting work has been done on the Romantic reader in a more abstract sense as audience, most notably in the British context by Jon Klancher. One can also find studies of actual, individual readers; for example, John Brewer's work on the English Anna Larpent or Robert Darnton's on the Swiss Jean Ranson.[3] While the ideal might be to combine both approaches, unfortunately real readers as a group do not generally leave a record of their activity, and they are statistically very difficult to pin down. Surveys of literacy rates, for example, are available for this period at least in Great Britain and France, but their value in gauging the progress of a literary marketplace is very limited. Just because a person can read, after all, is no guarantee that he or she will pick up Wordsworth and Coleridge, for example, or Mme. de Staël.

Still, there is a sense of a sharp rise in readership around the time we associate with Romanticism, although exactly at what point, in what terms, and to what effect is a matter of some debate. In *Popular French Romanticism: Authors, Readers, and Books in the 19th Century* (1981), James Allen Smith argues that in France it is a larger, new, and more socially diverse audience that provides readers both for French "high" Romanticism and then for the more truly popular literature that succeeds it. In *The English Common Reader* (1957), on the other hand, Richard D. Altick does not see a real change in the class makeup of British readership until midcentury, when we find both the tremendous commercial success of Charles Dickens and also the rise of a mass literature aimed specifically at these new readers. Even Altick, however, dates the rise of an upper-class anxiety about lower-class readers to the 1790s, and he also notes Scott's phenomenal sales beginning with *The Lay of the Last Minstrel* in 1805, which would argue that something relevant at least to "high" literature was happening sooner.

The same class anxiety can be traced in the German context at approximately the same time, although again the implications are unclear. Starting in the 1780s a cry is raised against what writers variously call the *Lesesucht* (reading epidemic), *Lesewut* (reading mania), or *Vieleserei* (much-readingness) that had apparently overtaken the lower levels of the population, a protest that some scholars have taken to reflect a real change in both the quantity and quality of readers. Rolf Engelsing has famously coined the term "*Leserevolution*" to describe a shift not just in the numbers and class status of readers but also in the way German readers read. According to Engelsing, in the late eighteenth and early nineteenth centuries an increasingly democratic readership makes the transition from a traditional, "intensive" style of reading one or two books over and over again to our contemporary, "extensive" style of reading many books once.[4]

While the idea of a "Leserevolution" has proven very influential, still there are more recent sociological studies that would qualify any claims to an increased readership. In his article "Reconsidering the Reading Revolution" (1999), for example, Joost Kloek does not attempt to deny that changes in reading production and consumption took place in the course of the eighteenth century, but he does question our understanding of them. According to Kloek the problem is in part that while a great deal of research has been carried out, the results "are fragmentary . . . open to various interpretations, and at times . . . even contradictory," and certainly his own numbers fail to support the notion of a change in the class affiliation of readers. More important, Kloek also notes the circularity of the entire enterprise. The writers' cry of "Lesewut," as will be noted below, was in fact far from disinterested, and in any case, to look for a *Vieleserei* in late eighteenth- and early nineteenth-century Germany is only to seek support for an assumption we already hold. We are back where we started when Kloek notes that "[t]he idea that from around 1750 onwards there was a marked growth in the size of the reading public and that at the same time the nature of reading changed is not by any means a new one. It actually dates back to the eighteenth century itself."[5]

In light of the fragmentary, debatable, and even contradictory evidence offered, we are perhaps safest in assuming that reading in Western Europe remained a largely middle- and upper-class activity in the Romantic period. Our preconceived sense of change, however, may reflect the fact that that class of readers itself read more or even expanded. Klancher, for example, argues that what marks the English Romantics as writers is the lack of a "single, unified 'reading public'" to whom they could address themselves, and he connects this loss of a unified readership to a loss of intimacy among real readers and writers: according to Klancher the English Romantics no longer knew their audience in a more abstract sense because they no longer knew their readers in a more literal one. The reading public, he claims, had grown in size and its relationship to literature had accordingly changed. As opposed to the more intimate world of the eighteenth-century coffeehouse where a smaller group of readers and writers could and did meet face to face, Klancher writes that "[b]y 1790, the public sphere had . . . become an image to be consumed by readers who did not frequent it."[6]

Given that the socioeconomic and cultural situation of Russian readers in the early nineteenth century differed a great deal from that of their Western European counterparts, it is striking that the picture Klancher paints of a new and more anonymous readership finds a reflection in Russian literature only a few decades later. Records of literacy rates are even less useful in the Russian context simply because there are none, although the assumption is always that literacy in prerevolutionary Russia was staggeringly low. It is only in 1897 that the census began to address the question, at which point 21 percent of the population of the Russian Empire was literate; scholars seem to agree that that number must have been much lower prior to the educational reforms associated with the emancipation of the serfs in 1861.[7] In *Literacy and Education in Pre-Revolutionary Russia and in the USSR* (1963), I. M. Bogdanov offers few hard facts prior to the 1897 census, but he does note the results of two studies of literacy rates among two peasant populations, the first in Kostroma province in 1867 and the second in Moscow province in 1869, indicating a literacy rate among the peasant class of 8.6 and 7.5 percent, respectively—numbers that are too high, according to Bogdanov, to be relevant to other, less industrialized parts of Russia.[8] The earliest figures Bogdanov includes come from a survey of male literacy rates among the various sorts of serfs, the *meshchanstvo* (petty bourgeois), and the merchantry taken in the Saratov province in 1844, which found a total literacy rate across these classes of 4 percent.

Bogdanov's pre-1897 surveys unfortunately leave out the one class that we know did read, the *dvorianstvo* or gentry, and while scholars generally assume that it was only the gentry who were reading at the start of the century, it is not at all clear how much of the gentry actually did.[9] Russian literature through the 1820s has generally been read as an intimate conversation between a small group of readers and writers who were often one and the same, and other indications would support the notion of a highly limited readership. Lending libraries never played as significant a role in Russia as they did in Western Europe, nor did coffeehouses, which means that readers in Russia were more generally also purchasers of books. There is considerable disagreement as to the actual cost of books in Russia in the first third of the nineteenth century, and it seems evident that prices varied. Still, as elsewhere in Europe, high prices seem to have been an obstacle for all but the very wealthy, and S. Ia. Gessen in his *Book-Publisher Alexander Pushkin* (1930) makes a detailed case that even the gentry reading public was sharply limited by the high cost of books and by the high cost of living generally.[10] Some scholars argue that book buying and even library collecting became something of a fad among the gentry in the early nineteenth century despite the cost, although M. N. Kufaev makes a distinction between gentlemen who only bought books and gentlemen who actually read them. According to Kufaev, the "serious readers" of the time were to be found only among that subgroup of the gentry who later became Decembrists, which perhaps explains why we have so many studies of the Decembrists' reading habits in particular.[11]

The notion seems to be widely shared that this socially and economically circumscribed reading public began to break out of its confines by the early 1830s, although the evidence that would support this argument, as we saw in the Western European context, is a little elusive. What is clear, above all in the work of William Mills Todd III, is that Russian writers by the 1830s had begun to feel a strong sense of change in their own ranks (see below) and a corresponding change in the reader.[12] The often ferocious debates that engaged Russian writers in the 1830s derived from an anxiety that a literary world, which even into the 1820s had been characterized by handwritten and oral exchanges in the confines of an aristocratic salon, was giving way to a more anonymous sort of literature in which the reader was no longer a friend or even an acquaintance, but merely a source of profit. The problem with trying to actually quantify this change in readership, however, is another kind of circularity, as much of our information derives from a somewhat suspect source.

It is noteworthy that many of the references we find even in twentieth-century scholarship seem to either pertain to or actually emanate from the *Library for Reading*. For example, both André Meynieux in his *Push-kin: Man of Letters* (1966) and the editors of *Books in Russia and the Soviet Union* (1991) write that the Russian readership at least quadrupled in the decade from 1824 to 1834. The latter support this claim with only the bare statement that "it was estimated by the contemporary journalist O. I. Sen-kovskii that readers had quadrupled between 1824 and 1834."[13] Meynieux offers no evidence at all, but then goes on in a footnote to refer to an article published by Senkovskii in the *Library for Reading* in 1836 that describes a dramatic increase in readership.[14] Neither notes that while the assertion of such exorbitant growth may well be true, it is also one in which their source had a great deal invested. After all, the most striking evidence we have of a marked increase in readers in the early 1830s is the subscription rate to the *Library for Reading* itself. As scholars of Russian literature never tire of pointing out, while the typical circulation for a periodical from the eigh-teenth century on ranged from 600 to 1,200 copies, the *Library for Reading* almost immediately achieved an estimated 5,000–7,000 subscribers, a truly astounding number on which much of Senkovskii's notoriety rests.

Because this new readership is so closely associated with the *Library for Reading*, our understanding of its social makeup is also shaped by the ideo-logical controversy that still surrounds the journal. Smirnov-Sokol'skii, for example, speaks admiringly of "new cadres of readers" won over by the *Library for Reading* and quotes at length from a contemporary account that describes how the reading public had noticeably increased, how the "mass of the public" cried: "Let us read! Make the acquisition of books acces-sible to us!" and how, on the appearance in St. Petersburg of a "brilliant, splendid book depot that made itself the subject of honest commerce and not of speculation," the "public" immediately took to it.[15] It is not just Smirnov-Sokol'skii's Soviet context that colors his analysis, however, but also his source. The contemporary account that he quotes, as the reference to the "brilliant book depot" might suggest, is taken from the preface to an 1858 collection of essays in memory of A. F. Smirdin, the well-known and recently deceased bookseller and publisher of the *Library for Reading*. Given the intent of the book as a whole, the author of the preface again had a clear motive for possible exaggeration.

In any case, in a still semifeudal empire ruled by an autocrat, the sort of large-scale social upheaval that phrases such as "the mass of the public" imply simply could not have been under way, and the changes in readership marked by the *Library for Reading* are perhaps more accurately rendered by the opposing camp. Gogol, for example, in a letter to Pogodin in 1834 disparaged Senkovskii's antics in his new journal by describing the responses of his various readers: "The chiefs of sections and the directors of departments read and split their sides laughing. Officers read and say: 'son of a b . . . ! how well he writes!' Provincial landowners buy and subscribe and probably will read it. Only we, sinners, put it aside for reading at home."[16]

In other words, much as we saw in Western Europe, this new readership perhaps included the lower levels of the gentry and possibly even the higher echelons of the still small merchant class, but probably no more than that.[17] The authors of *Literature and Commerce* also draw on a 1903 history of the Glazunov publishing firm to describe Smirdin's readers as "not the aristocracy and the merchant class" but "military men and for the most part provincial landowners." Given the social and political exigencies of the Russian situation, this more conservative approach to the change in the Russian reading public is perhaps radical enough.[18]

WRITERS

What is especially striking in the Russian context is the sense that new readers did not create a demand for a literary marketplace but were rather themselves created by new writers, and above all, as the quotes above would suggest, by Senkovskii. But as Meynieux points out, "[c]'est l'histoire de l'oeuf et de la poule," and our belief in the importance of writers may simply derive from the fact that their activities are so much better documented.[19] Still, there is a widespread notion at this time of a new professional writer across Europe, even, for example, in Great Britain, where it would seem that a professional class of writers had existed at least since Alexander Pope. The difference between Pope and his later compatriots, however, is the loss of intimacy that Klancher describes and which, when it comes to the writers, can more clearly be derived from real numbers.

When Peter Murphy seeks to explain the phenomenon of *Blackwood's Magazine*, for example, he writes: "During the romantic period (from 1760 to about 1830, say) the world of publishing changes slowly but surely from a small familiar world, full of friends, friends of friends and enemies, to a world like ours today: full of anonymous faces, large profits, and mass markets."[20] Of course, truly "mass markets," in Altick's terms, had not yet come into being, even in England and even by 1830. Still, the unprecedented commercial successes of figures like Scott, Byron, and Hugo offered an entirely new idea of what it could mean to be a writer. Starting with the publication of *The Lay of the Last Minstrel* (1805), Scott's financial rewards were so large and so seemingly guaranteed that it is hardly any wonder that he decided, in the words of his son-in-law, John Lockhart, that "literature should form the main business of [his] life," which it did, the *Waverley* novels as well as the earlier narrative poems famously providing the fortune that Scott used to buy his mansion at Abbotsford and set himself up as a Scottish laird.[21] In France, Victor Hugo also profited greatly from his writing, after 1838 commanding upwards of 30,000 francs a year from his booksellers and garnering an average of 40,000 francs in annual royalties from one of his plays alone, the hugely popular *Ruy Blas*. Hugo was also far more fortunate in his investments than Scott and died a very wealthy man.[22]

That writers like Scott and Hugo could in fact make literature "the main business" of their lives also reflects a changed relationship between the writer and his or her text that was increasingly enshrined in law. It is not just that writers in the Romantic period began to receive much larger honoraria for their work, although they did. More important, their rights to compensation for their work were guaranteed by new copyright laws that Romantic writers themselves vigorously advocated. Martha Woodmansee has argued that this advocacy both derived from and also shaped a concept of art that we associate with figures like Kant and Schiller. According to Woodmansee, throughout the eighteenth century the German literary elite strove to bring reading to the masses and to create a market for literature, only to find by the end of the century that these new readers read the wrong sorts of books, consistently choosing lowbrow literature over the works that the *Aufklärer* themselves wrote. Without purchasers for their own works, the purveyors of high art found themselves in a difficult situation. Not only could the copyright laws that they had strongly supported with a new concept of authorial originality not do them any material good, but even the literary value of their writings, now tied to the presence of actual readers, came under attack.

One possible response to this new state of affairs was offered by Wordsworth, who in the somewhat more advanced literary culture of Great Britain fought for ever-longer periods protected by copyright in hopes that the ideal audience would eventually appear to support him materially and to validate the worth of his writings, and while he argued initially for perpetual copyright, Wordsworth finally settled in 1842 for forty-two years of protection or, if the writer survived that, life plus seven years. More to Woodmansee's point, however, is the example of Schiller, who like many turned back to patronage and to the university to support himself and along the way helped develop our modern theory of art as "an autonomous object that is to be contemplated disinterestedly."[23] As Woodmansee explains, it is only once the evaluation of the artistic work is taken back out of the literary marketplace, either temporarily, in the case of Wordsworth, or forever, in the case of Schiller, that a writer can safely claim as "good" works that the average reader had no interest reading.

In the meantime writers like Schiller could and did decry what they saw as an undiscriminating *Vieleserei* while also taking advantage of copyright laws that were first established in Germany in 1810. While France had some form of copyright protection as early as 1777, in 1793 the revolutionary regime instituted copyright protection for the lifetime of the author plus ten years, and in 1810 Napoleon's government extended private claims on a text to the life of the author, his widow, and their children for twenty years after their deaths.[24] Copyright law came into being in Russia for the first time in the Romantic period, and its initial formulations in 1828 and then its extension to fifty years in 1857 are also strongly associated with a quintessentially Romantic figure: Alexander Pushkin.[25]

Pushkin was actively engaged in the professionalization of writing for most of his career. He is well known for his pragmatic approach to the money he always needed, not only in the ironic terms of the poem "A Bookseller's Conversation with a Poet" (1824) but in any number of comments he made on his *torgovlia stishistaia*, or "verse commerce"—for example, his famous aside to his friend Prince P. A. Viazemskii: "I write for myself but publish for money and not at all for the smiles of the fairer sex."[26] While the point of Pushkin's importance in the commercialization of Russian letters has often been made, still our understanding of his role is a little vexed, largely because that role does not quite square with the general representation of literary commerce we find in the writing of the time.

As was noted above, the main reason why we see Russian writers as changing in the 1830s is that they saw themselves in the same way, and the tensions over this change erupted in what William Mills Todd III has called the debates over "literary aristocracy" (1828–31) and "literary commerce" (1835–36).[27] Both of these debates took place largely in the pages of the new periodicals and reflected a good deal of discomfort with what writers of the day viewed as an increased professionalization of letters. We usually understand these debates as pitting the already established, more traditionally aristocratic writers such as Pushkin or Princes Viazemskii and Odoevskii against a new group of lower-class literati who wrote for a living, such as Senkovskii or Bulgarin. As many scholars have pointed out, including, for example, Todd and also Timothy Kiely in his unpublished dissertation "The Professionalization of Russian Literature: A Case Study of Vladimir Odoevsky and Osip Senkovsky" (University of Michigan, 1998), this opposition does not completely hold up.

Well before Senkovskii shocked the Russian literary world by accepting 15,000 rubles a year to edit the *Library for Reading*, Pushkin was not only setting new precedents for high honoraria but also openly advertising the fact.[28] As Gessen explains, after complicated and relatively unsuccessful financial dealings over the publication of his first two narrative poems, "Ruslan and Liudmila" (1820) and "The Prisoner of the Caucasus" (1821), Pushkin entrusted the publication of his third, "The Fountain of Bakhchisarai" (1824), to his friend Viazemskii. Again Viazemskii's dealings with the publisher were convoluted, but he nonetheless gained two important victories for Pushkin. The poem came out in record time, and where Pushkin had earned a mere 500 rubles for the first edition of "The Prisoner of the Caucasus," he received 3,000 for the first edition of "The Fountain of Bakhchisarai."[29]

Viazemskii did not merely settle for the money, however, but also went on to publish the fact of the 3,000 rubles in a piece entitled "On 'The Fountain of Bakhchisarai' Not in Literary Terms" (1824). Viazemskii's essay began: "The appearance of 'The Fountain of Bakhchisarai' is worthy of the attention not only of lovers of poetry but also of those who would follow our successes in intellectual production"; as Gessen notes, Viazemskii's intent was clearly to set a precedent. Pushkin expressed to his brother wary satisfaction with the fact that Russian booksellers were "for the first time acting like Europeans [*po-evropeiski*]," and went on to negotiate still better conditions for a collection of shorter poems published in 1825, this time clearing the still more impressive sum of 8,000 rubles. Pushkin's successes then raised his expectations for the publication of *Eugene Onegin*. As he wrote to Viazemskii already in the beginning of 1824, "Slenin is offering me whatever I want for Onegin. What about Russia, it's in Europe after all—and I thought it was just a mistake of geography."[30]

Pushkin's efforts to increase his remuneration "like Europeans" were often severely hampered by the lack of any real copyright law in Russia, however, and Meynieux spells out the consequences for us in his explanation of what he calls the "Ol'dekop affair." Less than a year after the original publication of Pushkin's "The Prisoner of the Caucasus," a German translation in verse was published in St. Petersburg. The translator, Aleksander Evstaf'evich Wulfert, at no point sought either Pushkin's advice or permission to publish his translation, nor did he offer him part of the proceeds. In Russia in 1822 copyright protection did not exist, and translations of this sort were regarded not as the appropriation of someone else's work but as a compliment to its literary value.

While Pushkin may have been flattered the first time around, his reaction was quite different when, in 1824, Evstafii Ol'dekop, the St. Petersburg postal censor and publisher of the German-language *St. Petersburg Journal,* announced plans to publish the translation again, this time together with the original Russian. It was an entirely different matter for someone else to republish Pushkin's original text, particularly considering Pushkin's hopes of himself publishing a second edition of the poem. In 1824 Pushkin was in exile and apparently initially unaware of Ol'dekop's intent, but in the meantime his father, Sergei Lvovich Pushkin, immediately petitioned the censor to forbid the publication of any of his son's works without the express permission of either the son or the father. The Censorship Committee ruled that there was in fact no law that the Ol'dekop publication would violate, which was true, and that accordingly their permission stood. The Committee also noted, however, that neither of the Pushkins had previously petitioned the Committee to ask that permission for such publications be denied, as if to suggest that even in the absence of copyright law the Committee would be willing to defend Pushkin's rights to his own work in the future. The Committee finally also sent a copy of the complaint to Ol'dekop, an act that suggested a moral if not legal reprimand.

Pushkin's friends were not prepared to give up so easily, even with the edition ready for distribution and amid rumors that Pushkin the father had cut some sort of deal with Ol'dekop; as Viazemskii wrote to the poet V. A. Zhukovskii: "We can't let them rob Pushkin. It's enough that they oppress him." Pushkin by this time had found out about the proposed publication and, in answer to Viazemskii's question about a possible exchange of money between his father and Ol'dekop, expressed his opinion of the whole matter quite succinctly: "Ol'dekop stole and lied!" Despite their strong sense of moral rectitude, Pushkin's friends had no legal standing to stop the sale of the books, as Pushkin himself admitted when he finally wrote to Viazemskii, "I'm sick of Ol'dekop. Spit on him and we're quits."[31]

Pushkin had learned a lesson for the future, however, and on his return from exile he sent a memo to his official contact at the court, Count Benckendorff, detailing the problems he encountered in the Ol'dekop affair. On Benckendorff's pointing out that in fact no law had been broken, Pushkin responded vigorously:

> If . . . we allow that in Russia a translation gives the right to republish the original, then it will be impossible to protect one's literary property against the attack of a predator. In presenting this opinion to your Excellency's consideration, I suggest that in the establishment of permanent rules for the safeguarding of literary property the question of the right to republish a book together with its translation, commentary, or preface is highly important.[32]

The following year, on April 22, 1828, the new censorship regulations included five new articles devoted to the topic of authors' rights, three of which gave authors exclusive right to the sale and publication of their own works; the heirs were also granted this exclusive right for twenty-five years after the death of the author. In 1830 another twenty-five years were added in the event that the heirs published a new edition within five years of the expiration of the first twenty-five-year period. Finally in 1857, due largely, as S. Pereselenkov has argued, to the petitions of Pushkin's widow, Natalia Nikolaevna, the initial period of rights was extended to fifty years. By comparison, at this time the standard period in Western Europe was thirty years.[33]

The 1828 establishment of copyright law in Russia marked a signal victory for Pushkin personally and an important step in the development of the literary marketplace. It did not, however, bring that marketplace fully into being. Unfortunately, while the establishment and enforcement of strict copyright laws are essential to the development of a literary marketplace, on their own they are no guarantee that writers can make a living in that marketplace, and in Russia in the 1820s and 1830s it is hard to say that any purveyor of high literature did so, even Pushkin. What we find instead, both before and after 1828, is a curious mix of a new professionalism with an older structure of literary patronage.

A contemporary recalls, for example, that K. F. Ryleev and A. A. Bestuzhev started the almanac *The Polar Star* (1823–25) "with the intent of turning a literary enterprise into a commercial one," which they did, the success of their sales enabling the two publishers not only to pay their friends for their literary contributions but also themselves to clear 2,000 rubles in profit each. The newer reward of hard cash, however, was somewhat jarringly combined with rewards of a more traditional kind. As Faddei Bulgarin grandly informed his readers:

> The publishers of "The Polar Star" had the happiness of presenting copies of this issue to their excellencies the Majesties the Empresses and were favored with the highest consideration. K. F. Ryleev received two diamond rings and A. A. Bestuzhev a gold snuff-box of beautiful workmanship and a diamond ring. It is also very pleasant for us to announce that "The Polar Star" was just as favorably received by the public; *in three weeks it bought up 1,500 copies: this is a unique event in Russian literature, for, excluding Mr. Karamzin's "History of the Russian State," not one book and not one journal has had a similar success.*[34]

Bulgarin's italics would seem to emphasize the importance of the second half of his note, and indeed, as the authors of *Literature and Commerce* point out, the presentation of diamond rings and golden snuffboxes at this point sounds more than a little anachronistic. Bulgarin himself would be the recipient of imperial rings in the early 1830s, but the practice became increasingly rare, not because patronage disappeared but because it took on new forms.[35]

Pushkin, for example, in addition to the income generated by his writing could draw on the proceeds of the estate he inherited at the time of his marriage and which his father claimed would furnish him with 4,000 rubles a year. These two sources together, however, were never sufficient to maintain the extravagant style of life both Pushkin and his wife demanded, and much of the story of Pushkin's interactions with the Tsar in the 1830s is his repeated requests for more financial help. The Tsar was never particularly forthcoming, and there is a strong sense that he was more interested in increasing his control over Pushkin than in actually helping him. Still, Pushkin was the recipient of a loan of 20,000 rubles in 1834 and again 30,000 rubles in 1835, and he was appointed to a sinecure in 1831 when he was made a quasi-official court historiographer at an annual salary of 5,000 rubles. The Tsar also paid off Pushkin's debts at his death, and while such a gesture may seem too little too late, since they have been estimated at a staggering 138,988.33 rubles, it probably didn't seem quite so mean to Pushkin's family.[36]

A more successful beneficiary of Tsar's largess in the 1830s and after was Gogol, who also found himself unable to make his living by his writing and who, unlike Pushkin, had no estate to fall back on. As Donald Fanger explains, particularly in his later years Gogol was supported largely at court expense, with grants ranging from 500 rubles in 1841 to 3,000 rubles in silver (the equivalent of 10,000 rubles in paper) in 1845.[37] Of course Gogol, like Pushkin, was exclusively a practitioner of "high" literature, and in the 1830s writers with somewhat less lofty aspirations did make their living by their writing, most notably Senkovskii and also Bulgarin. Again, though, to offer these last two as proof of a more fully functioning marketplace is problematic on a number of levels.

As pointed out above, there is first of all the fact that hack writers by definition always made their living by their writing, even in Russia, and Grits et al. note in particular the example of Fedor Emin, whom they describe as "one of the first professional writers of the eighteenth century."[38] Second, even hack writers in the 1830s did not survive entirely without government intervention, as the example of Bulgarin makes especially clear. The commercial success of his *Northern Bee* (1825–59) was infamously guaranteed by the fact that it was at the time the only privately published journal granted the right to publish political news, a privilege Bulgarin allegedly received in exchange for his reports to the secret police. Hack writers as well as the more elevated sort were also paid not by the public directly but by publishers who themselves were not always left to the mercy of the marketplace, and even Smirdin, as will be noted below, was a belated beneficiary of a state subsidy.

If these qualifications make it difficult to speak of a professionalization of writers in Russia in the 1830s despite the clear gains we traced in the case of Pushkin, still we should consider the extent to which a "real," fully functioning professionalization of writers remains something of an illusion, or at least a very vaguely defined concept, anytime, anywhere. Even the important financial successes of Scott and Byron in the most advanced literary marketplace of the day alluded to earlier, for example, were made possible by an enormous amount of financial failure, as Nigel Cross argues in his *The Common Writer: Life in Nineteenth-Century Grub Street* (1985). As Cross points out, for the vast majority of the even relatively well-known British writers, the literary marketplace throughout the nineteenth century offered only very meager rewards, and writers' incomes were necessarily supplemented by other sources.[39]

Many writers, along the lines of Thackeray, worked also as journalists and men of letters more generally, while others combined writing with work in other fields, most notably Trollope at the Post Office. Many more were forced to seek charity, as the annals of the Royal Literary Fund, established in 1790, attest, and in 1856, for example, none other than Charles Dickens himself spoke before the Fund asking that its trustees dispense their money rather more freely and if need be to the same deserving recipients over and over again.[40] Starting in the 1830s, Civil List pensions were also a possibility for struggling writers and even for those who were in less than dire straits; although Wordsworth, for example, like Pushkin and also Byron, began with a private income, still in 1842 he was awarded a generous one. Finally, we should note that even in our own day this somewhat ambiguous situation has not exactly been resolved, as writers both in the United States and Great Britain have increasingly found some measure of financial security in college writing programs, thereby achieving what Cross describes as the nineteenth-century "prerequisites for literary success": "education, social status, and monied leisure."[41] Even in our era of high capitalism the idea of "writing for a living" remains a far from straightforward one.

INTERMEDIARIES

While the case for new writers is perhaps more compelling than that for new readers, especially in the Russian context, it may be that the development of a literary marketplace in Russia was dictated by neither but rather by the changes in the various book-related industries and institutions that mediated between the two. Many scholars have noted that the early nineteenth century saw considerable advances in publishing technology; for example, in the distribution and availability of books, in the role of censorship, and even in the person of the publisher himself. Once again, however, these changes are hard to quantify. The date of the appearance of the Stanhope press, for example, does not necessarily correspond to the moment of its significance, and while print runs and overall production of written material do increase, if irregularly, in Russia over the first third of the century, scholars do not all agree as to when and how much. The role of a new sort of publisher is also unclear, although we often have a sense of new business practices in operation.

As Balzac rendered them in *Lost Illusions* (1837–43), those new business practices included rapacity and a brutal indifference to actual literary quality, and if to read Balzac's novel as a historical record is another example of the circular thinking that seems to plague our discussions of the literary marketplace, still, *Lost Illusions* is a touchstone for scholars that is perhaps not without relevance to the Russian context. For by the 1830s Russia, too, is popularly supposed to support a new kind of publishing industry driven by money and geared toward the lowest common denominator, although interestingly enough, the blame for this apparently unfortunate state of affairs is never seen to rest with the single most important publisher of the time, A. F. Smirdin.

Smirdin's centrality to Russian literature in the 1830s was established as early as 1834 when V. G. Belinskii in his essay "Literary Reveries" labeled what he saw as the fourth and current era of Russian literature the "Smirdin period." Still, Smirdin in this essay as elsewhere is consistently exonerated of responsibility for what commentators usually see as the low level of Russian publishing and journalism. The villains of the piece are always the three journalists known to literary historians as the "unholy triumvirate": Bulgarin, N. I. Grech, and Senkovskii, while the well-respected Smirdin is left to occupy an anomalous position in the history of Russian letters. Scholars of Russian literature tend to make a distinction in the early nineteenth century between usually older, well-educated, independently wealthy gentry-class publishers who are described variously as "culturally motivated," "*kulturträgers*," or "publisher-Maecenases," and, on the other hand, "a new purely commercial type," the "publisher-merchants."[42] Despite scholars' devotion to this divide, Smirdin is always presented as both. Certainly Smirdin made his living as a publisher and bookseller, which would argue that he was a "publisher-merchant." The great number of testimonials to the love of literature that supposedly on more than one occasion trumped Smirdin's business instincts, however, suggests that he was something more or, in terms of the rise of the literary marketplace, something less.

Aleksander Fedorovich Smirdin (1795–1857) was born in Moscow into a merchant family of modest means. He received only a very minimal formal education, and while there is some debate over the extent of his literary abilities, his clear dependence in later life on his editors lends credence to the oft-quoted claim that "he wrote fairly incorrectly, with many orthographic mistakes, and never entered into the inner content of the books offered to him for publication, instead satisfying himself with the author's explanation."[43] What Smirdin did have was a great deal of experience in the field of publishing and bookselling, starting from age twelve when he went to work as a clerk in the bookstore of his uncle, P. A. Il'in. He had reached the rank of shop assistant when Napoleon's advance in 1812 forced Smirdin to flee temporarily to St. Petersburg, where he was fortunate enough to meet a prominent Petersburg publisher and bookseller, V. F. Plavil'shchikov. After the liberation Smirdin returned to Moscow to work another four years for yet another bookseller, A. S. Shiriaev, and in 1817 he moved to St. Petersburg to take up a position as Plavil'shchikov's chief shop assistant. Plavil'shchikov's business included a press, the largest bookstore in St. Petersburg, and a reading library that by 1817 contained 3,000 volumes, and upon his death in 1823 he left the entire enterprise to Smirdin.[44]

Among Smirdin's early achievements as a publisher and bookseller, perhaps most notable were his purchases of the aforementioned edition of Pushkin's "The Fountain of Bakhchisarai" in 1824 for 3,000 rubles, and a second edition of his "Ruslan and Liudmila" in 1828 for 7,000 rubles. In 1829 he scored an enormous success with the publication of Bulgarin's best-selling novel *Ivan Vyzhigin*; scholars estimate the unusually large print run at anywhere from three to five thousand copies, all of which sold out in three weeks, and Smirdin became known for his large editions, low prices, and generous honoraria. In 1830, for example, he bought the rights to I. A. Krylov's fables for 40,000 rubles, a far cry from the 3,000 rubles Pushkin had received for "The Fountain of Bakhchisarai" a mere six years earlier, and Smirdin promised to publish the *Fables* in editions totaling 40,000 copies over the next ten years.[45] Whether this represents a good business practice or not, by 1831 Smirdin was already offering copies at reduced rates. In another example, in the same year he purchased the rights to all the published work Pushkin would produce over the next four years for a monthly payment of 600 rubles in silver, a sort of salary (as Pushkin himself called it) that Grits et al. describe as a "significant resource" for the ever-struggling poet.[46]

Toward the end of 1831 Smirdin relocated his enterprise from Sinii Most to Nevskii Prospect, paying the fabulous sum of 12,000 rubles a year for his fashionable new quarters, and in 1832 he celebrated the opening of his new lending library above the store with a dinner famously attended by all the literary lights of St. Petersburg and itself later celebrated with the 1833 publication of the anthology *Housewarming*. While the move to such a central location was a measure of Smirdin's commercial success, it also paradoxically removed the taint of business from the whole proceedings, creating a strange hybrid. Smirdin's store now became, in the words of Grits et al., "a sort of literary salon," and something of the awkwardness of the conjunction of store and salon can be felt in the *Northern Bee*'s "puff" for the new establishment:

> A. F. Smirdin, who has won the respect of all right-thinking literati for his honesty in his affairs and his noble striving for literature's successes, and gained the trust and love of the public for his rich and inexpensive editions of the works of their favorite authors, old and new, and for his accuracy in the fulfilling of his responsibilities . . . has decided to give appropriate shelter to the Russian mind and has founded a book store such as has never been seen in Russia. Fifty or so years ago, Russian books lacked even stores. Books were kept in basements and sold on tables, like rag dealers' merchandise. The activity and intelligence of Novikov, who is unforgotten in the chronicles of Russian enlightenment, gave a new direction to the book trade, and book stores were founded in Moscow and Petersburg, [but] along the lines of ordinary stores. . . . Finally, Mr. Smirdin has secured the triumph of the Russian mind and, as they say, settled it in our first place: on Nevskii Prospect, in a beautiful new building . . . can be found the book trade of Mr. Smirdin. . . . One's heart is comforted at the thought that finally our Russian literature has entered into honor and from basements has relocated to mansions.[47]

A store that is not a store is an interesting notion, and the praise for Smirdin's "inexpensive editions" and "accuracy" sits a little oddly next to "the triumph of the Russian mind." The cultural aspirations that are associated with Smirdin's "beautiful new building," however, almost entirely disappear when we turn from the real library for reading to its literary manifestation, the *Library for Reading*.

In a scathing article Senkovskii's contemporary S. P. Shevyrev described the *Library for Reading* as a "stack of banknotes, turned into articles," and it is certainly true that the journal, apparently as opposed to the building, was firmly based on the exchange of money.[48] Meynieux, for example, dates the appearance of the literary marketplace in Russia precisely to 1834 and the launching of the *Library for Reading*, and it would seem that Smirdin's journal was the first to operate on an entirely professional footing. At the time, despite the advances in the professionalization of writing described above, honoraria for work published in journals were still not quite a given, so that a frustrated Pushkin, for example, could receive absolutely nothing for his contributions to the *Moscow Herald* for the entire year of 1828.[49] The *Library for Reading*, however, paid generously and promptly, and Smirdin even offered special deals to certain privileged writers.

He made an agreement with Pushkin, for example, that the poet would publish his latest poetry only in the new journal but at the high rate of ten rubles per line, a deal resulting in 1,200 rubles for rights to the poem "The Hussar," while Denis Davydov was offered in advance 300 rubles for each printer's sheet appearing in the *Library for Reading*. Money flowed to other aspects of the business, too, as Smirdin paid Senkovskii the princely sum of 15,000 rubles annually to edit the journal and gave Krylov 9,000 rubles simply for the use of his name on the masthead; in 1835 Smirdin even offered Pushkin 15,000 rubles to undertake *not* to publish a rival journal, an offer that Pushkin turned down in some disgust. Finally, the large sums out seem to have implied large sums in. While again prices and their significance are in some dispute, given the size and frequency of the *Library for Reading*, its subscription price of 50 rubles a year is at least reasonable; in any event, the journal's truly impressive circulation argues for its commercial profitability and in fact puts it in an entirely different category from any of its rivals.

If by the mid-1830s the commercial success of the *Library for Reading* would seem more significant than the cultural enlightenment purportedly offered by Smirdin's "salon," he is nonetheless remembered more for the latter, perhaps in part because after his early business successes Smirdin failed rather spectacularly. Smirdin was already in financial trouble by the end of the 1830s, and some of his bolder initiatives began to go awry; for example, the attempt to purchase both Bulgarin's *Northern Bee* and Grech's *Son of the Fatherland* that, apparently due to the underhanded dealings of the two editors, eventually resulted in large losses for Smirdin.[50] In 1839 he also began publishing a lavish multivolume anthology called *One Hundred Russian Writers* which was poorly received. In the early 1840s Smirdin tried to raise capital through a series of lotteries, a practice pioneered by the struggling French publishing industry, but in 1845 he was forced to move from his elegant establishment at Nevskii Prospect. Smirdin's last real achievement was the publication, beginning in 1846, of a small-format

Complete Collection of the Works of Russian Authors priced at the very low figure of one ruble per volume, which he financed with the help of a government subsidy.[51] In the early 1850s he declared bankruptcy, and when he died in 1857 he was completely destitute.

Smirdin may have simply outlasted what turned out to be only a small window onto the possibilities of the literary marketplace, as Grits et al. claim: "if the 1830s can be called the years of the blossoming of the book trade, then, on the contrary, the beginning of the '40s is the epoch of its sharp decline."[52] Scholars suggest a number of possible reasons for the apparent abrupt reversal of the gains of the preceding decade. The editors of *Books in Russia and the Soviet Union*, for example, note an overproduction of books by the late 1830s, a monetary reform in 1839 that further decreased the already low prices of books, and also a series of poor harvests beginning in 1838 that brought on a wider economic depression. *A Brief Sketch of the Book Trade and Publishing Activity of the Glazunovs for One Hundred Years* (1903), on the other hand, puts the blame on the "fat" journals that put book publishing out of business, and finally almost everyone notes the tightening up of censorship in the wake of 1848. For a great many of Smirdin's contemporaries and subsequent historians, however, the issue was not the collapse of the Russian book business as a whole but rather that Smirdin himself was simply a poor businessman.

The editors of *Four Hundred Years of Russian Book-Publishing* (1964) offer a sobering view of Smirdin's career. Despite "enabling the dissemination of Russian literature," they write: "Smirdin failed to understand the real possibilities of the market for books. Large editions sold out slowly, debts grew. In paying high honoraria, Smirdin overestimated the importance of capital in literary creation."[53] Smirdin was also done in, they add, by Senkovskii, Grech, and Bulgarin, who "put commercial interests in first place," whatever the cost to literature and fair business practices. Kufaev says, "[t]he disinterested and generous Smirdin turned out to be a poor businessman," a judgment that Beaven Remnek echoes when she refers to "the legendary generosity of a man who placed literature above profit."[54] In the end the most significant figure in Russian publishing and bookselling in the first half of the nineteenth century is cast as a gentle lover of literature who both failed to understand the marketplace and was victimized by the unscrupulous writers who did; in Pushkin's words, Smirdin was not just a "fool" but also a "*Libraire gentilhomme.*"[55]

It is instead the unscrupulous writers who are once more cast as the agents of the whole process, above all because the great achievement of the nascent Russian literary marketplace, the *Library for Reading*, has always been associated not with its universally respected publisher, Smirdin, but with its universally despised editor, Senkovskii. The praise we read of the former is almost always offered as a counterweight to the condemnation of the latter, so that Gogol, for example, in his 1835 attack on the *Library for Reading*, "On the Movement of Journalistic Literature in 1834 and 1835," makes careful and repeated distinction between "the bookseller Smirdin, already long known for his activity and conscientiousness" and the real culprit, Senkovskii;[56] according to Pushkin, while Smirdin is a "fool," Senkovskii is a "beast."[57] With admiration for the publisher serving as a sort of trope in the attacks on the editor, criticism of Senkovskii's commercial tactics ensures that Smirdin enjoys an entirely positive but also diminished role in the history of the literary marketplace.

It is much more difficult to put writers in charge of the most anonymous aspect of a new publishing industry—the technological advances that made larger editions both possible and affordable over the course of the nineteenth century—and in the account Lee Erickson gives in *The Economy of Literary Form: English Literature and the Industrialization of Publishing, 1800–1850* (1996), writers would seem to play a fairly passive role. In Erickson's argument, the Fourdrinier papermaking machine, in operation from 1807, together with Stanhope's stereotyped printing method, first used in 1804, dramatically lowered the cost of producing books in Great Britain; in the case of paper alone, the cost of demy (the kind of paper most commonly used in printing books) dropped from thirty-two shillings a ream in 1810 to twenty shillings a ream in 1835. According to Erickson, the total effect was staggering:

> The advances in printing technology led inexorably to both a democratization and a stratification of literary culture in England, as books and periodicals became available to all classes of readers and an economy of scale came into being. The technological changes propelled the expansion of the publishing industry and forced a reordering of the relationships among literary forms. In particular, the rise of the periodical format created powerful competitors for poetry's audience in the forms of the short story and serialized fiction, which together were eventually to drive poetry from the marketplace.[58]

What is especially striking in Erickson's stark account, however, is that while it downplays the role of writers as well as readers in the creation of literature, it at the same time enshrines the account of the rise of the literary marketplace given by one writer of the day in particular, once more Balzac and once more in *Lost Illusions*.

The novel that traces Lucien de Rubempré's rise as a would-be poet and subsequent fall as a contributor to the very sort of periodicals that Erickson describes also famously begins with an account of Jérôme-Nicolas Séchard's outdated printing operation and its sale to Séchard's son David. David himself, a former apprentice at the well-known Paris printing firm of Didot, then over the course of the novel devotes himself to the invention of a cheap method of paper manufacture, eventually ruining himself in the process. As Erickson's work would suggest, Balzac's tale reflects actual changes in publishing technology, and the story of David Séchard's unfortunate efforts to invent a new method of paper manufacture, for example, echoes that of Nicolas-Louis Robert, a one-time supervisor at the real Didot paper mill who worked for a number of years to develop a papermaking machine. Robert first applied for a patent for his idea in 1798, only to be forced by financial need to sell the patent to Didot. When Didot failed to make payments, Robert was able to resume the patent in 1801. In the meantime, in an example of truly Balzacian double-dealing, Didot described Robert's plans to his brother-in-law, an English papermaker, and a machine was eventually produced not by Robert but by the English manufacturers, Henry and Sealy Fourdrinier, who then gave their name to the papermaking process.[59]

If Balzac's fiction in some respects anticipates Erickson's history, however, its example also complicates the relationship between technology and the various workings of a literary marketplace that Erickson describes. There is again a hint of *l'histoire de l'oeuf et de la poule* when we consider that, whereas *Lost Illusions* with its rendering of writers for hire and cutthroat periodicals was set in the 1820s, at least as Albert Joseph George tells it in *The Development of French Romanticism: The Impact of the Industrial Revolution on Literature* (1955), the new technology that supposedly produced that literary world in fact had little effect in France before the 1830s. According to George, although the first papermaking machine started commercial operation as early as 1812, by 1827 there were only four such machines in all of France, and by 1833 only twelve. Other technological advances also first appeared in the late 1810s, including the Stanhope press in 1818, the American iron

Clymer press in 1820, and Ganal's invention of a roller for the speedy inking of type in 1817; but again, George argues, their full impact would not be felt for more than a decade.[60] Only by the early 1830s, George writes, were the factors in place "necessary for a mass literature," although, again, "mass" literature is not the same as the sale of "high" literature and these factors may or may not add up to the picture that *Lost Illusions* presents.

In the Russian context privileging technological advances in the rise of a literary marketplace is still more problematic, and in fact that story, whether as history or fiction, is never told. While the evidence offered in *Four Hundred Years of Russian Book-Publishing* is perhaps deliberately vague, in the area of paper production Russia seems to have done not too badly. Russians apparently produced an excess of their own paper as early as 1814, although as one contemporary wrote, the paper was "so thick and so rough, that from the wrinkles sometimes the letters would not print on it."[61] By 1825 there were throughout Russia eighty-eight paper factories with 8,272 workers producing 740,000 reams of paper, and by 1831, 808,621 reams. Unfortunately, *Four Hundred Years* gives us no information that would explain if this production answered the needs of the Russian publishing industry either in quantity or quality or how the Russian production of paper compared with that of Western Europe.

What is clear, on the other hand, is that Russia was seriously behind in the mechanization of the printing process. Both *Books in Russia and the Soviet Union* and *Four Hundred Years of Russian Book-Publishing* note that mechanized presses began to be constructed at the Aleksandrovskii factory in St. Petersburg in 1828–29 and that the first of these went into operation in Grech's typography for the printing of the March 19, 1829, issue of the *Northern Bee*. Throughout the 1830s, however, the transfer from hand to machine presses proceeded only very slowly, largely, both works argue, because of the pressure exerted on journal and newspaper publication by Nicholas's repressive regime. According to *Books in Russia and the Soviet Union*, by 1844 mechanized presses were installed in only six of eighteen Moscow presses, and "the full impact of mechanization was not realized until the late 1800s."[62] In other words, if we cast technology as our primary factor, then the various trappings of the literary marketplace, including new readers, professional writers, and commercially viable periodicals, could only come into being in Russia well after the generation of Pushkin, Senkovskii, and Smirdin was dead.

Literary Marketplaces Less Real

The concept itself is vague, the possible facts vast in number, and conclusive evidence of a literary marketplace in operation in Russia in the 1830s a bit lacking. What is clear is that accounts that would associate the rise of a Russian literary marketplace with the 1830s tend to circle back to the writer, who is both the source of much of the evidence and also either the hero or the villain of the piece. It may be that Russian writers of the 1830s truly did reach new readers, pull the wool over the eyes of trusting publishers, and overcome obsolete handpresses to create a literary marketplace and corresponding literature exactly like that of Western Europe. Whether they did or not, the whole discussion of the literary marketplace in Russia and elsewhere is necessarily trapped in a circularity of both sources and assumptions that itself demands our attention. The more immediate question is not what makes up a literary marketplace and whether Russia in the 1830s had one, but why a story of the literary marketplace is one Russian writers of the day chose to tell.

The easy answer is that Russian writers took their story from Western European writers, who in turn derived their story from their socioeconomic circumstances. The problem with this approach, however, is that it operates on two contradictory assumptions: while overall we seem to be saying that literature necessarily reflects reality, we at the same time are making an exception for Russian literature that is then apparently uniquely equipped to borrow someone else's reality or even create its own. Russian literature may indeed offer a special case, and in fact that argument has often been made. But it might also be that Russian representations of the literary marketplace drew not just on the real changes in readers, writers, and the production of books that were distributed unevenly across Europe, but also on the Romantic ideas of writers and readers that first appeared in the *Athenaeum*.

The particulars of these ideas are the topic of the next two chapters. For now suffice it to say that benefits of copyright were not yet available for the real authors of the *Athenaeum*, nor was the journal itself particularly financially successful, and with the exception of Ludwig Tieck, none of the Jena circle at that time or later made his living in the literary marketplace.[63] Novalis before his untimely death supported himself as assistant administrator of the Saxon salt mines, for example, while the university offered a haven for many, most notably Friedrich Schelling and also Friedrich Schleiermacher, who combined his work as a pastor with professorships in theology first at Halle and then in Berlin. August Wilhelm Schlegel also taught in various universities, including in Jena and eventually in Bonn, he gave lectures by subscription, and he also twice interrupted his academic career to join Mme. de Staël's retinue.

It is finally rather difficult to tell how Friedrich himself made his living, and in fact by and large he did not. According to Hans Eichner, Friedrich imagined himself especially early on as making his living as a freelance writer, but whatever intentions he had were thwarted not just by the exigencies of the marketplace but also by his own inability to follow through on his ideas. While he, like August Wilhelm, tutored and gave lectures, Friedrich then also failed in his attempts to find more permanent employment in the academy.[64] In 1809 he became an Austrian civil servant and in 1815, First Secretary of the Austrian Legation to the Diet of Frankfurt. In 1818, however, Metternich officially recalled him, and for the remaining years of his life Friedrich lived largely on his state pension and on whatever income he derived from various projects, dying in 1829 as he lived, deeply in debt.

The response of the Schlegels and their friends to their sometimes grim situation, however, at least in the years 1798–1800, was very different from those of Wordsworth and Schiller described above. The *Frühromantik* neither imagined a real and more appreciative reading public of the future nor abandoned the literary marketplace altogether. Instead, an awareness of and interest in the literary marketplace in its various institutions and implications runs through the works associated with the *Athenaeum*. These references are sometimes very slight, for example when Antonio in the "Letter on the Novel" notes in passing that Amalia gets her books from the lending library; over much of Europe lending libraries were one of the main engines of an emerging literary marketplace, hence the *Library for Reading*. Other mentions of the literary marketplace are much more obvious, and we find in and around the *Athenaeum* direct references to the author as a producer of goods, to the notion of the reading public, and above all to the fact of publication.

Athenaeum Fragment 62, for example, tells us that "[p]ublishing is to writing as the maternity ward is to the first kiss," as if Jena believes that without the act of publication the work remains incomplete.[65] Of course, the Romantic work is intended to be incomplete, but then, as we see in an unpublished dialogue Novalis intended for the *Athenaeum*, it is also publication that turns the single, completed work into the multiplicity of infinite copies. In his dialogue, Novalis's B. unhesitatingly refers to books as *Handlungsartikels*, business commodities, and gleefully compares the wealth of the German printing presses to that of the Peruvian silver mines. In dismissing A.'s fears of the famous "book epidemic," B. also expresses the wish "to see before me a whole collection of books from all arts and fields of knowledge as the work of my spirit," suggesting that the completed and published book is in turn but one part of that great whole that is the unfinished and unfinishable collection of all books of all times.[66] In *Athenaeum Fragment* 367, Friedrich Schlegel is equally blunt in his choice of words:

> People often think they can insult writers by comparing them to factories. But why shouldn't a real writer be a manufacturer as well? Shouldn't he devote all his life to the business of shaping literary substance into forms that are practical and useful on a grand scale? How well many bunglers could use only a small fraction of the industry and precision that we hardly notice anymore in the most ordinary tools.[67]

For Friedrich Schlegel as for Novalis there are real possibilities in the representation of the writer as the producer of a product just like any other.

While all these allusions to the various institutions and aspects of publishing are themselves significant, the most important reference the *Athenaeum* makes to the literary marketplace lies elsewhere: in the extent to which the "Romantic kind of poetry," as a space where readers and writers half-real and half-imaginary meet to "create" literature, prefigures the space that is the literary marketplace itself. If we have struggled in much of this chapter to define it, it is because the literary marketplace is a strange and paradoxical sort of space in much the same way as is the ideal Romantic form. The literary marketplace is both real, especially when reality is measured by monetary worth, and imaginary, in the sense that it does not point to any real space in the world. It is a forum where real writers earn real money, but do so by projecting an image of themselves as author that often and intentionally takes on an existence of its own. It is finally also a space where real readers spend real money and so collaborate in the creation of literature in a very basic sense, while at the same time making up that amorphous reading public that Friedrich Schlegel described in *Critical Fragment* 35 when he wrote: "One sometimes hears the public being spoken of as if it were somebody with whom one had lunch at the Hôtel de Saxe during the Leipzig fair. Who is this public? The public is no object, but an idea, a postulate, like the Church."[68]

In other words, Romanticism comes with something like a theory of the literary marketplace already included in the very form of the "Romantic kind of poetry," a fact that perhaps renders the later reality of the literary market-place, whatever it may be, a little redundant, or that perhaps simply makes it very difficult to distinguish that later reality from its literary representation. The *Athenaeum* closed after six issues in 1800, but the ideas the journal put into circulation went on, its vision of Romantic form shaping our under-standing of the literary marketplace even as that marketplace itself appar-ently came into existence, above all in the pages of the *Library for Reading*.

While O. I. Senkovskii was in fact not the first Russian to do so, he noto-riously did make his living from a literary marketplace that he is at the same time often held to have invented in his journal, and in the confusion of the half-real and half-imaginary that thus marks his career, we find a striking demonstration of the collision of Romantic irony with the literary market-place. The genre of the periodical all on its own is a fragmentary subject always under construction; it also figures the interactions between writer and reader in a particularly tangible way. When the literary magazines start selling in large numbers, as they seem to do over the course of Romanticism not just in Russia but also in much of Western Europe, the interactions between writer and reader that in the *Athenaeum* might be associated with Romantic irony alone then appear considerably more complicated and even contradictory.

On the one hand the argument could be made that the literary market-place serves to rein in the free play of Romantic irony. When we talk about the new readers who subscribed to the *Library for Reading* in record num-bers, after all, we would seem quite clearly to be talking not about literary personae but about real bodies in the world. It would also seem that the fact of being paid for one's literary output by one's readers would tie a given author to a given book not just in a particular persona but in his or her real person, the person, that is, who tries to keep food on the table with the money produced by writing. In this sense a rising literary marketplace does not just "meet" with Romantic irony but puts an end to it, and Senkovskii has long been credited with exactly this sort of anti-Romantic and, indeed, antiliterary energy.

Oddly enough, however, as we will see in the next two chapters, many of the pioneers of literary professionalization are also among the most noted practitioners of Romantic irony, including Scott in the *Waverley* novels and perhaps most especially Pushkin. The *Library for Reading* for all its dependence on apparently real readers and writers is also stunningly and even oppressively rich in the invention of fictional writers and readers. In the face of this profusion of reader- and writer-personae we might be tempted to reverse ourselves and argue instead the opposite, that it is the new literary marketplace that actually lends itself to a Romantic play of authorial identity, even as early as the *Athenaeum,* as it is only the increase in the number of readers and in the distance between author and audience that makes impersonation possible. Here again is Klancher's notion of an expanding public sphere, and if in England the transformation to a more anonymous literary world would apparently just predate Romanticism, in Russia it appears halfway through. By 1836 Belinskii could express genuine surprise on learning that Baron Brambeus and Tiutiun'dzhiu-Oglu were not real (if pseudonymous) writers, but rather the products of Senkovskii's fertile brain, and his astonishment was widely shared.[69] It would seem that Senkovskii could hardly have achieved this degree of separation between his person and his personae even ten years earlier, when a smaller and more elite Russian Romantic reader- and writership could still expect to encounter one another in the Moscow and Petersburg salons.

Particularly given the uncertainty of the actual facts of the literary marketplace, especially in Russia, it may finally also be that the relationship between Romanticism and the literary marketplace is a good deal more fluid than either of these arguments taken alone would allow. The socioeconomic realities of Russia in the first third of the nineteenth century were very different from those of Great Britain, France, or Germany, just as circumstances in those three nations differed considerably one from another. What is nonetheless remarkable is the extent to which, in their writing in and about the literary marketplace, Russians still sound the same notes as their European counterparts, and they do so because while literature can directly reflect reality, it does not have to. Literature, after all, can enjoy a very indirect relationship to reality; it can even render our understanding of what reality is extremely problematic. Romantics, as we will see, specialize in rendering our understanding of reality problematic, and Senkovskii does so only in a particularly disturbing fashion, as his literary practice is not at all the affront to Romantic sensibilities it is often claimed to be. The

Library for Reading instead illuminates an admittedly extreme end of what is nonetheless a Romantic spectrum, a "Romantic kind of poetry" stripped to its essentials in an imitation of the space that Senkovskii wants very much to bring into being: a literary marketplace where virtual readers and writers gather under the control of that one reader who is at the same time a writer, the all-powerful literary critic Senkovskii himself.

2. Romantic Writers

As the editor and chief critic of the *Library for Reading*, Senkovskii developed a peculiar brand of literary criticism in which two features quite regularly occur. Almost all of Senkovskii's work is marked by a strong sense of personality, so strong in fact as to seriously annoy many of his readers, especially those in the literary establishment. At the same time this personality is often not quite Senkovskii's own, since it tends to be embodied in a series of personae, most famously Baron Brambeus but also including, for example, Tiutiun'dzhiu-Oglu, O. O. . . . O!, the three landowners from Tver, Kritikzada, A. Belkin, and even (in a review on the use of mineral waters) Doctor Karl von Bitterwasser. The widespread critical distaste for Senkovskii then and now is certainly due to the blatant interest in making money detailed in the last chapter. The critics have been equally disturbed, however, by the often astonishing insincerity that Senkovskii displays in the jarring combination of so-called "personal criticism" with a personality not his own.[1]

Senkovskii's utter lack of integrity would seem to exclude him from consideration as a real writer and especially as a real writer of the Romantic variety. As Monika Greenleaf comments in her *Pushkin and Romantic Fashion*: "When we think of Romantic subjectivity we tend to think of the Rousseauist or Wordsworthian 'authentic self in nature,'" only "secondarily vitiated by its dealings with other men in society and the necessity of mediation through an inherently corrupt language."[2] Senkovskiian subjectivity, in contrast, is strikingly *in*authentic, one that transparently exists only in language and not in nature at all. As for any sort of "secondary

vitiation," its origins in cold hard cash would suggest that the Senkovskiian self starts out so corrupt as to be unable to sink any lower. Still, Greenleaf herself has a very different notion of Romantic subjectivity than the
one she summarizes above, and this chapter will follow her lead to return
Senkovskii to the ranks of another kind of Romantic writer, one who
wields various and even contradictory forms of authorship to deliberately
blur the distinction between real and imaginary, both obscuring the individual writing subject and considerably complicating the interactions of
writer and reader.

While few are as brazen as Senkovskii, there are a great many Romantic
writers who deliberately construct inauthentic, insincere, or fragmentary
selves and in fact, as we will see, despite their reputations even Rousseau
and Wordsworth partake of a certain bent in this direction. This tendency
reaches its peak in the periodical press of the 1830s, as Senkovskii's particular
style of "personal criticism" finds echoes of all kinds in the critical writings
of the day, including in Russia the *Northern Bee*, the *Moscow Observer*, and
the *Telescope*, and in Great Britain *Blackwood's* and *Fraser's*. Those whom we
might call "writers" as opposed to "critics" also participate in this instability of identities, however, and not only in terms of their own ventures into
journalistic literature. Pushkin, for example, engages in a complicated play
of ideas of authorship not just in two key critical articles he publishes in 1831
in the *Telescope*, but also in his contemporaneous but more "literary" work,
The Tales of the Late Ivan Petrovich Belkin. Not only are *The Tales of Belkin*
presented as merely published by "A. P." and actually authored by Ivan Belkin, but the editor's preface also indicates that Belkin in fact collected rather
than composed his five tales.[3]

This image of the writer as a collector or an editor is one familiar to readers of Romanticism, especially those who regularly read prefaces.[4] Different
sorts of editor-types figure most prominently in the critical apparata with
which Romantic writers from Scott and Constant to Pushkin, Gogol, and
Odoevskii tend to surround their works, and wherever they appear a basic
function of these authorial constructs is to collapse the distinction between
literature and literary criticism, putting Senkovskii's Brambeus and Pushkin's Belkin on the same spectrum. In the hands of these personae, both literature and literary criticism become the shaping or presenting of someone
else's words, an approach with various and perhaps contradictory implications. On the one hand, all this borrowing, whether by an author who is

only an editor or by a critic who quotes copiously from the work under re-view, would seem to lend to a text an authenticity and even a documentary-like quality. At the same time, borrowing undermines the authenticity of the text's purported author, who then becomes at best a passer-on of words not his or her own, a pretender, or even a plagiarist.[5]

It is easy and no doubt accurate to attribute the persistent personifica-tion of an unstable writing self to the rise of the so-called literary market-place and an increased distance between writer and reading public that led, in Peter Murphy's words, to a "nearly obsessive interest in the interaction, attachment and slippage between authors (published names) and persons (bodies indicated by names)."[6] That this fascination with author-constructs could also flourish in Russia, where, as discussed in the last chapter, a "real" literary marketplace was more or less lacking, suggests another possibility entwined with the first. In the absence of the apparently necessary socioeco-nomic reality, Russian writers could certainly always imitate the representa-tions of writers and their interactions with readers that they found in the works of their Western contemporaries, and they clearly did. At the same time, both Russian and Western European writers, including Senkovskii, could also draw on another source, not the apparent realities of the British or French literary marketplace but the aesthetic theories of German Ro-manticism, particularly as expressed in the *Athenaeum.*

Attributing the presence of insistent and even obnoxious writer-critic personae to the exigencies of the literary marketplace reminds us of the extent to which commercial concerns impinged on even the most appar-ently disinterested of Romantic writers. My intent in making the presence of a literary marketplace felt is not to sully Romanticism, but rather to emphasize an aspect of the irony that makes Romanticism both deeply plea-surable and more than a little disquieting. Leaving the apparent demands of the literary marketplace behind, however, to associate Romantic writer-critic personae instead with the theory that drives the movement as a whole, serves a still more valuable function. While, as I argued in the last chapter, the actual historical reality of a commercialized high literature will always elude us, the juxtaposition of the later literary periodicals, in particular the *Library for Reading*, with the tenets of the *Frühromantik* makes at least one fact startlingly clear. It becomes evident that the aim of Romanticism was always critical omnipotence, and it is precisely critical omnipotence that the later periodicals, above all the *Library for Reading*, achieve.

The Writer as T.-O., O. O. . . . O!, and Baron Brambeus

In the very first issue of the *Library for Reading* Senkovskii concludes an article in praise of the young poet Kukol'nik with an announcement of the principle of personality on which his literary criticism would rest. Senkovskii describes his criticism as the readings of what he calls his own "critical thermometer," literally a record of what makes him hot and what leaves him cold, and he defends this apparent subjectivity with the somewhat more elegant claim that "[c]riticism in our day has become the picture of the personal feelings of each person—of each person who is endowed by nature with a clear feeling for the ways and means by which the beautiful can produce a complete and pleasant effect on the heart and imagination of a man."[7] Given the extravagant admiration of Kukol'nik's less-than-successful *Torquato Tasso* that fills the preceding pages of the review, this first critical manifesto might seem nothing more than a last-minute defense of an obviously unorthodox view. In a review of Bulgarin's *Mazepa* in the very next issue of the *Library for Reading*, however, Senkovskii states his principle of personality still more emphatically.

Senkovskii prefaces his comments on *Mazepa* with a lengthy defense of the current state of criticism in Russia. "Criticism? . . . You are expecting from me Criticism?" he begins, "Excuse me: we don't have any Criticism! So assert many of us, many of our confrères." Russian literary critics, he continues, have also claimed that in the last year not one book came out, that in Russia it is not worth interesting oneself in literature, that there is no unity in Russian literature, that there is no Russian literary world, that there is no criticism and even that there is no Russian literature at all. Senkovskii dismisses these claims one by one, typically by making recourse to a more material understanding of the matter under consideration. In response to the cry, "We have no literature!" for example, he asks, "then what do the 12,000 titles of Russian books in the catalogue of our book trade mean?"[8] When it comes to the claim of the absence of criticism in Russia, however, Senkovskii shifts gears and argues that the problem is only that the average Russian critic does not understand what criticism is.

As he repeats the mantra, "We have no Criticism!" Senkovskii descends to again typically heavy-handed sarcasm:

> Yes! What can we do, we have no Criticism! . . . In France, in Germany, in England,—that is a different matter: there there is Criticism!—Criticism infal-

lible, like the Pope himself, dispassionate as an inkwell,—Criticism that, on taking up the pen, hides its heart in its pocket, throws its prejudices out the window, orders the lackey to keep its passions outside the gate, elevates its mind to the seventh degree of magnetic clairvoyance, and writes,—writes and judges,—judges and never makes a detour; Criticism, of which you can ask whatever you like and from all typographies, from all desks and drawers . . . it will answer you in one word, like the echo in caves set out in a row, never contradicting itself; in a word, perfect, real Criticism—something in the way of ideal beauty. . . . Where is it? Show us such Criticism in Russia!

They must have such Criticism in Europe, Senkovskii continues; after all, they have wine and oysters. "Germans! Englishmen! Frenchmen!" he cries, "give us Criticism! Ten quarters of bread for Criticism! Fifty poods of hemp for good Criticism! . . . A whole load of raw hides for Criticism, for a part, for a small piece of Criticism!"[9] If Senkovskii's point were not already clear, he then becomes very explicit. No one answers his call, Senkovskii says, because there is no such criticism, and he draws on his truly wide reading to prove his point, referring to *The Edinburgh Review*, *The Quarterly Review*, *The Westminster Review*, and *Journal des Savans* and quoting at length from the *Blätter für literarische Unterhaltung*.

That there is no such thing as infallible, dispassionate, unified criticism, however, is not to say that there is no good criticism but rather that Russian critics do not understand what criticism is, and Senkovskii goes on to give a definition: "True Literary Criticism is a personal gift, an individuality, like true poetic talent." A budding critic has to be born with a great many talents, including strong poetic feeling, a fiery imagination and firm logic, and he must then receive a "proper education," ornament his mind with "diverse information," and, above all, "acquire the skill of judging with his own head" and "thinking his own thoughts." In other words, for Senkovskii a work of criticism is the expression of the individual critic's personality complete with all its quirks, passions, contradictions, and even mistakes, as he says any critic is bound to make some; at least ideally, though, the critic's own personality would be such that even the mistakes themselves were useful. Senkovskii does not make the claim that he himself can offer such ideal criticism, since that would be to claim that he is an "extraordinary person," but he does say that we will find "something in the way of Criticism" in his writing: "You will find," he promises, "my personal opinion, and in my opinion proof of the literary independence of the editors of this journal."[10]

At this point Senkovskii's idea of criticism, as William Mills Todd III points out, sounds not unlike what the writer and historian Nikolai Karamzin had said some two decades earlier.[11] Senkovskii's definition of criticism as personality and personal opinion takes an odd turn, however, when we reach the end of his two articles and find that they are not signed "O. I. Senkovskii." The review of *Torquato Tasso* is signed instead "T.-O.," initials that at least some of Senkovskii's readers would recognize as belonging to Tiutiun'dzhiu-Oglu, a persona adopted by Senkovskii for one of his most successful and scandalous scholarly works, the "Letter of Tiutiun'dzhiu-Oglu-Mustafa-Aga, actual Turkish philosopher, to one of the publishers of the *Northern Bee*" (1827), while the review of *Mazepa* appears over the mysterious "O. O. . . . O!" That Senkovskii would base his critical authority on his own personality while at the same time undermining the notion of his own personality with the use of pseudonyms is of course very funny. More important, it also suggests that Senkovskii's criticism operates on the principle of the simulacrum as Jean Baudrillard defines it.

Baudrillard's essay "Simulacra and Simulations" (1981) is an attack on his more or less current phase of capitalism that, according to Baudrillard, has disrupted an originally more "natural" relationship between signified and signifier, reality and representation. In fact, Baudrillard claims, what capitalism has done is to erase the difference between the two, as the "age of simulation . . . substitut[es] signs of the real for the real itself."[12] In the current absence of the real, Baudrillard argues, this endless chain of signifiers is marked by "a proliferation of myths of origin and signs of reality . . . of second-hand truth, objectivity and authenticity" and by an "escalation of the true, of the lived experience"; authenticity in the simulacrum can only be mythical because the simulacrum is a self-sufficient sign, a sign that exists without any referent.[13] The post-Modernist disease of simulation that Baudrillard diagnoses with such horror, however, is also strikingly anticipated by Senkovskii's critical practice. Just like Baudrillard's simulacrum, Senkovskii's criticism pretends to an authority and an authenticity that its signs of authorship undermine, ultimately blurring the distinction between the real and the fictional. After all, "my personal opinion" means something quite different when we understand that the "my" and the "personal" refer not to a person (Senkovskii) but to a persona (T.-O. or O. O. . . . O!), or it may be that it no longer means anything at all.

What Senkovskii promises in these two articles is what we get in the

Library for Reading, criticism that is filled with "personality" in almost every sense of the word: a definite tone is established, strong opinions are expressed, veiled personal attacks are made, and personae of the most colorful sort are created. The strong presence of personae, however, guarantees that the one personality that would seem to be largely missing is the one actually attached to a body, Senkovskii's own, and if this absence is already a little disturbing, what is still worse is that while playing with a set of signs with no clear "real world" referents, Senkovskii at the same time insists on the importance of making those associations in the most concrete sense, so that the proof that Russian literature exists lies in the 12,000 titles listed in the catalogue of the book trade. As T.-O. and O. O. . . . O!'s declaration of principles would seem to announce, it is this contradictory and highly problematic twofold practice that becomes the trademark of literary criticism in the *Library for Reading*, especially when signed by the infamous Baron Brambeus.

Although Brambeus is the quintessential personality of the *Library for Reading*, he, like Tiutiun'dzhiu-Oglu, actually predates the journal's founding and even Senkovskii's turn to literary criticism. A king in Tiutiun'dzhiu-Oglu's "Letter" and in Senkovskii's favorite Turkish folktale, the "Tale of Frantsyl the Venetian," Brambeus reappeared as a Baron and as the author of a number of works in Smirdin's anthology *Housewarming* (1833) and only then became the leading literary critic of the *Library for Reading*. Brambeus's works from the very beginning are marked by a chatty, intimate tone and a great deal of apparently personal detail. As a general rule Brambeus at least purports to share the facts of his own life in a sort of literary criticism-as-autobiography; for example, in his 1834 attack on *l'école frénétique*, "Brambeus and the Young Literature."

This article begins with an account of its own origin as the result of an apparently imaginary postprandial conversation. While dozing after dinner Brambeus hears his friends condemn him and especially what they see as his hypocritical stance against the new French writing, only to wake with a start and realize that it was all a dream.[14] Even if imaginary, however, and it is not entirely clear that it is, the accusation still bothers Brambeus, and while he claims to know that his friends "in reality" said no such thing, he feels the need to defend himself against "even those reproofs that are cast at [him] in his dreams by their hazy phantoms, for [he] esteem[s] not only them, but also their shades, images, phantoms,—all that reminds [him] of their presence in the world," and accordingly he writes the article that follows.[15] Having thus prefaced his comments on the new French writing with the description of a private dinner party and the presumably even more private world of his dreams, Brambeus then goes on in the main part of his piece to still more intimate revelations: he explains the difficulties faced by the average reader in resisting the onslaughts of the new French literature by showing their effects on his wife, the Baronessa.

The Baron casts his Baronessa as an obvious fiction, nothing but a device created midway through his article to illustrate his point. Still, with Brambeus as with O. O. . . . O! there is a constant slippage between abstract and concrete. The Baronessa rather unexpectedly arises from Brambeus's argument that what the new French writing threatens is what he claims to be the founding principle of contemporary European literature, the idea of Christian marriage. Once she has appeared on the scene, however, the Baronessa promptly turns out to have a greater degree of materiality than we might expect. "Say that I'm fat," says the Baron, "and that my Baronessa, as luck would have it, is not overly thin: together we form a broad and fleshy mass of humanity that, in the event of need, can offer to any revolutions a decent expanse of resistance." Where in the beginning of the article presumably real friends were revealed to be phantoms, with the creation of the Baronessa the phantom of the reading public is made more real and then ever more material, first as a sturdy moral defense is represented by a large expanse of flesh and then as Brambeus forms his marriage into a castle keep, the better to defend it against the onslaughts of the crafty new French literature. Just before the article ends the garrison of the castle mutinies and Brambeus is forced into one last embarrassing personal revelation: in the face of Literature's merciless attack, all he can do is mortgage his estate and use the proceeds to carry "one ardent lady reader" off to Karlsbad.[16]

For a literary figure without a body the Baronessa proves remarkably solid, and the same might be said of the Baron who bases the "truth" of his literary criticism on what he presents as the facts of his own life. In a sort of Senkovskiian tautology, the life and the literary criticism stand as guarantors of each other's authenticity while in fact being one and the same, and accordingly Brambeus gains a kind of self-sufficiency. It is this circular existence that gives rise to the comical oscillation between metaphor and its realization in "Brambeus and the Young Literature" and, beyond this one article, to a further proliferation of personae, for once Brambeus has constituted himself as a free-floating sign he allows for an endlessly unfolding confusion of referents.

As in O. O. . . . O!'s review of *Mazepa* and Brambeus's attack on the new French writing, Senkovskii's tendency is always to ground critical authority in what is more or less obviously a simulation of personality and of authentic life experience, a move that undermines the relationship of signifier to signified on which literary practices such as literary criticism would seem to depend. To accept the truth of the criticism is to accept the reality of the personae, which in fact is to elide any sort of distinctions between fiction and reality. But such distinctions must be made, above all by Senkovskii himself as he actually makes his living at this writing; whether he signs his articles O. O. . . . O!, Baron Brambeus, or even Dr. Karl von Bitterwasser, the check must be written to him, O. I. Senkovskii. The situation that Senkovskii has thus created for himself is contradictory and even alarming, but despite the impression given by his many detractors then and now, it is far from unique. As it happens, complicated and even problematic forms of authorship were in fact widely practiced in Romanticism, both in the critical works that often attacked Senkovskii's own writing and in the literature that Senkovskii as critic reviewed.

The Writer as Editor

Romanticism offers a dizzying array of directions in which signs of authorship might point. There are what we might call celebrity authors, for example Byron and Constant, whose conflation of author and hero turns the text into a titillating glimpse of the writer's own life; anonymous authors, above all in the case of the "Author of *Waverley*," a.k.a. the Great Unknown; and fascinating and messy collaborative enterprises, not just in the periodicals from the *Athenaeum* on, but also in the famous example of Wordsworth and Coleridge's joint production of the *Lyrical Ballads* (1798). Most notably for our purposes, in Romanticism we also quite frequently observe the phenomenon of colorful authorial personae who are often only very tenuously connected to actual physical bodies in the world and even to the texts that may or may not bear their names.

A great number of Romantic works come with a persona who may present his name as that of the author but nonetheless goes on to describe himself not as the writer of the text but as someone responsible for the text in a more indirect fashion. In the case of Pushkin's *Tales of Belkin* (1831) mentioned earlier, the title itself offered Belkin as author, while "A. P." styled himself only as the publisher. "A. P." even goes so far as to offer evidence for Belkin's reality in a preface that includes a letter from an alleged neighbor detailing something of the author's life and his interest in literature. Interestingly enough, however, in a footnote "A. P." also reveals that the five stories that make up the collection are not actually of Belkin's own making, a fact that would seem to considerably diminish the value of the information contained in the letter. Readers interested in attaching the text to a person might rightfully want to know more details not of Belkin's life, but of the four sources whom Belkin is said to have identified in the margins of his manuscript only by initials and rank: A.G.N., a titular councilor; Colonel I.L.P.; B. V., a steward; and the maiden lady K.I.T.

Critics have produced a great deal of work on the *Tales of Belkin* as allegories of reading, and we will turn to these interpretations in the next chapter. If the prefatory material to the *Tales* helps figure different ways of reading, however, it also serves to undermine the integrity and even the authority of the author, and we find the same sort of subversion at work in two other well-known collections of stories that appeared at nearly the same time, first Gogol's *Evenings on a Farm Near Dikan'ka* (1831) and then Prince V. F. Odoevskii's *Motley Tales* (1833). Gogol published his *Evenings* under the auspices of the Ukrainian beekeeper Rudyi Pan'ko, and Odoevskii published his *Motley Tales* as the work of Irinei Modestovich Gomozeiko, Master of Philosophy and Member of Various Scholarly Societies. While there are significant differences between the personalities and their presentation, what is remarkable is how with Pan'ko and Gomozeiko as with Belkin, the initial personae lend themselves to ever more layers of narration.[17]

In his preliminary comments Rudyi Pan'ko lists the various storytellers from whom he gathered his tales, including an unnamed young man and the deacon Foma Grigor'evich. While readers are left to guess which stories are by the young man, the deacon's stories are identified as such at the start of each, and the penultimate story in the collection, "Ivan Fedorovich Shpon'ka and His Auntie," begins with a brief note from Pan'ko describing its teller, Stepan Ivanovich Kurochka, and explaining why in its present form the story lacks an ending. *Motley Tales* offers at the beginning three separate frames, first a note "From the Publisher" explaining that it was only

Gomozeiko's obvious and great financial need that persuaded the publisher to present these stories to the public. We then come to the "Writer's Foreword" where Gomozeiko describes himself and the excessive shyness in society that has driven him to reach out to others through the medium of print. Finally the first story, "The Retort," is a first-person account of how the narrator, presumably Gomozeiko, found himself turned into a story along with a crowd of other unfortunates. Magically restored to his original human shape, the narrator escaped with various of his colleagues stuck in his pocket still in story form, and it is these stories that he now presents to his reader.

Both Gogol and Odoevskii clearly sensed the parallels between their proliferating personae and Pushkin's, as they even suggested to Pushkin in 1833 that Belkin, Pan'ko, and Gomozeiko jointly publish an almanac that they proposed calling *The Three-in-One*. As critics have since noted, the particular forms of authorship all three writers employed also owed a great deal not just to Pushkin but through Pushkin to Sir Walter Scott, the great publishing phenomenon of the early nineteenth century who famously published the *Waverley* novels first anonymously and then along with a whole host of related personae, including Jedediah Cleishbotham, Lawrence Templeton, Dr. Dryasdust, Capt. Clutterbuck, and Chrystal Croftangry.

Sir Walter Scott began as a Scottish lawyer and antiquarian, and he first achieved critical acclaim and even greater commercial success with his narrative poems, beginning with "The Lay of the Last Minstrel" in 1805. For most of the next decade the poetry business proved quite profitable, and Scott was enabled to buy his estate at Abbotsford and embark on a series of ambitious and seemingly endless renovations. Just as Byron was beginning to eclipse his success as a poet, however, Scott changed genres and names in 1814 and published *Waverley* anonymously, becoming an international sensation as the Great Unknown.

The *Waverley* novels eventually came to include twenty-two different works, and as time went on the novels came with an ever-more elaborate critical apparatus attached, including not just footnotes but also communications back and forth from various imaginary persons. This critical apparatus reached its final form starting in 1829 when, faced with bankruptcy, Scott was able to recoup some of his losses by revealing his identity and republishing all twenty-two novels under his own name in a special edition with additional introductions and notes written by himself. Readers who skip over the commentaries, and many do, lose an essential aspect of Scott's work: its irony. In their quasi-documentary status, the prefaces and notes, like the genre of the historical novel itself, undercut Scott's plots as they elide the distinctions between history and poetry. Scott's communities of authors also undermine Scott's own authority as author, most strikingly in the note to the reader that prefaces *The Heart of Midlothian* (1818).[18]

The Heart of Midlothian is particularly noteworthy because of its influence in Russia and because it was in fact published not "by the Author of *Waverley*" but as the second part of a series called "Tales of My Landlord" purportedly edited by one Jedediah Cleishbotham.[19] Scott published the first novels in this series in 1816 apparently out of a desire to tease his readers yet again and see if they would recognize the Author of *Waverley* in Jedediah Cleishbotham, which many of them promptly did, and much of Cleishbotham's note prefacing this, the second series of "Tales of My Landlord," is devoted to protesting his own entirely separate existence. Cleishbotham then adds that those who have accused him of counterfeiting his own existence have gone still further, for, as he says, "[t]hese cavillers have not only doubted mine [sic] identity, although thus plainly proved, but they have impeached my veracity and the authenticity of my historical narratives!"

The "Tales of My Landlord" are all set in Scotland since the union with England and so deal with still touchy issues of religious civil war, and here Cleishbotham makes his ultimate claim for the objective truth of his work. Where one side has accused him of leaning too far toward the cavaliers and the other of supporting the Cameronians, Cleishbotham is sure of his complete impartiality: "For, O ye powers of logic! when the Prelatists and Presbyterians of old times went together by the ears in this unlucky country, my ancestor (venerated be his memory!) was one of the people called Quakers, and suffered severe handling from either side, even to the extenuation of his purse and the incarceration of his person."[20] In a note he added to the 1830 edition, Scott reveals Cleishbotham's claim to objectivity to be his own as Scott explains that he really did have a Quaker ancestor. Even this "real" ancestor, though, cannot guarantee the truth of Cleishbotham's work both because Cleishbotham, as he himself insists, is in fact not Scott, and because Cleishbotham is not even the author of the "Tales of My Landlord."

The "Tales of My Landlord" are rather purportedly written by one Peter Pattieson and only published by Cleishbotham, and even Pattieson himself in *The Heart of Midlothian* claims not to be a writer but only the recorder of tales heard one evening from three men, all of whom had actually spent time in and around the heart of Midlothian, a.k.a. the Edinburgh jail. In other words, just as in O. O. . . . O!'s claim of critical independence or in Brambeus's explanation of the dangers of the latest French writing, as in the case of Belkin and his co-authors or Pan'ko and his, these layers of personae serve to create an entirely spurious authenticity based on entirely fictional personalities.[21] Cleishbotham cannot ground the truth of his narrative in his Quaker ancestor and in Peter Pattieson's having taken the tales right from the source both because the two explanations are mutually exclusive and because neither the Quaker ancestor nor Peter Pattieson, nor the three men at the inn nor even Cleishbotham actually exist, and no one thinks that they do.

While Scott's practice of multilayered and contradictory signs of author-ship was extremely influential, especially in Russia, it was nonetheless not his invention either. The idea of the author as a kind of editor or collector of someone else's words is fundamental to the epistolary novels that were so popular at the end of the eighteenth century, for example, and as Robert Darnton suggests in his "Readers Respond to Rousseau: The Fabrication of Romantic Sensitivity," the notion is equally problematic there. Darnton's point in this piece is to show how real readers, and one real reader in partic-ular, Jean Ranson, a merchant from La Rochelle, sought to connect through Rousseau's extraordinarily successful novel in letters, *Julie* (1761), to the man whom Ranson never met but nonetheless always referred to in his letters as "*l'Ami* Jean-Jacques." While Darnton focuses on real readers in search of a real Rousseau, however, he also carefully outlines the extent to which Rous-seau misrepresents his own relationship to the text.

Rousseau's name appeared on the cover of *Julie*, and in a second preface attached to the second edition of the novel the author makes much of this fact. When his imaginary interlocutor "N." suggests that "R." would do better to disclaim any responsibility for *Julie*, R. proudly answers that he will not hesitate to claim the book as his own:

R. Own it, Monsieur? Does an honorable man hide when he addresses the Public? Does he dare to print what he would not dare to acknowledge? I am the Editor of this book, and I shall name myself as Editor.
N. You will name yourself? You?
R. Myself.
N. What! You will put your name on it?

R. Yes, Monsieur.
N. Your real name? *Jean Jacques Rousseau,* in full?
R. *Jean Jacques Rousseau* in full.[22]

R.'s proud assertion "*Jean Jacques Rousseau* in full" would seemingly establish a direct connection between Jean Jacques Rousseau the man and *Julie* the book so that, as Darnton puts it, "author and reader [might triumph] together over the artifice of literary communication."[23] The unmediated communion of writer and reader nonetheless eludes us, not just because the conversation between N. and R. is itself an obvious example of the "artifice of literary communication," but because R.'s open claim of responsibility as editor of these letters obscures the fact that he is really their author.

When Rousseau in *Julie,* then, in Darnton's words, "broke down the barriers separating writer from reader," he paradoxically did so by creating other sorts of obstacles, including first an "editor" who is both a literary construction and something of a liar.[24] Whereas Scott's readers tend to skip his prefaces, Rousseau's readers in Darnton's account are truly remarkable for their determination to understand the words of his novel as those of real people and above all of a real writer, and we find something of the same desire to pierce through layers of personae in the response to two last examples of Romantic texts framed by the author as editor and/or collector, Constant's *Adolphe* (1815) and Lermontov's *A Hero of Our Time* (1841).

It is an odd fact that even before its publication *Adolphe* was read as some kind of authentic rendering of Constant's own romantic entanglements, perhaps with Mme. de Staël or with Anna Lindsay or with someone else, odd because Constant seemingly insulates himself from his hero by means of an editor, his correspondent, and the tale of a found document, and because Adolphe himself, eventual first-person narrator though he may be, is so strikingly insincere and inauthentic. In our current climate of post-Modernism, however, readers have begun to focus instead on the ways in which Constant's frame texts problematize the novel's confessional aspect. As Martha Noel Evans argues, where a confession would seem to demand a judgment, Constant's frame texts, including an exchange of letters between the purported "editor" and an unnamed "friend," "provide us with such inconsistent attitudes toward the hero and his story that the possibility of unambiguous identification with any of these postures, including the author's, seems impossible."[25]

Lermontov, with evident knowledge of *Adolphe,* uses a similar layering of texts to create much the same sort of ambivalence in *A Hero of Our Time.*[26]

Again the reader is tempted to associate Lermontov's hero with his creator, although in an attack on his own supposedly unsophisticated readers, the author of *A Hero of Our Time* appends to his text an ironic preface that reinforces the identity of writer and hero only by emphatically and insultingly rejecting it. Readers have also long noted the dizzying set of resemblances in the chapter "Princess Mary," wherein Grushnitskii as a parody of the hero Pechorin in turn reflects the real Lermontov, whose death in a duel in the Caucasus at the tender age of twenty-six Grushnitskii's own tragic end foreshadows. The distance between the writer and his eventual first-person narrator is nonetheless marked by a frame narrator who first recounts a story about Pechorin as told to him by a chance travel companion, Maksim Maksimich, then tells of his own eyewitness encounter with Pechorin, and finally passes on to us three selections from Pechorin's diaries. As many commentators have noted, this movement from talking about the hero to encountering him and finally to the hero's own words brings us ever closer to the "real" Pechorin. As Pechorin's diary reveals our hero to be a contradictory, inconsistent, and even untrustworthy narrator of his own thoughts, however, it is also true that the "real" Pechorin never entirely coincides with himself, an ironic absence that is emphasized by Lermontov's *Adolphe*-like layering of storytellers.[27]

The Writer as Plagiarist

A persistent figuring of the Romantic writer is in itself an interesting phenomenon, one we might associate with the mulling over of what it might mean to be a writer in the new conditions of a literary marketplace. What is especially significant, however, is that these representations cast the writer not as an actual writer but as the shaper or presenter of someone else's words. There is a certain slipperiness or even dishonesty attached to the idea of appropriating another's story, whether that appropriation is acknowledged or not, and this shaper or presenter may actually be the usurper of someone else's words. Lermontov's frame narrator suggests the problem when he prefaces his excerpts from Pechorin's diary with the excuse: "Not long ago I heard that Pechorin had died on his way back from Persia. I was delighted, since it means that I can print his notes, and I readily take this opportunity of putting my own name to somebody else's work. I only hope that the reader won't blame me for this innocent deception."[28] In the face of the increasing emphasis put on the notion of literary property by the struggle detailed in the last chapter for the establishment of copyright law, borrowing another's words may actually look less "innocent" and more like plagiarism, and in fact that accusation was frequently made.

Senkovskii was notorious for his tendency to alter submissions to the *Library for Reading* without permission, and his free-and-easy way with others' words on at least one occasion descended to what would seem to be actual plagiarism. A number of critics at the time noted that a story Senkovskii published in *Housewarming* (1833) as Brambeus, "Satan's Great Ball," looked suspiciously like Balzac's "The Devil's Comedy"; and in an article in the *Moscow Observer* the somewhat mysterious N. P—shch—v openly accused Brambeus of stealing from Balzac, backing up his charge with a fairly devastating point-by-point comparison of passages taken from the two authors. While Senkovskii's flexible standards might seem particularly unattractive, once again he was far from alone in either his relatively free appropriation of others' texts as editor or even in his actual plagiarism, particularly in the more advanced literary culture of Great Britain.

The most famous example of Romantic plagiarism is of course Coleridge, who was first accused of the act immediately following his death in 1834.[29] With the publication of Norman Fruman's magisterial *Coleridge, the Damaged Archangel* (1971), the list of Coleridge's at best questionable publications has grown to include any number of his shorter poems as well as large chunks of *The Watchman* (1796), the *Biographia Literaria* (1817), the *Philosophical Lectures* (1818–19), his Shakespearean criticism, and his posthumously published *Hints Towards the Formation of a More Comprehensive Theory of Life* (1848). Coleridge's original accuser was Thomas De Quincey, who has himself been revealed to be a plagiarist by later critics, and Coleridge, too, seems to have complemented his compulsive borrowing with the regular leveling of the accusation of plagiarism against any number of other writers, usually falsely.[30] He did seem to have some grounds in protesting what he saw as Sir Walter Scott's appropriation in "The Lay of the Last Minstrel" (1805) of his own at the time unpublished "Christabel," as at any rate Scott was willing to cheerfully acknowledge Coleridge's influence in a note he appended to the 1830 edition.[31] The literary plagiarist most thoroughly exposed by the 1830s, however, was Laurence Sterne, who had been shown as early as 1791 to have taken from other writers any number of passages offered as his own in *Tristram Shandy*, most amusingly the comments on plagiarism that he lifted from Burton's *Anatomy of Melancholy*.[32]

While plagiarism in a literary world marked by the institution of copyright might seem an obvious crime, in fact plagiarism is especially problematic only because it is not altogether different from the normal conditions of Romantic authorship, as again the example of Coleridge now together with his alter ego Wordsworth would suggest. It is always Wordsworth who is juxtaposed with Coleridge as the "real" poet who emerged from their poetic and personal collaboration with his identity as a writer fully formed, while Coleridge was left a mere shadow, a writer whose life in letters, as his own *Biographia Literaria* depicts it, was validated only by the success of his friend. In a fascinating article on the respective fates of Wordsworth's poem "Michael" and Coleridge's "Christabel," however, Susan Eilenberg questions not only the victimization of Coleridge, but also the integrity of the being apparently thus created, namely Wordsworth.

The history of the *Lyrical Ballads* is a complicated one. The first edition published anonymously in 1798 and consisting of nineteen poems by Wordsworth and four by Coleridge was not a great success, and in December of 1799 Wordsworth expressed to Coleridge his "thankfulness that the first edition of *Lyrical Ballads* did not have his name attached to it, instructing [him] to 'take no pains to contradict the story that the *Lyrical Ballads* are entirely yours. Such a rumour is the best thing that can befall them.'"[33] At the same time Wordsworth seems to have attributed the book's lack of success largely, if not entirely, to Coleridge's part in it, and he was soon interested in publishing a second edition of the work that, while still marked by the significant help of his friend, would nonetheless be more unambiguously Wordsworthian.

The first volume of the new *Lyrical Ballads* contained all of the 1798 version with only a few changes, most notably to "The Ancient Mariner." Although Wordsworth had initially intended to drop the poem from the collection entirely, he in the end asked Coleridge only to eliminate some of the "old words" he particularly disliked, then appended a "Note" distancing himself from the work of his unnamed "Friend," and finally moved the poem from first to twenty-third place. At Coleridge's urging, Wordsworth also added the famous preface. The second volume was to contain new poems written by Wordsworth in Germany and also Coleridge's "Christabel," but at nearly the last minute "Christabel" was dropped, perhaps because, as Wordsworth wrote to his sister Dorothy, "I found that the Style of this Poem was so discordant from my own that it could not be printed along with my poems with any propriety."[34] Wordsworth then wrote "Michael" to take the place of "Christabel," in hopes, as he wrote his new publisher, Longman, that the new poem would be "highly serviceable to the Sale."[35] While Wordsworth failed to convince his publisher to accept a new title, he did with some difficulty prevail on Longman to put his own name on the cover, and in January 1801 the two volumes, which still included five pieces by Coleridge, appeared as "Lyrical Ballads, with *Other Poems. In Two Volumes. By W. Wordsworth.*"

It may seem evident that this creation of "W. Wordsworth" as the sole author of the 1800 *Lyrical Ballads* comes largely at Coleridge's expense, and it is certainly in the wake of the *Lyrical Ballads* that Coleridge's genius seems to fade. The sort of instability of writerly identity that the very project of collective creation sets into motion is not easily arrested, however, and in her article Eilenberg focuses on the last-minute substitution of "Michael" for "Christabel" to paint a very different picture of the two poets' interaction. Eilenberg points out the many moral, thematic, and structural parallels between the two poems, above the theme of (dis)possession, by demons in "Christabel" and of fields in "Michael," and she connects this theme to the idea of literary property and to Wordsworth's notion quoted above that the publication of "Christabel" together with his own poems would offer an offense against "propriety."

Eilenberg's point is not that Wordsworth lifted a great deal from the poem he sought to exclude, although that no doubt is true. More important, she also suggests the extent to which "Christabel" insinuated itself into the poem written to replace it. As Scott, too, would later find, there is something about "Christabel" that destabilizes the whole notion of originality, and in the case of "Michael," Eilenberg argues, "Wordsworth's poem can save the proprieties that "Christabel" menaces only through an act of literary violence that, paradoxically, mimics the objectionable impropriety of its victim." In Eilenberg's account both poems tell a tale of ventriloquism, as Coleridge's Geraldine casts her voice into Christabel and Wordsworth's Poet appropriates the story of Michael, and so both tell the story of the *Lyrical Ballads.* As Eilenberg concludes:

> "Michael" acts as both usurper and usurped, taking on—like "Christabel"—
> the features of what it undertakes to exorcize, its poetic purity corrupted by the
> object of its cathartic intentions. Who is to say whether Coleridge fell victim

to Wordsworth's story or Wordsworth to Coleridge's? Who even will insist it is necessary to apportion blame? The two poems, each one a Geraldine to the other's Christabel, take mutual possession of one another, undermining the very notion of exclusive poetic property.[36]

I would only add that while "Michael," like "Christabel," undermines the very notion of exclusive poetic property, still it was written to create just that, as part of an attempt to make the *Lyrical Ballads* more Wordsworthian and Wordsworth more saleable, and that Wordsworth (if we can call him that) achieved with "Michael" the latter seemingly at the expense of the former may not be coincidental. It would seem instead from the examples of often highly commercially successful books given above that what sold in Romanticism was a writer whose "originality" lay in his apparent ability to appropriate other people's stories, whether we are speaking of Sterne and Coleridge or of Scott, Rousseau, and Constant. In this sense Russian literature with its wholesale borrowing from the West becomes the most Romantic of all literatures, above all in that quintessentially Russian, Romantic, and intertextual text, Pushkin's *Eugene Onegin.* In an apparent paradox *Eugene Onegin* is brilliantly original precisely because it is a pastiche of references to other texts and other writers, and openly, insistently so, as Pushkin teases us with complicated layers of imitation in every aspect of his text, from the epigraphs to the characters' well-detailed reading habits to Tatiana's realization that Onegin may be nothing more than, in the narrator's words, "A Muscovite in Harold's cloak."

The Writer as Critic

If a writer who casts himself as an editor or collector of someone else's words may suggest, or actually be, a plagiarist, there is another, perhaps more palatable option: he may instead be a critic. In Friedrich Schlegel's *Dialogue on Poetry* published in the *Athenaeum* in 1800, his Antonio expresses the need for a theory of the novel that would itself be a novel, a formulation that would exactly describe all the literary works discussed above. Central to these works' explicit theorization of their own interpretation is this writerly persona whose words and recorded deeds provide a map for our own reading, although a map that, as Martha Noel Evans notes regarding *Adolphe,* may or may not actually lead us to an actual destination. The critic as he appears in the literary periodical of the 1830s performs exactly the same function, as he too collects or arranges another's words; for example, in the form of a review in which his words direct our reading of another text made present by often extensive quotations. This framing then lends itself to the same slipperiness of writerly identity, an insincerity that is emphasized by the literary critic's pointed rendering of his own "personal" opinion as that of another or even of others, not just in the *Library for Reading* but also in other popular periodicals of the day, most notably *Blackwood's Edinburgh Review* (1817–) and its later offshoot *Fraser's* (1830–).

As always, any resemblance between Senkovskii and his Western European counterparts quite likely derives from what may seem the simple fact of imitation, and the fact that Senkovskii offered actual excerpts from *Blackwood's* in the *Library for Reading* makes his familiarity with at least that journal abundantly clear.[37] As we have seen, however, imitation is not a simple fact, and certainly not in the context of *Blackwood's*. *Blackwood's* eventually became a staple of the Victorian literary establishment, an eminently conservative journal that lasted well into the 1890s. It began, however, in Peter Murphy's words, as "a kind of extended language-experiment . . . conducted by a group of highly unstable, relatively mean-spirited but also brilliant and entertaining young men."[38]

At the head of this group were John Wilson and John Lockhart, the latter later Scott's son-in-law and official biographer, but neither called himself the journal's editor, leaving that role to a created persona, Christopher North. North contributed his own pieces to the journal and he also served as author and host of the *Noctes Ambrosianae*, a series of largely imaginary conversations where various of the regular contributors to the journal met to discuss literary issues usually over dinner at the real Ambrose's tavern.[39] The various contributors here, as in their own writings, tended to appear under regular pseudonyms, so "the Ettrick Shepherd," for example, referred to James Hogg and "Ensign Odoherty" to William Maginn, later the editor of *Fraser's*.[40] North, however, was a different sort of persona for, unlike his collaborators, he himself corresponded to no one person and so, according to Murphy, proved especially trying to his contemporaries.

North was no one and so, in a sense, could not be called to account. As Murphy writes, "criticism of him flies off into some no-man's land of discourse, the verbal equivalent of a dead-letter office."[41] This sort of game is just what Senkovskii loved to play, only in reverse, for where the fictional

North corresponded to no one real person, Senkovskii corresponded to no one persona. In a brief 1835 review of a recent translation of Allan Cunningham's *Life of Sir Walter Scott* (1833), for example, Senkovskii devoted all his attention to the criticism directed against Baron Brambeus in the translator's preface. The translator, known only as "Miss D.," whom Senkovskii imagines as "one of those young, pink, lovely creatures . . . with a pure brow, a burning heart, a languid blue eye, a smile and a sigh on her lips . . . and, most important, a recent graduate of boarding school," has accused Brambeus of attacking Sir Walter Scott. "O, hundred times fortunate Brambeus!" writes Senkovskii: "This sudden enmity seems to us very suspicious. You'll see—we'll answer with our heads if it doesn't end in the most romantic passion, and if before next Shrove-tide we don't hear—'Baron Brambeus, deadly enemy of Walter Scott, is marrying Miss ***, ardent defender of that same Walter Scott.'"

The problem is, Senkovskii explains, that Miss D. can only be referring to the criticism of Scott contained in the review of *Mazepa* that, as we already know, is signed not "Brambeus" but "O. O. . . . O!," and so he is able to dismiss her criticism entirely. As if no one could or should confuse Brambeus and O. O. . . . O!, Senkovskii assures us that Miss D. would be incapable of making such a gross mistake without some sort of ulterior motive, and he knows what that motive is: "Women always begin wars this way when they want to be conquered."[42]

Despite precisely this slippery kind of impersonality, however, what North was most often criticized for was in fact a focus on personalities. North was well known for the attention paid to the personalities of the authors reviewed in *Blackwood's*, as Odoherty explains in 1822 in the first of the *Noctes*. In response to the question, "Do you disapprove of personality?" Odoherty answers: "No, no. I am not quite fool enough to sport that; least of all to you. In reviewing, in particular, what can be done without personality? Nothing, nothing. What are books that don't express the personal characters of their authors; and who can review books, without reviewing those that wrote them?"[43] What this focus on personality meant in practice were vicious personal attacks, most notably on Keats and the Cockney School, a tendency that Christopher North mockingly defended in the October 1820 issue when he wrote:

[I will] take notice of one supposed feature of our character which our enemies represent as excessively unbecoming, but of which our friends entirely deny the existence—we mean, our PERSONALITY. We do not surely intend, in one sense, to deny personality as an attribute of ours: we have a personal existence, and our name is North. But our enemies assert that our style of writing is *personal,* and that we make too free with people's names and characters—nay, some people have gone the length of saying we are impertinent—slanderous.[44]

North denies one type of personality while acknowledging another, that is, his own, and indeed the very vehicle of the *Noctes* suggests the importance of the critic's personality for the criticism of *Blackwood's.* As J. H. Alexander writes, "the Ambrosians saw criticism not as a formal activity detached from the personality and everyday life of the critic, but rather springing directly from it."[45]

If North freely dispenses with the appurtenances of personality, then, he also depends on them, not only for his authors whom he attacked in personal terms but even for himself, an entirely contradictory stance that gave rise to some very odd situations. Among them most notable is the tragicomic duel that forms the focus of Murphy's article "Impersonation and Romantic Authorship in Britain." In 1820–21, apparently enraged by Christopher North's assertion of personality quoted above, John Scott, the editor of another London magazine and no relation to Sir Walter, wrote two articles essentially accusing *Blackwood's* of committing fraud. While one might argue that Scott simply lacked a sense of humor, what is truly amazing is Lockhart's response: he challenged Scott to a duel. Lengthy negotiations ensued in which Scott demanded that Lockhart deny being an editor of *Blackwood's,* which Lockhart refused to do. After a long stalemate the duel finally was fought and Scott was killed, but not by Lockhart. After Lockhart had given up on the whole affair, his friend James Christie took up his cause and killed Scott in his place.

At given moments, then, North and Lockhart behind him are ready to defend the strict association of fictional personalities with physical bodies that their criticism in other respects seeks to subvert, and Senkovskii was ready to do the same; for example, in an attack he made on Pushkin. Unlike Christopher North, Senkovskii was actually forbidden by the Tsarist regime to engage in personal attacks, and so his anger and anxiety at Pushkin's plans beginning in 1835 to launch the *Contemporary* had to find a more indirect outlet. Fortunately for Senkovskii, Pushkin made a misstep in 1836 when he unwisely lent his name in an effort to help a struggling friend, so that the friend's rather poor translation of one of Wieland's verse narratives, *Vastola, or the Heart's Wishes,* appeared as "Published by A. Push-kin." The *Tales of Belkin* had been "published" by Pushkin a mere two years earlier. With great glee and more than a little hypocrisy, Senkovskii now chose to understand *Vastola* as "published" in the same way, explaining in his review that while he was astonished at the poor quality of the verse, he was nonetheless utterly unable to believe that Pushkin would so deceive the reading public as to lend his name to someone in the hope of increasing sales. This affair, too, almost ended in a duel, although again not between Pushkin and Senkovskii but between Pushkin and a Senkovskii surrogate, a young man so unfortunate as to mention Senkovskii's article to Pushkin at a party.[46]

Like Senkovskii, the *Blackwood's* people attach and detach signifiers from signifieds at will, and we play along only at our own risk; as Murphy writes, "[i]ntimacy is held out as the basis of *Blackwood's* games, but intimacy always eludes the reader, and is destroyed by the games themselves."[47] The combination of personality and personae ensures that we never really know who these critics are, but then a confusion of identities is precisely the intent of a Romantic authorship whereby authors fail to correspond either to real writers or to the texts for which they front. Figures like Cleishbotham and Belkin are certainly less mean-spirited than North and Brambeus, but their function is essentially the same, and the important question is then why Romanticism apparently so needs this function to be performed.

It might be, as Murphy argues, that this peculiar troping of the writer-critic reflects an emerging literary marketplace, that is, mimics a sort of reality that is all the more strongly felt in the necessarily more commercially oriented periodicals. Certainly Baudrillard claims that the urge to simulate is driven by the demands of capitalism, as: "it was capital which was the first to feed throughout its history on the destruction of every referential, of every human goal, which shattered every ideal distinction between true and false, good and evil, in order to establish a radical law of equivalence and exchange, the iron law of its power."[48]

While Baudrillard's darkly ominous reference is largely to his own era of late capitalism, the Romantic period might do, as the literary marketplace creates a space between reader and writer that is then bridged by the chameleonlike figure of the writer as editor, plagiarist, and/or critic.[49] We might also complicate this argument, as Kevin McLaughlin does in his *Writing in Parts: Imitation and Exchange in Nineteenth Century Literature* (1995), by arguing that the Romantic obsession with the figure of the writer-critic not only reflects, but also responds to the changing conditions of writing by offering a homeopathic remedy to the commercially tainted situation in which writers increasingly find themselves. The homeopathic approach is especially effective for those writers whose writing we feel somehow exceeds the demands of the marketplace. Senkovskii's own homeopathic practice, however, problematizes this argument, as do the actual socioeconomic realities of Russia as we know them.

After all, the notion of Romantic literature as a reflection of or response to a given historical situation assumes an objective and original reality that can then be imitated. For Baudrillard there is the originally more pure relationship of signified to signifier that post-Modernism has allegedly compromised, while for McLaughlin in a more Romantic era there is both an original "good" literature free of commercial concerns and also an original "bad" literature that right-minded authors like Balzac and Dickens can imitate and so cast out. Where Chapter One suggested that any sort of objective, historical reality may not be accessible either then or now, however, this chapter has gone on to render the whole question of originality moot, at least as it pertains to the figure of the writer-critic. Accordingly it may be worthwhile to depart if only momentarily from the ambiguous or even contradictory realities of early nineteenth-century Europe as we know them and instead consider one last possibility. It may finally be that the persona of the writer-critic offers an expression of a Romantic aesthetics that only simulates a literary marketplace while in fact giving rise to critical omnipotence, most strikingly in the *Library for Reading*.

The Writer-Critic as Literary Capitalist

The impressive flow of money that marked the *Library for Reading* made Senkovskii's commercial aspirations very evident to his contemporaries, in fact overwhelmingly so. His many critics never failed to portray him as a creature of the literary marketplace, whatever other faults they might find. In the 1835 article he published in Pushkin's *Contemporary*, "On the Movement of Journalistic Literature in 1834 and 1835," Gogol seems to attack the *Library for Reading* in aesthetic terms, for the journal's lack of a consistent editorial voice. He strikingly casts that criticism, however, in language that keeps ever-present Senkovskii's underlying problem. Gogol's emphasis is always on the commercial aspects of things, for example when he always, even twice in the same sentence, refers to Senkovskii's employer as the "bookseller Smirdin," and when he pointedly describes a strong editorial presence as the source of a journal's "credit." As editor of the *Contemporary*, Pushkin evidently felt that Gogol had overstated the case, and in the next issue he disassociated his journal from Gogol's anti-Senkovskii stance although, typically enough, in a (fictional) letter to the editor signed "A. B. from Tver." Still Gogol seems quite restrained compared to S. P. Shevyrev, who founded *The Moscow Observer* largely to attack the *Library for Reading*, which he did unremittingly and with a notable lack of subtlety.

In his very first issue Shevyrev took on the *Library's* tendency to publish "personal" criticism with no name attached. In "On Criticism Generally and Here in Russia" (1835) Shevyrev explains that he is not entirely comfortable with the notion of criticism as the record of the critic's personal impressions, for the simple reason that such infinitely individual criticism in fact obviates the need for the critic altogether. If one is to write personal criticism, he continues, then at least one rule should be observed, and he demands: "That any criticism be authenticated by the signature of the name of the Reviewer." While Shevyrev's solution is offered in general terms, the particular critic whose practice he disparages is the obviously pseudonymous Tiutiun'dzhiu-Oglu, whom he describes in a loaded choice of words as nothing but a "Tatar attack," a new "[Mongol] Horde" imposing an "Asiatic tone" on Russian literature.[50] Again intertwined with this problem of Senkovskii's inauthenticity, though, is the problem of money, as Shevyrev reveals in the next issue when he rails at the *Library for Reading* as nothing more than a "stack of banknotes, turned into articles."[51]

Both Gogol and Shevyrev accuse Senkovskii of an insincerity and lack of integrity that can be understood on a number of levels. For the sake of money, they seem to be saying, Senkovskii is willing to be all things to all people, a splintering of the self exactly expressed in his play of personae, and it is certainly true that the lure of money plays havoc with more than a few writerly identities. Wordsworth and Coleridge, for example, seem to have embarked on the entire project of the *Lyrical Ballads* largely with financial considerations in mind. In the account rendered by the editors of *Lyrical Ballads and Other Poems, 1798–1800* (1992), the first inklings of what would become the *Lyrical Ballads* came in November 1797 when Wordsworth and

Coleridge, only fairly recently acquainted, came up with the idea of raising the money for a walking tour by writing a ballad together, a plan that eventually resulted in Coleridge's later much-maligned "The Rime of the Ancient Mariner." Over time and through various poetic and personal vicissitudes, the need the money was intended to answer changed. Still, Wordsworth's focus on the financial end of things continued to color even his reactions to the generally poor reviews accorded the 1798 edition, as in his plaintive response to Robert Southey's criticism: "Southeys [sic] review I have seen. He knew that I published those poems for money & money alone. He knew that money was of importance to me. If he could not conscientiously have spoken differently of the volume, in common delicacy he ought to have declined the task of reviewing it."[52] Not for nothing did Wordsworth hope that the addition of "Michael" would be "highly serviceable to the Sale" of the 1800 edition.

While money interested a great many other Romantic writers, from Byron to Pushkin and Hugo, none illustrates the association of writer-critic personae with the literary marketplace more vividly than Scott, again above all in the preface to *The Heart of Midlothian*. As noted above, Cleishbotham begins his comments with a tongue-in-cheek denial of his identification with "The Author of *Waverley*" or, as he puts it, the identification of "thy friend and servant with I know not what inditer [sic] of vain fables; who hath cumbered the world with his devices, but shrunken from the responsibility thereof." "Truly," Cleishbotham says, "this hath been well termed a generation hard of faith: since what can a man do to assert his property in a printed tome, saving to put his name in the title page thereof, which is description, or designation, as the lawyers term it, and place of abode?"[53]

Of course, no one knew better than Scott that a man certainly can assert his property in a printed tome without putting his name in the title page thereof, and it is property that matters, not just to Scott but also to Cleishbotham. Before turning to the issues raised by his association with "I know not what inditer of vain fables," Cleishbotham explains to his reader that the purpose of his "prolegomenon" is to "unload my burden of thanks at thy feet, for the favour with which thou has kindly entertained the Tales of My Landlord." In a move that Richard Waswo describes as characteristic of Scott's many prefaces, Cleishbotham then goes on to convert the "favour" author and audience bestow upon one another "from a feeling to its physical manifestation in objects of ascribed and exchange value."[54] The first series having done so well, Cleishbotham explains, he and his readers "lie, in respect of each other, under a reciprocation of benefits":

> Certes, if thou has chuckled over their [the Tales'] facetious and festivous descriptions, or hast thy mind filled with pleasure at the strange and pleasant turns of fortune which they record, verily, I have also simpered when I beheld a second story with attics, that has arisen on the basis of my small domicile at Gandercleugh. . . . Nor has it been without delectation, that I have endued a new coat (snuff-brown, with metal buttons), having all nether garments thereto.

As the benefits received by Cleishbotham have been, as he puts it, "the most solid," he feels his thanks should be "expressed with the louder voice," and "not in words only, but in act and deed." "It is with this sole purpose," he adds, "and disclaiming all intention of purchasing that pendicle or poffle of land called the Carlinescroft, lying adjacent to my garden, and measuring seven acres, three roods, and four perches, that I have committed to the eyes of those who thought well of my former tomes, these four additional volumes of the Tales of my Landlord."[55]

Needless to say, Cleishbotham clearly does intend to buy that "pendicle or poffle of land called the Carlinescroft," and he knows perfectly well that a "new house" is not more solid than a "new tale," as the whole thrust of his note is to equate the two by showing what one is worth in terms of the other. A book is for Cleishbotham not just "words" but also "act" and "deed," as published words gain solidity because they are worth something, which is to say that commercialization creates a simulation of reality, making more "real" a literary world that once might have been called imaginary. If the self-mocking reference is to Scott himself busily writing more novels to finance the expansion of Abbotsford, it is equally suggestive of Senkovskii's often frustrating critical practice. It is, after all, Senkovskii's own sense of the literary marketplace that drives his play between different levels of reality, starting from O. O. . . . O!'s offer to exchange fifty poods of hemp for "good Criticism," and ending with the whole game of personae that both exist and do not exist so that Senkovskii, like Scott, can lay claim to his property precisely without putting his name in the "title page thereof."

The curious thing, though, is that the propensity to equate value-added words with things is not limited to those writers who aspired to commercial success. The phenomenon seems instead to be quite a bit more widely spread, encompassing even Senkovskii's greatest detractors. Gogol, for example, famously also wrote *Dead Souls* (1841), a deeply ambiguous exploration of the worth and corresponding reality of words, while Shevyrev's very notion of the *Library for Reading* as a "stack of banknotes, turned into articles" derives from the same play of different levels of reality.[56] In the case of those writers so adamantly opposed to the literary marketplace, though, it may be that they adopt Senkovskii-like tactics deliberately, turning the weapons of the marketplace against the market itself in order to cure literature of the disease that ails it with a dose of homeopathic medicine.

The Writer-Critic as Homeopath

In *Writing in Parts* Kevin McLaughlin applies a sophisticated notion of homeopathy to a reading of Balzac and Dickens that draws on Marx, Adorno, Benjamin, and Derrida in "Plato's Pharmacy." McLaughlin's starting point is the commodity form in Marx's *Capital*, which he describes as the "perfect impostor" since "it looks exactly like a labor product, conforming in every visible detail to the ultimately irrelevant physicality of the human product it has replaced." The function of this imposter, in McLaughlin's words, is to produce "in its beholders the false belief that its 'meaning' derives from its physical identity with a labor product," when its "'true' meaning [lies] in its social *character*—in its capacity to write or prescribe for humans, in a godlike fashion, their social movement."[57] While this "imposter" in itself already suggests the person as well as the product of Brambeus and his friends, what is particularly relevant here is McLaughlin's discussion of how Marx's rhetorical strategy with regard to the commodity form he so loathes is exactly reflected in the writings of Balzac and Dickens.

McLaughlin borrows from Derrida the notion of writing as *pharmakon*, as not just poison but also as remedy, to argue that in *Capital* Marx deliberately mimics "commodity language" in order to "define it as a sign, to denaturalize it and subject it to a certain kind of reading," a reading that "will prove lethal." Marx's writing is then "good" writing that serves to destroy the "bad," as *Capital* attempts to overcome capitalism by citing it, only most obviously in the title of the book. As McLaughlin points out, this rhetorical strategy "parallels the mimetic character of revolution throughout [Marx's] work"; for example, in his famous call to compel the "petrified relations of German society . . . to dance by singing them their own melody."[58]

McLaughlin identifies the same attempt at a homeopathic cure for the disease of specifically literary capitalism in Balzac and Dickens, and Russian literature of the 1830s would seem to offer similar remedies. In much the same fashion, for example, we can see Pushkin turning his own weapons not against Senkovskii, but against a sort of Senkovskii stand-in, the other émigré Polish journalist who played an important role in Russian literature in the 1830s, Faddei Bulgarin, editor of *The Northern Bee*. Pushkin usually steered clear of journalistic polemics, both because of his own personal inclinations and because of his delicate position vis-à-vis the Tsar. In 1831 he made an exception to his usual rule, however, and published two articles attacking Bulgarin in Nadezhdin's *Telescope*, "The Triumph of Friendship, or Aleksandr Anfimovich Orlov Justified" and "A Few Words About Mr. Bulgarin's Little Finger, and About Other Things," both under the jokingly provincial pseudonym Feofilakt Kosichkin.

J. Thomas Shaw suggests that Bulgarin earned the honor of being the target of Pushkin's most important foray into personal and personae-ridden criticism by virtue of the very public and very personal nature of his own attacks on the poet, including scurrilous jabs at Pushkin's parentage.[59] It is also useful to consider, though, the extent to which Bulgarin presented many of the same dangers to more mainstream Russian writers as did his compatriot Senkovskii. While Belinskii labeled the two together with Grech as the "unholy triumvirate," current scholarship finds little evidence that Bulgarin and Senkovskii actually were literary allies; with the publication of Bulgarin's police files, it also seems today that it was only he who reported to the secret police, and not Senkovskii as well.[60] Both these villains of Russian literature, however, practiced different but nonetheless parallel kinds of imposture that were criticized by their contemporaries in different but nonetheless parallel ways.

There always was and continues to be a personal aspect to criticism of Senkovskii, whose underlying pretense in the eyes of his contemporaries was his pose as a Russian writer when he was only a Pole who traded in literature. Still, since the most immediate difficulty they faced was connecting the Baron et al. back to their maker, his detractors tended to criticize Senkovskii's imposture more in literary than in personal terms. Criticism of Bulgarin, on the other hand, pertained almost entirely to the details of his actual biography. These details included not only such savory items as Bulgarin's current situation as another émigré Pole attempting to dominate Russian literature and a spy, but also his performance in the Napoleonic wars when he first fled the Russians and fought against them for the French and then changed sides just in time for the Russian victory. The sordid facts of Bulgarin's life were so well known that Pushkin could publish an unsigned review of the memoirs of the French police spy, turncoat, and journalist Vidocq in 1831 with the expectation that his fellow writers would recognize Bulgarin as his real subject, and those few who missed it were shortly enlightened by an epigram addressed to "Vidocq Figliarin [Mountebank]."[61] It is in the two articles purportedly by Kosichkin, though, that Pushkin was at his most crushing, as with complete inconsistency he attacked Bulgarin's real-life impostures while at the same time supporting a literary imposture practiced at Bulgarin's expense.

At issue were a series of unauthorized sequels to Bulgarin's *Ivan Vyzhigin* written by one A. A. Orlov. In an 1831 defense of his friend's nonetheless highly successful novel, Grech had referred to "two extremely stupid books that had appeared in Moscow . . . composed by some A. Orlov."[62] Given his activity on behalf of his own intellectual property, one might expect Pushkin to be equally dismayed at Orlov's appropriation of Bulgarin's plot and characters. Instead he chose to respond to Grech's article in a way that mocked both Bulgarin's novel and Bulgarin himself as well as a literary collusion that Bulgarin and Grech disguised as simple friendship.

Posing in his turn as a friend of Orlov's, Feofilakt Kosichkin, Pushkin argues in "The Triumph of Friendship" that the literary value of Orlov's work should be measured by the five thousand copies it had sold, which put it on a par with Bulgarin's. He then goes on to a detailed comparison of the two novels' strengths that again would suggest that Orlov had as much right to the title of author as did his rival. Along the way Kosichkin notes the apparent aspersions cast on Moscow by Grech's mention of where Orlov's book was published. He writes: "It is not the first time that we have noticed in the editors of *Son of the Fatherland* and the *Northern Bee* this strange hatred toward Moscow. It is painful for the Russian heart to hear such opinions about mother Moscow, Moscow built of white stone, Moscow, which suffered from the Poles in 1612 and from all kinds of riff-raff in 1812."[63]

If Pushkin's references to Bulgarin's life were not already clear, Kosichkin then describes Moscow writers as for the most part "native Russians, not immigrants or displaced persons for whom: *ubi bene, ibi patria*, and it's all the same whether they flee under the banner of the French eagle or shame everything Russian [while writing] in the Russian tongue, as long as they have enough to eat."[64] After an indignant published response by Grech, Pushkin came out with "A Few Words About Mr. Bulgarin's Little Finger, and About Other Things," a piece that concludes with a prospective table of contents for Kosichkin's own sequel to *Ivan Vyzhigin*. Kosichkin proposes to call his novel *The Real Vyzhigin*, and his absolutely outrageous table of contents includes such gems as "Chapter II. Vyzhigin's first libel. The Garrison"; "Chapter IV. Friendship with Evsei. The Frieze Coat. Theft. Flight"; "Chapter V. Ubi bene, ibi patria"; "Chapter VII. Vyzhigin deserts"; and "Chapter XVI. Vidocq or Down with Masks!"[65]

In appropriating Bulgarin's own style of attack and along with it something of his slipperiness and insincerity, Pushkin would seem to be fighting fire with fire. We find the same phenomenon in much of the criticism directed toward Senkovskii, not just as written by Gogol and Shevyrev but also as produced by another of his archenemies, Nikolai Nadezhdin. Nadezhdin was an ally of the Pushkin crowd who was also completely committed to the apparently antithetical principles of personal criticism, personal attacks, and personae. Starting with his work in the late 1820s in the *Herald of Europe* and moving on to his editorship of both *Telescope* and its companion publication, *Rumor*, Nadezhdin made his critical name not as Nadezhdin but as the "Ex-Student Nikodim Nadoumko," resident of Patriarch's Ponds, and Nadoumko in turn tended to couch his criticism as dialogues with a number of regular participants, including his friends Tlenskii and Fliugerovskii and that personification of the common man, Pakhom Silich. Despite its apparent similarity to Senkovskii's own critical practice, however, Nadezhdin operated from behind the bulwarks of precisely this combination of personae and personality in waging his own war against the *Library for Reading*.

In an 1834 review of O. O. . . . O!'s review of Bulgarin's *Mazepa*, for example, Nadezhdin objects to the critic's apostrophes to the real Bulgarin as "comical mystifications," when Nadoumko's addresses to the fictional Pakhom Silich could be little else.[66] He also complains about a lack of principle, substance and above all, "good conscience," when his own habit of layering his "own" opinions gives rise to ethical questions in turn, for example in a review of *Ivan Vyzhigin* in which Nadoumko and Pakhom Silich respond critically to an anonymous review that was published in the journal *Atenei* and that, as only much later scholarship has revealed, was in fact written by Nadezhdin, too. In "Common Sense and Baron Brambeus" (1834) Nadezhdin notes that Brambeus's style is "highly infectious," for "our worthy Orientalist Mr. Professor Senkovskii, in his research on *Scandinavian Sagas*, just as the no less worthy aristarchs of the *Library for Reading*, Effendi Tiutiun'dzhiu-Oglu and Mr. O. O. . . . O!, in their critical articles, demonstrate a marked similarity to Brambeus' way of thought and means of expression."[67] It is not clear whether Nadezhdin, too, has caught the infection, or whether he intends to pass it on with deadly effect, for example in his 1834 letter to the editor of *Rumor*, "More Claims About Baron Brambeus's Last Name," which attacks Senkovskii in a pointedly Senkovskiian fashion.

The issue again is the use of pseudonyms, and the point of this brief note is to dismiss the derivation of Brambeus's name that Grech had offered in the *Library for Reading* by explaining first that there are no Barons in Spain and then that the "Spanish" King Baram-Bei-Iusuf was in fact Mauritanian. At the end the author of the letter then appears to lend weight to his claim by styling himself as a "militant Spanish archeographer," "Don Juan-Alonzo-Salveto-Kverera-Estremaduro-Velasko-Gvadalkviviro-Ponso, native-born Spanish Nobleman."[68] Nadezhdin's very joke, though, would seem to undermine his own aim. Having begun by criticizing Senkovskii's tenuous connection to reality, Nadezhdin ends by creating a simulacrum of his own, a persona freighted in just the same way with the "proliferation of myths of origin and signs of reality . . . of second-hand truth, objectivity and authenticity."[69]

This move may be intentional, part of a plan to turn Senkovskii's own writing back on its source and so purge Russian literature of the disease of inauthenticity. Given that Nadezhdin's literary success just slightly predates Senkovskii's, however, it may be that he is the one who fell sick first, or at best, as in Eilenberg's reading of Wordsworth and Coleridge, that this play of personae offers instead a more muddled "mutual possession of one another."[70] In his discussion of Balzac and Dickens, McLaughlin is also aware of this sort of ambiguity, and he writes in his conclusion of the difficulty in distinguishing between simple imitation of the "literary industry" and a dialectic movement that would represent and so cancel it. When we consider Senkovskii in particular, this confusion over whether writers are actually attempting a homeopathic cure or not is especially marked. As it turns out, this "bad" writer, the apparent target of a cure by "good" writers, is himself engaged in the practice of homeopathy, and one that operates on a still more fundamental level.

When Derrida in "Plato's Pharmacy" (1981) develops the notion of the *pharmakon*, he is not talking about the kind of writing produced by one set of writers or another but of writing generally. Derrida begins by noting that in the "Phaedrus" Plato several times refers to writing as a *pharmakon*, a word that, depending on the context, is generally translated as either "poison" or "remedy." Derrida points out that in fact *pharmakon* means both "poison" and "remedy" at the same time, and in the ambiguous, double meaning of the word he sees the ambiguous, double place of writing in Western civilization. While there is, Derrida argues, only writing, we tend to base our epistemologies on an arbitrary distinction between what we call writing and what we call speech. The former is seen as an evil, a counterfeit leading to the blurring of distinctions, and we cast it out for the sake of the latter, an imaginary original that gives us the ability to make any distinctions at all. As a counterfeit or imitation, writing poisons our world with ambiguity. When we label something as writing in order to cast it out and thereby give order to our world, however, that poison becomes a remedy, a homeopathic cure. According to Derrida, Plato can then present his own writing as uniquely "good" because it offers itself as a remedy, and it is just such a remedy that Senkovskii's writing offers as well.

The term itself appears at least twice in Senkovskii's criticism. In his "Literary Chronicle" for January 1838, Senkovskii's retelling of the *Arabian Nights*, his writer-critic figure Kritikzada has recourse to what she herself calls "homeopathic means" when her husband, the dread Piublik-Sultan-Bagadur, falls ill simultaneously with a hernia and the plague and she finds a recently published work on hernias and one on the plague and cures her husband merely by summarizing their contents. With his substitution of Kritikzada for Scheherezade, Senkovskii openly acknowledges that the function of the critic generally is homeopathic, as the critic cites or imitates in order to correct. In yet another direct reference to homeopathy, this time in "The First Letter of Three Landowners from Tver to Baron Brambeus" (1837), Senkovskii also addresses specifically the distinction between writing and speech.

When he was not busy advocating for and against particular writers, Brambeus saw his mission as improving the state of the Russian literary language generally by making it more closely approximate actual educated

Russian speech, and he famously claimed to have single-handedly elimi-
nated archaisms like *sei* and *onyi* from the contemporary written language.
In a wonderful Senkovskiian play of personae, the fictional "Three Landowners from Tver" write to Brambeus to dispute his claim, but only by
taking credit for themselves. "Here something isn't right, Baron Stepan
Kirillovich," the landowners solemnly state: "Petr Afrosimovich says, and
we agree, that there is no one in the world with the power to destroy, in the
language of an immense people, a single truly existing word." Of course,
the landowners continue, such a change has taken place in the Russian literary language, but not because of the efforts of any mythical Baron Brambeus. Indeed, they say, it's not Brambeus who caused the disappearance of
sei and *onyi*, but the landowners themselves, or, as they also say "our, Tver
province" by which, as they explain later, they mean "all intelligent provinces, all of Russia."[71]

Writing as the three landowners Senkovskii makes the case for speech over
writing not just in his insistence that the latter change to reflect the former,
but also in the pretense to orality that marks all of his writing. On behalf of
Brambeus the three landowners, for example, transcribe entire conversations
amongst the three of them and also with their neighbor Father Pansii, complete with his friendly call, "but it's time to drink vodka!" while the "Literary Chronicle" for January 1838 is couched almost entirely in the form of a
conversation whose participants include, besides Kritikzada and the Sultan,
Kritikzada's sister Ironizada and her father, Brambeus-Aga-Bagadur. We un-
derestimate Senkovskii, however, if we see a contradiction in the fact that
his condemnation of writing, like Plato's, is itself written. The three landowners' letter in fact begins: "Dear Sir, Baron Stepan Kirillovich: Nikolai
Nikolaevich, Petr Afrosimovich and I, although not acquainted with your
honor, find ourselves compelled to write to you decisively; only we don't
know about what—about the Russian language or about homeopathy? Both
subjects are extremely interesting to us."[72] That the three then settle on the
first question does not mean that the second is not answered, for the two
questions are really one. Brambeus's criticism of the Russian language *is* his
homeopathy, as his writing escapes his own blanket condemnation of writing because it is a sort of hair-of-the-dog-that-bit-you, a cure for the ills of
writing by means of a dose of writing.

Like Pushkin and Nadezhdin, Senkovskii can posit his own writing as
"good" because as criticism it is not just poison but also remedy for the

diseases that infect Russian literature, Russian language, and even writing in its most abstract sense. That Senkovskii, too, can cast himself as a homeopath, however, renders the whole notion of homeopathic criticism absurd. In "Plato's Pharmacy" Derrida argues that the distinction between original and imitation is an arbitrary one, for in Derrida's world there is only writing. The same is true of a Romanticism in which critics imitate other critics and writers other writers, and the two functions become one in the figure of the writer-critic. The entire homeopathic enterprise is undermined when we can no longer clearly distinguish between original disease and cure-by-imitation, and Senkovskii's example makes it plain that we cannot. Unfortunately for the budding homeopath, Brambeus's ironic practice of the same opens us onto a *mise-en-abîme* of "bad" writing, leaving us without even the original and authentically "bad" writing on which any homeopathic criticism depends.

If arbitrary, still this distinction between "bad" and "good" writing has nonetheless long been made, and literary historians are quite sure which sort Senkovskii's is. I would argue, however, that labeling Senkovskii's writing as "bad" and as "other," non-Russian, and un-Romantic is not only not correct but in fact serves another purpose. As reproduction or doubling, writing is a poison that threatens to "slip . . . out of the simple alternative presence/absence" altogether, erasing difference.[73] At the same time, however, writing serves as a remedy for the very problem it causes when it is cast out in order to create an imaginary opposition of writing to speech, and in this sacrifice of the *pharmakon* Derrida sees a sort of ritual expulsion analogous to the ancient Athenian sacrifice of the *pharmakos*.

Derrida quotes scholarship to the effect that the Athenians "regularly maintained a number of degraded and useless beings at public expense," poison to the community that in time of need, in the face of a drought, for example, or a famine, could be put to death, thereby becoming a remedy. Just as the expulsion of writing draws tidy lines between presence and absence, creation and reproduction, original and imitation, the expulsion of the scapegoat allows the community to clearly distinguish between self and other, as the city "reconstitutes its unity . . . by violently excluding from its territory the representative of an external threat or aggression," the one who "represents the otherness of the evil that comes to affect or infect the inside by unpredictably breaking into it."[74] To cast Senkovskii out as a sort of *pharmakos* is then to reconstitute a wholeness that perhaps neither Russian nor Romantic literature actually ever had. To return him is to acknowledge instead that a fragmentary, insincere, and inauthentic writing self is fundamental to both, a product not just of a tainted literary marketplace, but of the theory that may be seen to have launched the whole Romantic enterprise in the first place.

The Romantic Construction of Critical Identity

In Germany in 1798, in the relative absence of commercial concerns, the Schlegels' concept of authorship is already a profoundly unstable one that both emphasizes a personal attachment of writer to text and at the same time ironically undermines it. On one hand, and perhaps most obviously, Friedrich and his friends incarnate themselves in their writings to an extraordinary degree. While we may not completely agree on the identity of the various participants, both authors and audience, of the *Dialogue on Poetry*, for example, still our readings always rely on our knowledge of the existence of this group of friends, and the most basic pronouncements of the Jena circle would seem to encourage this sort of one-to-one correspondence.

In the long middle part of the famous *Athenaeum Fragment* 116, Friedrich writes of the "Romantic kind of art" or "novel" that "there still is no form so fit for expressing the entire spirit of an author: so that many artists who started out to write only a novel ended up by providing us with a portrait of themselves"; he goes still further in the *Critical*, or, as they are often called, the *Lyceum Fragments,* published a year earlier in the *Lyceum*. In *Critical Fragment* 78, for example, Friedrich directly says that "[m]any of the very best novels are compendia, encyclopedias of the whole spiritual life of a brilliant individual," and in *Critical Fragment* 89 he asks, "[i]sn't it unnecessary to write more than one novel, unless the artist has become a new man?"[75] It is again the idea that the form is somehow commensurate with the spirit or personality of the author that prompts Antonio in "The Letter on the Novel" to claim that "true story is the foundation of all romantic poetry" for "what is best in the best of novels is nothing but a more or less veiled confession of the author, the profit of his experience, the quintessence of his originality."[76] Indeed, as Friedrich once wrote to his brother of his own aphoristic style, "I can give no other 'echantillon' of my entire ego than such a system of fragments because I myself am such a thing."[77]

But if the Schlegels et al. "are" their writings, they also are not, and the case of Friedrich's *Fragments* is particularly revealing: readers in search of an authentic Friedrich Schlegel will nonetheless find themselves at a loss to understand just what sort of a "thing" this particular "system of fragments" might be, for the simple reason that Friedrich did not actually write all the *Fragments* himself, nor did he put his name to any of them. In fact, despite the obvious and important connections to the "real world" described above, the identification of Jena's writings, especially in the *Athenaeum*, as the essential expressions of actual people is fundamentally problematic, largely because of the *Frühromantik* notion of "sympoetry." "Sympoetry" or "symphilosophy" (Jena uses both terms) is the idea of collective creation that is both simulated, for example in the various pseudo-Platonic "dialogues" of the *Athenaeum* and in the dialogue that is the *Athenaeum* as a whole, and also enacted, most notably in its first two collections of aphorisms.[78] The *Fragments*, if we strongly associate them with Friedrich, were nonetheless composed by various members of the group and published in the journal anonymously, while *Grains of Pollen* appeared pseudonymously, as the work not of Friedrich von Hardenburg but of Novalis.[79]

While an apparently paradoxical desire for "sympoetry" obscures the attachment of Jena's own texts to any real writer in the world, Friedrich's notion of the *Charakteristik* also compromises that connection for any writer anywhere. As Friedrich defines it in his essay "On the Essence of Criticism" (1804), the *Charakteristik* is the most basic item in the Romantic critic's toolbox, a seizing of the essence of the work through the reconstruction of its historical development. In Schlegel's words: "And so one can only then say that one understands a work, a spirit, when one can reconstruct its movement and formation. Now this fundamental understanding that, if it were to be expressed in a particular word, is called characterization [*Charakterisieren*], is the true calling and inner being of criticism."[80] While this act of "characterization" that should lead us to the work's "spirit" and ultimately to the "more or less veiled confession of the author" may come in some sense from outside the work, it is nonetheless inherent in it. As Walter Benjamin explains, criticism from the outside "is, as it were, an experiment on the artwork, one through which the latter's own reflection is awakened, brought to consciousness and to knowledge of itself"; accordingly for the Romantics, he continues, "criticism is far less the judgment of a work than the method of its consummation."[81]

This "consummation" more often than not is presented as the achievement of a special sort of reader, the professional critic who edits journals, for example, and who writes the reviews that Novalis calls "the complement of the book" or the "good preface" that Friedrich Schlegel describes as "at once the square root and the square of the book." More broadly, however, characterization is the function of any reader who, when confronted with the disparate pieces of the "Romantic kind of art," creates of it a single whole. Either way, as Benjamin's notion of "consummation" implies, what the Romantic reader learns the Romantic work already at least dimly knows, and in this sense the sort of reviews published in the *Athenaeum* or the *Library for Reading* perform a reading and writing that ideally have always already happened. It is on the one hand, as the quotes from Schlegel above would suggest, that the writer once "read" some aspect of him- or herself and then wrote it into a text that is now available to our reading and writing. Still more important is that in Schlegel's theory this "original" critical act of writing is also an ongoing process, as the Romantic text itself in every reading performs for us an act of characterization, characterizing its creator and so itself.

In other words, if Schlegelian criticism would seem to point outward as a characterization of a "real" writer, as a process by which the text actually characterizes itself, the *Charakteristik* points inward, so that the text becomes in a sense self-sufficient, not just an object for our perusal but also a subject producing readings in its own right.[82] The two poles, subject and object, are opposed to one another and yet also derive one from the other, for it is the very act of mimesis fundamental to Romantic criticism that at the same time creates of that criticism a self-sufficient sign. As Lacoue-Labarthe and Nancy write: "A character, or a character sketch, is a subject produced through *mimesis*, and capable (undoubtedly *for this very reason*) in its presentation or staging of re-producing or re-constructing the Subject, a Subject that is auto-constituting, auto-mimetic, auto-ironic, or in short, auto-fantastical. . . . and that auto-imagines, auto-*bildet*, auto-illuminates itself: the Subject-Work." As the Subject-Work, the "character is what characterizes *itself*," not what characterizes something else presumably real, so that what Romanticism in fact initiates, in Lacoue-Labarthe and Nancy's words, is literature not as imitation but as a "*critique* of imitation."[83]

Instead of Plato's poetry as imitation at a third remove, the Schlegels and their friends offer literature as literary criticism, a form that in their rendering is both mimetic and a subversion of mimesis.[84] According to Lacoue-Labarthe and Nancy, from the point of Romanticism on, "the genuine identity of art (of the work, of the artist) no longer depends on the relation of resemblance to another given identity (or on veri-similitude), but on the construction of *critical identity*."[85] In this understanding the *Charakteristik*, or the sign of the artist that the Romantic work of art embodies, is not intended to point to any real figure, although it is then not quite correct to understand it as imaginary. What we are left with instead is once again the simulacrum, or writing self-consciously as what Derrida calls "writing."

The *Frühromantik* zeroes in on a writer not so much *of* as *in* the text, and while the two are clearly connected one to another, the terms of their relationship are entirely at the mercy of the Romantic critic, that all-powerful reader-writer who seeks not the identification of the real person in the world who expressed him- or herself through a given text, but instead his or her reconstruction. Whether from a point within the text, as in the case of a writer-persona, or from without, as in the case of criticism as more conventionally understood, the Romantic critic's aim is not the imitation of reality, but its replacement with something the critic has him- or herself created. In pursuit of that goal it might be the critic who absorbs the writer into him- or herself or the writer who divides him- or herself in order to become the critic of his or her own work. In either case the Romantic writer-critic's self-sufficiency more often than not is figured in the form of a persona.

Critical Omnipotence

Critical omnipotence gained at the expense of the authenticity and integrity of the writerly self is not an accidental by-product of Friedrich's vision of the Subject-Work, and certainly an all-powerful critic sounds a great deal like Senkovskii. As we have seen, too, Jena's reformulation of literature as literary criticism, or the construction of critical identity, was a basic component of the literary world in which Senkovskii operated. Still, as we move across the time and space that separates the *Athenaeum* from the *Library for Reading*, we cannot help but sense some sort of change, perhaps a raising of the stakes or at least of the temperature. It is hard not to perceive in later and more extreme versions of Romantic theory a reality that has only gradually manifested itself, as if the possibility of real writers making real money renders Friedrich Schlegel's idea of literature as literary criticism all too real, above all in the pages of the *Library for Reading*, where Senkovskii's criticism could swallow up anything, even Pushkin. But as we have seen, despite our temptation to believe in it, still that reality remains less than tangible and its exact contours difficult to determine.

Baudrillard's "radical law of equivalence and exchange" means that for Jedediah Cleishbotham a story in a book and a story on a house are the same, a claim that is disturbing not so much because it represents the commercialization of art but because it blurs the lines between what we call "fiction" and "reality": it is no longer clear on what level "story," in any of its various meanings, belongs, or if any kind of distinction between "fiction" and "reality" can even be made. It is this unstable and uncomfortable situation that the expulsion of Senkovskii from the annals of literary history is intended to rectify, and returning him to the world that he once dominated may seem to generate only more confusion. Certainly for Baudrillard simulation is an utter dead end, as a simulacrum is not an imitation of something that already exists in the "real world," a particular kind of Western European writer or critic or trade in literature, for example; nor is it an imitation of something that could exist in the "real world," for example a belated Russian version of any of the above. It is instead a self-sufficient sign, "not unreal, but a simulacrum, never again exchanging for what is real, but exchanging in itself, in an uninterrupted circuit without reference or circumference."[86]

Returning Senkovskii to his own context clarifies at least this much, however: that it is precisely Baudrillard's notion of simulation, with or without financial remuneration, that marks Romanticism from start to finish, and over the course of the thirty years or so traced in this chapter, it is even practiced by more or less the same cast of characters. Friedrich Schlegel may withdraw into a very different career in the Austrian civil service and Lermontov dies young, but Coleridge reappears as the patron saint of *Fraser's* and Scott as the mentor of *Blackwood's*, while Pushkin and Gogol continue to publish works not just like and about but even in the *Library for Reading* throughout the 1830s. Senkovskii's combination of critical personae with a personality not his own is just one more manifestation of Romantic simulation, although the particular cynicism that marked his various performances is still significant. Irony is a difficult stance to maintain, and it also comes in very different flavors, from the joyful to the nihilistic, and it does seem that over time, whether under the pressures of the market or of simply sustaining its own virtuosity, Romanticism finds itself tending more toward the latter variety.

While the Schlegels may leave their readers frustrated, they often also leave them marveling at the glimpse of the Absolute that their irony at its best affords. Senkovskii's readers, on the other hand, have more often been simply offended by a view of writers and writing so darkly ironic as to appear dismissive. The *Library for Reading* would certainly seem to express a disdain for writers in every way imaginable, from Senkovskii's transformation of Scheherezade into Kritikzada to his habit of altering submissions, and Senkovskii compounds his crime against writing by what may seem a vulgar catering to the desires of real readers, the new and largely provincial reading public that Senkovskii is famously held to have discovered. Where this chapter has suggested that Senkovskii is not quite as unfair to writers as it may seem, however, the next will argue that neither is he quite so interested in real readers. Senkovskii's readers, as it happens, are only partly real and largely imaginary, for Romanticism simulates not just writers but also readers and the relationship between the two. It is to the latter half of this equation that we now turn.

3. Romantic Readers

In his famous article "What Is an Author?" (1969) Foucault announces the imminent disappearance from literature of what he calls the "author function." Instead of the author-oriented questions "Who really spoke? Is it really he and not someone else? With what authenticity or originality? And what part of his deepest self did he express in his discourse?" Foucault says, we might soon find ourselves turning to the text with other, more open-ended questions: "What are the modes of existence of this discourse? Where has it been used, how can it circulate, and who can appropriate it for himself? What are the places in it where there is room for possible subjects? Who can assume these various subject functions?"[1]

For Foucault, power, it would seem, falls to one of two camps. Either it is in the hands of the author, an entity that Foucault defines as "a certain functional principle by which, in our culture, one limits, excludes, and chooses: in short, by which one impedes the free circulation, the free manipulation, the free composition, decomposition, and recomposition of fiction," or the author is dead and the text's "various subject functions" are up for grabs.[2] As my last chapter has indicated, however, at least within the confines of Romanticism authorship is a far more complicated phenomenon than Foucault's brief article would suggest, one that paradoxically facilitates the "free circulation" of fiction even while impeding it. It is also a "functional principle" that, rather than shutting down readings, in fact brings particularly complicated readings and readerships in its wake.

While Foucault tends to speak in generalities, still he does clearly associate the appearance of this "author function" with a point "at the end of the eighteenth and the beginning of the nineteenth century" when "a system of ownership for texts came into being, [and] strict rules concerning author's rights, author-publisher relations, rights of reproduction, and related matters were enacted." Foucault also suggests the ambiguities of Romantic authorship when he explains that along with these rules came the possibility of their transgression, "as if the author, beginning with the moment at which he was placed in the system of property that characterizes our society, compensated for the status that he thus acquired by rediscovering the old bipolar field of discourse, systematically practicing transgression and thereby restoring danger to a writing which was now guaranteed the benefits of ownership."[3] Yet any opening up of the space of literature for other voices would still seem to be a matter for Foucault's future, after the notion of the author has been cleared away, and Foucault's article anticipates the shift toward the reader that much post-Structuralist literary criticism would take.

Once again, however, Romanticism was there before us; for the voices of Romantic readers, as variously understood, clamor for attention and always have. There are first of all the real readers of Romanticism, the allegedly more numerous and more democratic reading public that in Russia included the at least 5,000 subscribers to the *Library for Reading*. This sort of Romantic reader comes with a body attached and has long been of interest not just to scholars seeking to ground Romantic ideals in a real spread of reading across real class lines, but also to the Romantic writers themselves who wrote into their texts their eagerness to please their new customers. Romanticism is also known for another sort of real reader, the close friend or associate of the writer to whom the piece is in some way addressed. The *Athenaeum*, for example, is filled with dialogues in which the participants in some way reflect the real members of the circle at Jena, while English Romanticism notably offers the "conversation poem" as addressed by Wordsworth to his sister Dorothy, for example, or by Coleridge to his friend Charles Lamb.

This second sort of reader might seem even more tangible than the first for pointing to a real and truly intimate relationship in the world. At the same time, though, as scholars have long recognized, these supposedly real addressees are also stand-ins for the reader in general, figures not just of the reader but of the act of reading with which Romantic theory is deeply engaged. We have already seen that for the German *Frühromantik* there is no work without the reading that the ideal Romantic text itself incorporates, and Tilotamma Rajan devotes *The Supplement of Reading* (1990) to demonstrating in the British context "how the activity of reading is narrated in a wide range of romantic texts and how the role of the reader is projected and complicated by romantic theory itself."[4] This Romantic reader, then, as simultaneously both a real audience and an element of the text itself, is already quite a complicated beast. Romantic readers and reading can take still more extreme forms, however, above all in the *Library for Reading*.

Not unlike other Romantic writers, Senkovskii was popularly supposed to have discovered or even created a new real reader largely in the Russian provinces and among a slightly less educated class, and the *Library for Reading* reflects its dependence on this readership on a number of different levels. There is the apparent redundancy of the journal's title that so offended Prince Viazemskii, as if Senkovskii were pointedly reminding us that any library is for reading and not, say, for writing; there is also Senkovskii's famously bad treatment of the writers whose work he criticized and absorbed into his own. Most strikingly, while Senkovskii's slapstick comedies of criticism usually star the personified writer-critic, these writer-personae, often to their chagrin, appear only alongside any number of equally vivid reader-personae: the Baron has his Baronessa and also the three landowners from Tver, for example, while Kritikzada operates only under the watchful gaze of her dread spouse, Piublik-Sultan-Bagadur. Few Romantic writers can match Senkovskii for the literalness with which he represents the role of the reader in the creation of literature. Senkovskii's admittedly extreme rendering of readers, however, like his extreme rendering of writers, can serve to lay bare the tensions that underlie the work of his more mainstream colleagues as well.

It is never easy for critics to talk about readers, and the possible pitfalls are many. As Rajan puts it, while "reader-response theory is often accused of approaching the reader in an insufficiently materialist way," the opposite tack is also flawed, for "literalizing the notion of audience by identifying it with a specific historical group is equally essentialist."[5] Senkovskii's practice makes this choice particularly problematic, as while his reader-figures clearly point to the real readership he hopes to create and guide, the personalities with which he endows his personae at the same time lend to them their own individual existence. In a wonderfully Romantic paradox, the more Senkovskii materializes his readers in the pages of his criticism, the less those readers actually belong to the material world. While critics have often tended to focus on a certain kind of reader—historical, for example, or intended, implied, or model—what Senkovskii's example makes clear is that at least in the context of Romanticism we might best speak of the reader only as an amalgam of all of these at once. Like Rajan, we perhaps do better to define "audience as a blank that can be filled in more than one way" and "the audience-oriented text as an unstable compound of voices that can never quite be fixed."[6] We might even go a step further and consider the extent to which this instability serves to point not to a shifting readership but straight back to the critic.

For as Romantic readers ultimately always elude us, they leave us once more face to face with the question of critical power. Certainly Romantic theory imagines the ideal work as a collaboration between reader and writer, one that Senkovskii, like Friedrich Schlegel, casts explicitly as marriage. As Schlegel writes to his real reader and future wife in the essay "On Philosophy. To Dorothea" published in the *Athenaeum* in 1799, so Baron Brambeus addresses his wife the Baronessa, and Kritikzada her husband the Sultan, and these marriages have often been understood as a relationship between equals appropriate both to Jena's abstract ideas about subjectivity and also to Senkovskii's more concrete alliance with his provincial readership and against the literary elite of the capitals. As I hope to show, however, this apparently intimate sharing of interpretative control ironically devolves into the concentration of power in one side of the relationship alone, although I would argue that the entity with the upper hand is not the author function, or at least not the author function as Foucault defines it. For where Foucault seems to see only two camps, I see three, if a third that swallows up the other two. As we have already seen, Romantic authorship is really about critical omnipotence, and we will now see that Romantic readership is, too.

Readers in the Library for Reading

Much is made of the readers of the *Library for Reading*, that shadowy, new, and apparently mainly provincial reading public that subscribed to the journal in such large numbers. Perhaps because so few scholars today actually read the *Library for Reading*, however, a great deal less attention has been paid to the readers in the *Library for Reading*. In fact, readers make quite a spectacular appearance in the pages of Senkovskii's journal, as Senkovskii repeatedly portrays the creation of literature as a sort of puppet show where the main parts are played by the critic-writer and by his or her reader. I say "critic-writer" because Senkovskii's critic seems to have already absorbed the function of the writer into him- or herself; the critic's relationship to his or her reader, however, remains a little more complicated. The tales they tell in the *Library for Reading* strongly suggest that Baron Brambeus and Kritikzada are utterly dependent on their readers for their very existence, much as the real Senkovskii was on his. Still, Senkovskii was most often credited not with his dependence on his readers but with his creation of them. As Kaverin writes, the *Library for Reading* "was not just a magazine, but the discovery of the reader," and there is something of the same slippage at work in Senkovskii's fictional rendering of that relationship.[7]

The Baron is particularly good at hiding the perhaps unsavory secret of his own critical omnipotence; for example, in his "First Letter of the Three Landowners from Tver to Baron Brambeus."[8] Here Brambeus slyly casts himself as only the recipient of a letter that, while nominally addressed to him, even calls into question his very existence. But if Nikolai Zaezzhaev, Petr Zakusaev, and Ivan Mukholovkin claim that their own existence as the true transformers of the Russian language disproves Brambeus's, they at the same time emphatically lend their support to what they persist, despite their doubts, in calling "Brambeus' system" and "teaching about language," his attack on the Church Slavonicisms lingering in the literary language.[9] The three letter-writing readers from Tver see no contradiction in the two aspects of their argument. Indeed, according to the landowners, it is precisely the truth of Brambeus's ideas about language that proves his nonexistence. As the last chapter has argued, however, the three landowners cannot undermine Brambeus's person only to support his ideas because the two are one and the same. A still more basic flaw in their reasoning is that the landowners are themselves transparently the invention of Brambeus.

While the reader might well doubt the corporeal existence of a letter-writer named Mukholovkin (Fly-Catcher) without any prompting, the landowners also go out of their way to render their own reality absurd, particularly when the three compare the report that Brambeus is but a "fictitious person" to similar questions that, they claim, have already been raised with regard to Tver. While vigorously insisting that it is Brambeus who is the fiction, not Tver, it is also the landowners themselves who pointedly cast their town in entirely symbolic terms. Tver, they say, is located at the midpoint along the highway from Petersburg to Moscow, "at the very cross-roads of the ideas traveling there and back," ideas to whom, they continue, "Larivon Il'ich, the stationmaster, provides horses for the journey as long as they, that is, the ideas, not the horses, have legal orders."[10] The near confusion of pronoun antecedents in this quote speaks to the larger confusion that is the "Letter" itself. Not despite, but because of the landowners' claims to independent existence, the "Letter" suggests instead a mutual dependence of imaginary critics and readers and, behind them, real ones, whereby the two (or the four) can only exist and effect change in the literary language together. What Brambeus is really interested in, however, is a considerably more intimate relationship than any the three landowners can offer.

This more intimate relationship is marriage, and first of all the marriage of the Baron to his Baronessa in "Brambeus and the Young Literature." In this article marriage in fact operates on a number of different levels. Brambeus's overarching assertion is that while writers on their own can produce something, they nonetheless cannot produce what he calls "real literature." "Real literature," he says, is the child of the marriage of critic and reader. The more immediate target of Brambeus's piece is the latest French writing, and here marriage is also at issue. According to Brambeus, the problem with the new French writing is that its ultimately false notions of equality for women present an attack on public morality and in particular on the Christian institution of marriage, when without Christian marriage and the true equality for women that it offers, there can be no real literature.

Brambeus makes the rather extraordinary claim that the Greeks had no literature. They had no novels or stories to speak of, he says, their poetry was but "public entertainment" and their plays no more "literary" than the Roman battles of gladiators.[11] True literature, according to Brambeus, can arise only under the civilizing influence of Christianity whereby men are feminized and women masculinized, becoming what Brambeus calls "moral hermaphrodites," and then only under particular circumstances. Christianity is the necessary environment, but it is only when these newly created readers turn to the sheltering arms of critics that "real literature" is born.

Readers on their own are only barely better off than writers when it comes to creating literature, and Brambeus offers a revealing description of the "real" reading public when he explains that the:

> "literary public" . . . lives only when she [it] has nothing to do . . . she is born after the fastening of the last ribbon on the morning's toilette and after the

signing of the last business papers, rests during dinner and dies toward evening in the whirlwind of a noisy ball with the intention of being born anew tomorrow or the next day, at leisure. She is nowhere and she exists everywhere. There she said a word!—Over there, it would seem, she flashed past!—She is here! . . . She is there! . . . Count her,—she's a handful of individuals without their own opinion; and at the same time she is more numerous, stronger and more decisive in her feelings than we might suppose.

Evidently this shadowy and unfortunately stubborn reading public is made up of amateurs, part-time readers who are, Brambeus adds, incapable of independent thought, lacking even the time needed for independent thought, and yet desperately afraid of boredom, ever thirsting for "novelties, sensations, toys, events, shine, ready-made pleasures and ready-made thoughts."[12] It is, Brambeus says, the role of professional readers, critics, to then supply the reading public with the right sort of "ready-made pleasures and ready-made thoughts," the ones conducive to the creation of "real literature," and, to illustrate his point with regard to the latest snare set for the hapless reading public, the new French writing, Brambeus departs from the fleeting abstractions of a real reading public for the sake of something much more concrete. It is at this point in the article that marriage becomes an actual element of plot, as the Baron introduces a new character, his wife the Baronessa.

The portly Brambeus at first anticipates no difficulties in defending his equally plump Baronessa against the attack of "young literature." Unfortunately, however, even a wide expanse of flesh cannot fill all the chinks of free time, and there is still space for the seductions of "boredom" and its companion "literature" to slip behind their defenses. The Baronessa, of course, is the weak point in their marriage, as the Baron, sage critic that he is, knows better than to be caught by the wiles of the new French literature. To protect his weaker half, Brambeus forms their marriage into a fortress, with the Baron as the commander, the Baronessa the garrison. Undaunted, the new French literature immediately lays siege to their "bastion of marriage," launching missile after missile over their walls. The crafty "female infidel" or "basurmanka," as Brambeus calls her, insinuates that the institution of marriage is unnatural, that faithfulness is nothing but egoism, that virtue does not exist and that the commander of the fortress is deceiving the garrison. At the rallying cry, "freedom of the female sex!" the garrison mutinies, and Brambeus can see no other option than to beat a strategic retreat: "Harness up the carriage! I have to take my garrison to a watering-place in Germany," he calls as he whisks his Baronessa off to Karlsbad.[13]

If the Baron jokingly leaves the field to "young literature," however, he has not yet given up the battle. The article ends with a lecture on the proper uses of literature, as the husband is still determined to preserve his marriage to his wife and the critic his marriage to his reader without which "real literature" cannot exist. The Baron is nothing if not persistent, although his interest is in the institution of marriage per se rather than in any specific Baronessa. Indeed, as we see in the "Literary Chronicle" for January 1838, any and every reader will do, even of the male variety.[14] If calling his readers "hermaphrodites" would suggest that they are both male and female, Brambeus seems rather to mean that they are free to take either form. Accordingly, the sex of the readers' intended spouse, the critic, must be equally mutable, and in the "Literary Chronicle" Senkovskii transforms the *Arabian Nights* into a review of books in which the role of the reader is taken by the husband, the dangerously capricious Piublik-Sultan-Bagadur, and that of the critic by his lovely wife, Brambeus's daughter Kritikzada.

The power of Piublik-Sultan-Bagadur is immense: "his domains stretched from the sea to the ocean," we are told, "so that even the most learned of men . . . could not say with any exactitude where his realm began and where it ended." Piublik-Sultan-Bagadur seeks only to be entertained, and like the Baronessa, his taste is not at all discriminating. Still, when his entertainers fail to please him, the Sultan's punishment is terrible and swift: "as soon as Piublik-Sultan-Bagadur deigns to open his mouth wide and yawn, they disappear from the face of the earth,—they are beheaded, crushed into dust, burnt up, forgotten."[15] Despite his great power, however, Piublik-Sultan-Bagadur, again like the Baronessa, is unable to act in his own best interests and at the point the book review begins is so bored that he yawns nonstop, devastating the population of his realm. His ennui has reached such heights that even his faithful kapydzhi-bashi, our old friend Brambeus, is in despair, as the Sultan has taken it into his head to entertain himself by marrying a virgin every night and having her drowned the next day. To Brambeus's horror, his eldest daughter, Kritikzada, then offers herself as the next victim.

But Kritikzada has a plan, and armed with the latest books from the two distant, half-legendary cities of Moscow and St. Petersburg, she succeeds every night first in entertaining her terrible lord with her reviews and then in safely, without a single yawn, putting him to sleep. Kritikzada's road is not easy, and death tied up in the "sack of indifference" and drowned in the "sea of oblivion" often seems inevitable, for example on the fourth night when Kritikzada nauseates the Sultan with the review of three vulgar vaudevilles, or on the seventh when her exposition of the latest works in mathematics brings down upon the Sultan both a hernia and an attack of the plague. Thanks to her engaging and soporific recounting of a tale from a recently published almanac, however, Kritikzada is usually able to recoup her losses, and in the episode of the seventh night she has recourse to her "homeopathic means," as she receives a recently published work on hernias and one on the plague and cures her husband merely by summarizing their contents. Kritikzada's position remains precarious, but her hold over her powerful yet childlike husband is ever strengthened. On the fifth night the Sultan is already looking forward to their children, and by the eighth and final night he finally fills the "sack of indifference" not with Kritikzada but with her marvelous almanac, casting out the original text for the sake of his critic-wife's careful retelling.

The Romantic Context

The three landowners, the Baronessa, and the Sultan are so silly in their representation of readers and the reading public that generations of literary critics might be forgiven for their refusal to pay them any heed. Simply to read articles like the "Letter" or "Brambeus and the Young Literature" is to identify ourselves in some way with these other readers of Senkovskii, when few among us would appreciate the comparison. Surely most readers like to believe that they can think for themselves, and if the three landowners put up only a faint resistance, even the Baronessa and the Sultan ultimately accept the critic's "ready-made pleasures and ready-made thoughts." Whatever problems a simple reading poses, a critical reading is still worse, for we are then asked to identify in some way with both halves of the interaction, and literary scholars may be understandably reluctant to participate in the reduction of our critical vocation to a Keystone Kops comedy of reader manipulation.

Certainly critics in Senkovskii's own day felt a kind of horror at the story his criticism so often told. The reading public at large, however, did not share the critics' revulsion; in fact, just the opposite, as for reasons the critics could not quite fathom they instead subscribed to the *Library for Reading* in record numbers. It may be, as Belinskii argued, that Senkovskii's success derived from the fact that he had found a new and immature readership that truly was as ignorant and tractable as its various personifications in his criticism. What I will argue here, however, is that Senkovskii's way may also have been paved by the writing that went before and around it, including that of his fellow critics. The three landowners, the Baronessa, and the Sultan are indeed extraordinary beasts, but only in the degree of their exaggeration, for as we will see, highly ironic representations of readers and the act of reading ranging from the subtle to the downright insistent mark Romanticism in all its aspects, including both as an aesthetic theory and as a historical moment marked by the rise of the so-called literary marketplace.

REAL READERS AND FRIENDS

It is first of all a fact that what we might call real readers impinge on Romanticism in many important ways. There are, for instance, the numbers of subscribers to periodicals such as the *Library for Reading* or *Blackwood's*, and to lending libraries like Mudie's, and also the many effects that these numbers would seem to produce. The periodicals are often thought to have given rise to a new kind of literature, for example, while Mudie's is famously held to have used the fact of its large clientele to largely control the conditions of publishing in nineteenth-century Great Britain.[16] Real readers also appear in letters like the ones Robert Darnton found from Jean Ranson describing his enthusiastic reaction to Rousseau and his novel *Julie*, and even in diaries and memoiristic accounts. A particularly fascinating glimpse of an apparently real Romantic audience can be found in Benjamin Constant's diary where he recorded the often surprising reactions he received to his readings from various stages of *Adolphe*. These contradictory responses range from "Read my novel to Mme. de Coigny. Bizarre effect of the work on her. Revolt against the hero," to "Read my novel to Mme. Laborie. The women who were there all dissolved into tears," and even "Read my novel. Mad laughter."[17]

Constant did not read his work in progress to just anyone, although neither was the audience he found in various salons in both Paris and London made up solely of close friends or associates. A good many Romantic writers, however, did write both in and to a circle of friends, and these more specific and also more intimate readers have left their traces as well. There are, for example, the protocols of the meetings of the Russian literary group Arzamas (1815–18) which record the joking rituals that organized their gatherings and also the actual literature they read one to another. While these particular renderings of a group dynamic were not intended for publication, others were, most notably those produced by Jena.

The fact of the Schlegel brothers' circle of friends and lovers, readers and writers is made known to us through their copious correspondence, but it also spills over into their published work. The *Athenaeum* is filled with dialogues and conversations that reflect in various ways the actual lives of their authors, perhaps most notably in the case of Friedrich's *Dialogue on Poetry* (1800). Scholars still debate the exact identity of the various participants in Friedrich's *Dialogue*, although Lacoue-Labarthe and Nancy state without hesitation that Amanda corresponds to August Wilhelm's wife Caroline, Camilla to Friedrich's soon-to-be wife Dorothea, Ludovico to Schelling, Lothario to Novalis, Marcus to Tieck, Andrea to August Wilhelm and, "last but not least" Antonio to Friedrich himself.[18] What everyone seems to agree on, however, is that the *Dialogue* is a reflection not just of the circle in general but specifically of their real gathering in the fall of 1799 at August Wilhelm and Caroline Schlegel's house for what the real Tieck later called "a never-ending feast of wit, humor, and philosophy."[19]

READERS AND FRIENDS LESS REAL

When the apparent representation of real readers, whether taken in their more abstract form as the reading public or more concretely as specific and readily identifiable friends, moves into published, literary texts, real readers start to become but one aspect of a great attention to reading that Romanticism displays on any number of levels. As Rajan writes with regard to Coleridge's poem "This Lime-Tree Bower My Prison," nominally addressed to his friend Charles Lamb: "The extraordinary complexity of this poem stems from the fact that it is not simply a conversation poem but also a poem that thematizes reading," for "the intention of the poem as persuasive argument is greatly complicated by the fact that reading is not simply part of the poem's generic frame but also its subject."[20] It is the same phenomenon that Philip Martin addresses in his wonderfully sharp *Byron: A Poet Before His Public* (1982), or that Darnton touches on in his reading of readers as created by Rousseau's *Julie*. In the Russian context, too, an attention to and awareness of audiences of all kinds is rampant, in Rudyi Pan'ko's addresses to his readers and in those of Gogol himself, for example, or in the multilayered narration that makes up Lermontov's *A Hero of Our Time* (1841).[21] But perhaps the most thoroughly explored instances of the Russian Romantic thematization of reading are given by Pushkin.[22]

Eugene Onegin, for example, begins with a preface apparently addressing the work to Pushkin's real friend and publisher P. A. Pletnev, an extremely limited audience that is then flagrantly compromised by the narrator's tendency to refer repeatedly to readers and reading in various guises throughout the work. The readers referred to in *Eugene Onegin* are notably also the main characters, as Nabokov has famously read the novel as the clash of world views as both represented and created by the characters' reading habits: Tatiana as a reader of the Richardsonian sentimental novel understands Onegin only when she reads his Byron, while Onegin in turn has little patience for the idealism Lenskii has learned from Schiller. In the case of the *Tales of Belkin*, the many levels of narrators described in the last chapter are matched by many levels of narratees, and the various readings as well as writings offered by A. P.'s preface then frame readings of all sorts in the *Tales* themselves, usually wrong ones; for example, in Samson Vyrin's misapplication in "The Stationmaster" of the story of the Prodigal Son to his own daughter, or in Maria Gavrilovna's misunderstanding of the genre of her own life in "The Blizzard."

David Bethea and Serge Davydov argue that Pushkin's intent in the *Tales* is largely parodic, as "[a]t once both saturnine coffin maker and puckish god of love, A. P. weds his fortunate couples over the graves of stock heroes and weds Russian prose to a western European tradition over the graves of domestic poets."[23] For this parody to work readers *of* the text have to understand how readers *in* the text read wrongly and themselves read rightly. This "qualified reader" is then so fundamental to the achievement of the work's meaning that E. S. Afanas'ev can argue that what Pushkin offers in the *Tales* is "a different type of prose, at the center of which are found the relationships of author to reader."[24] While Afanas'ev does not give a name to this "different type of prose," we can. In this sense, just as in the question of originality that so marks *Eugene Onegin*, Pushkin's prose is quintessentially Romantic, a perfect example of the Romantic attention to reading that Rajan describes. If the *Tales of Belkin* offer a particularly apt example, however, still Pushkin's texts leave open the question of just what purpose this trope of reading might serve, and it is here that the work of his less subtle colleagues in the later literary periodicals proves especially useful.

READERS IN THE LATER LITERARY PERIODICALS

While scholars are familiar with the centrality of readers and reading to Romantic literary texts, they have paid less attention to the apotheosis of this theme as found in the critical works of the later periodicals. This critical gap is especially striking given that the example of the periodicals casts the Romantic reader in a very particular light. Afanas'ev's "relationships of author to reader" suggest some sort of exchange between two somewhat unstable entities who can connect in multiple ways. The literary periodicals render this instability of identity in such extreme and even comical terms, however, that it is no longer clear if there are actually two separate entities involved, and if not, the picture changes drastically, for if we are left with only one great writer-critic-reader, an apparent multiplicity of relationships collapses into no relationship with any other at all. Once more we find ourselves in a realm ruled by the critic alone, as critical omnipotence turns out to be the aim of an apparent focus on the reader all along.

What is most readily apparent in the later periodicals, however, is not a collapse into critical solipsism, but a tension stretched almost impossibly thin between the representations of different kinds of readers. On the one hand, Senkovskii and his journalistic brethren never let us forget that their readers are emphatically, tangibly real in the sense of the real customers who keep these unabashedly commercial enterprises afloat. At the same time, though, they intentionally make their readers real in an entirely different sense of the word, paradoxically representing a more or less obviously nonexistent reader in increasingly material terms. Belinskii once described the reading public as a "terrible invisible master."[25] In the process of the relentless reader personification undertaken by the later literary periodicals, Belinskii's "terrible master," for all his or her buying power, begins to look a great deal more like a pawn in the hands of the real power, once more the critic.

Just as there were other writer-critics in Russia of the 1830s who attempted to make their living at writing, so were there others who tended to stage a play of reading in their criticism. When Nadezhdin signs his letter to the editor of *Telescope* as "Don Juan-Alonzo-Salveto-Kverera-Estremaduro-

Velasko-Gvadalkviviro-Ponso, native-born Spanish Nobleman," for example, he is impersonating his readership in exactly the same way as Brambeus
does in his "First Letter to Baron Brambeus from Three Landowners from
Tver," while Nikodim Nadoumko's friends Tlenskii, Fliugerovskii, and
Pakhom Silich model reading just as do the Baronessa and the Sultan. In an
earlier exchange with the editors of *Son of the Fatherland and the Northern
Archive*, Nadezhdin also participated in a still more complicated rendering
of the reader in mock-realistic terms.

In 1829 Nikolai Grech and Faddei Bulgarin decided to combine what had
been two separate periodicals, Grech's *Son of the Fatherland* and Bulgarin's
Northern Archive, into one, and in the second issue of the newly joint enterprise the last section, "Miscellany," they introduced a new feature, "The
Box."[26] In a lengthy note the editors explain:

> At the doors of the typography where this Journal is published, there is a box
> into which proof sheets, letters, packages and so on can be tossed from the ves-
> tibule, so as not to have to open the doors all the time and bother the workers.
> The publishers happened to find in this box the most amusing things, delivered
> to them by certain parties who desire to maintain a strict incognito. At the
> present time they have conceived the notion of publishing certain of the articles
> received in this fashion, with the request the lovers of Literature henceforth
> make use of the *typographic box.*[27]

It just so happens that almost all of the "most amusing things" they find there
turn out to be criticism directed against Nadezhdin's alter ego, Nikodim
Nadoumko, and to the journal that at the time provided him his forum, the
Herald of Europe.[28] The first few, including one titled "Questions for Mr.
Ex-Student Nedoumko," are indeed published under the strictest anonymity.[29] A later attack on the overly hellenized spelling and style of the *Herald*, however, titled "A Letter to M. T. Kachenovskii," editor of the *Herald*,
is signed by the suspiciously overhellenized name (especially as spelled by
the *Son of the Fatherland and the Northern Archive*) Ippolit Filipsilofitinskii,
while a "Letter to the Publishers" on the same topic is signed "A Passer-By."

Nadezhdin was no doubt pleased to be the recipient of so much attention, as he quickly responded in kind. The "Miscellany" section in the seventh issue of the *Herald of Europe* for 1829 is headed "To the Typographic
box of Messrs. the Publishers of the *Son of the Fatherland and the Northern
Archive.*" The first item under this heading is a lengthy defense against the
attacks of Ippolit Filipsilofitinskii written by one Ippolit Mezhdometnyi, or

Ippolit Interjection; this piece is then followed by two shorter blasts from Nadoumko himself, responding to the attacks on his own person. By the ninth issue of the same year Nadoumko announces that the "Typographic box" has closed, to the apparent misfortune of the editors. "Now where will the industrious editors of S. F. and N. A. dig up trash and rubbish?" Nadoumko asks. "Where will they find the stones with which to take aim at their humble brethren and oppress passers-by with fear? . . . The poor passers-by, the poor investors in S. F. and N. A.!" Fortunately the journal has compensated for the loss of its "Box" by absorbing its function into the journal as a whole, turning itself into one great Box that devotes it-self to attacking "everything journalistic and newspaperly." Here, however, Nadoumko indicates a footnote, and when we turn our eyes to the bottom of the page we read: "Excuse me, but not *everything*; there are exceptions, although they change with the direction of the weathervane. *Noted by an unknown visitor to the Typography*."[30]

With this footnote Nadezhdin adds yet another layer of readership to what is already a many-leveled phenomenon. There are the various writers busily reading one another's work, then the alleged "ordinary" readers dropping their missives into the *Son of the Fatherland and the Northern Archive*'s box. Now the *Herald of Europe* has its own anonymous reader, one who apparently read Nadoumko's piece somewhere in page proofs. If this sort of performance of reading is not unlike what we find in Schlegel, for example, or in Pushkin, still the game as it is played in the *Herald of Europe* and *Son of the Fatherland and the Northern Archive* is a little different. As we attempt to attach meaning to the Romantic trope of the reader, the question of the amount or perhaps kind of these readers' reality makes a crucial difference. If Romantic reader-personae come joined to bodies in the world, or even if we are supposed to believe that they do, we might then understand their presence as reflecting some sort of shift in literary power away from real writers and toward real readers or the appearance of a literary marketplace. Certainly the Russian periodical press in Senkovskii's day has been associated with both of these phenomena. What we find in the later Romantic literary journals, however, is Romantic reader-personae who have instead been largely cut loose from what we might call the "real world" and turned into something of a joke.

It is hardly likely that we are intended to believe in the fleshly reality of an "unknown visitor to the Typography," let alone in "Ippolit Interjection" or "Don Juan-Alonzo-Salveto-Kverera-Estremaduro-Velasko-Gvadalkviviro-Ponso, native-born Spanish Nobleman," as Nadezhdin, like Senkovskii, seems to mock the possibility of reader-contributors rather than encourage, let alone defer to them. The more or less obvious artificiality of their reader-personae would suggest rather that we remain in a world ruled by the writer-critic alone, which in Russia would seem to be the case. As we have seen, despite the 5,000 subscribers to the *Library for Reading*, there is little evidence in Russia for any real rise of a literary marketplace nor for any corresponding changes in the makeup of the reading public. Once again, though, Russian critical practice may have less to do with the realities of the Russian socioeconomic situation, whatever they may be, than with the reading habits of Russian critics.

In fact, I would argue, the reader-personae we find in the Russian periodicals reflect Romanticism more generally, as for all their absurdity they display clear affinities for the apparent product of a very different socioeconomic climate, the British reader-personae who fill the pages of *Blackwood's* and *Fraser's*. Again, these affinities are most probably not coincidental, as we know that Senkovskii was familiar at least with *Blackwood's* regular feature, the *Noctes Ambrosianae*. The *Noctes* offered a parody of Schlegel's *Dialogue on Poetry* or a sort of mock Arzamas in which the various contributors to *Blackwood's* in their personified forms perform a writing and reading about literature over dinner and drinks at Ambrose's Tavern, all presided over by Christopher North. The famous "Election of the Editor" that announced the founding of the journal *Fraser's* offers another very funny example of the British tendency to represent readers on various and even contradictory levels, and one that indicates particularly well the critical purposes this sort of personification of the reader can serve. There may be real readers in Great Britain, and they may be paying the salaries of any number of journal editors. Still, the power that *Fraser's* hands over to these readers would seem to be largely imaginary, a democratic window dressing for what is in fact a very different form of government.

Romantic Politics

Fraser's Magazine for Town and Country launched its first monthly issue in February, 1830. The editor and guiding force of the magazine through the 1830s was William Maginn, formerly of *Blackwood's,* where he wrote under the pseudonym Sir Morgan Odoherty and also invented the *Noctes Ambrosianae* as another avatar of Christopher North.[31] At *Fraser's* Maginn gathered many of his old friends around him, in fact quite literally so, as the contributors met regularly for actual dinners in the back room of James Fraser's establishment at 215 Regent Street. These gatherings were immortalized in Daniel Maclise's January 1835 portrait of the "Fraserians," and also in Maginn's regular accounts in *Fraser's* of their "symposiacs." While both the pictorial and the literary forms drew on some form of reality, however, they also transformed that reality in significant ways.

In the case of Maclise's sketch, as Patrick Leary notes, some of the magazine's most prolific contributors are not pictured at all, while some of those who are pictured, for example Thackeray, published little or nothing in *Fraser's.* In Leary's reckoning:

> Of the twenty-seven men pictured, Lockhart may have written one page-long sketch of his friend Maginn, while Hook may have collaborated with Maginn on one spoof, and Brewster published three articles. Six others—Southey, Murphy, Coleridge, D'Orsay, Hook, and Jerdan—published nothing at all that subsequent scholars have been able to identify. For that matter, Coleridge, one of the magazine's patron saints, had died in 1834, the year before the depicted dinner was represented to have taken place.[32]

As for the "symposiacs," the problem is more that the participants are not all exactly of a fleshly kind. Maginn himself, for example, appears only in the form of O'Doherty, who is not himself presented as the editor of *Fraser's.* The editor of *Fraser's* and host of its dinners is yet another persona, one Oliver Yorke, and it is the circumstances of the alleged Yorke's alleged election to that lofty position that are most revealing of *Fraser's* aims.

While William Maginn, like Senkovskii, actually produced an astonishing amount of the material that filled *Fraser's,* both the "symposiacs" and Maclise's sketch served to promote the legend of the "Fraserians," the convivial group that supposedly produced the magazine together and was described in an 1837 account of the magazine as "a happy brotherhood," or "a little literary republic of themselves."[33] This "little literary republic," moreover, was allegedly made up not just of the various contributors all on an equal footing with the editor, but also of the editor together with his readers, as *Fraser's* presented itself as unique among British magazines for having an editor, Oliver Yorke, democratically elected by its readers. In the April 1830 issue a notice was issued:

Aux Lecteurs,
And the World at large:

As the Proprietors of "FRASER'S MAGAZINE" are resolved to have the Work conducted upon the most liberal and efficient principles, they have declined to listen to the various private Communications from the first literary men of the day, for appointment to the honourable situation of Editor. A work of such superior eminence, embracing all that is great and good, is entitled to be conducted by the very first genius, whom this, or any other nation, can produce. The Proprietors, therefore, have resolved to Poll the Country, aliens or denizens, rich or poor, young or old, people or peers, subject or prince, and select the individual who, from intrinsic worth and merit, has best claim to the important charge in question.

Therefore Notice hereby given

That all applicants for the Situation of Editor to "FRASER'S MAGAZINE" do attend at Freemason's Hall, at One o'Clock, on Wednesday the 14th day of April, of this present year—bringing with them their testimonials and documents on which they rest their pretensions—that then and there the individual best qualified may be selected and appointed as aforesaid. Parties who cannot personally be present, are requested to transmit their Name, Address, and Note of Qualifications, by letter POST-PAID—addressed to MR. FRASER, Bookseller and Publisher, No. 215, Regent-Street—before Twelve o'Clock of the day.[34]

Over the next several months beginning in the May issue, *Fraser's* then published an account of the proceedings of this supposed election.

According to "Mr. Gurney's short-hand notes, corrected by Mr. Alexander Fraser, of Thavies Inn," due to an unexpectedly large turnout, the election was moved from the Freemason's Tavern to Lincoln's-inn Square. There the meeting is called to order by Coleridge, who as the chairman "elected by acclamation" opens the proceedings with an apparently spontaneously composed "poetical address" quoted in its entirety.[35] The many candidates for the position of editor of *Fraser's* then stand up to make their cases, which generally consist of more or less open admissions of their intent to connive with the booksellers, for example, or to pocket the salary without doing the work. Among these candidates we meet many of the leading London literary lights of the day, both those who come attached to bodies in the world and those who do not.

Thomas Moore proposes himself, for example, as does the Rev. George Croly and also Sir Morgan O'Doherty. James Hogg, a.k.a. the Ettrick Shepherd, has his letter read aloud by Mr. William Jerdan, while Allan Cunningham reads a letter from Mephistopheles, who recommends himself strongly as "the counterpart of old Christy North."[36] Christopher North himself later appears to defend *Blackwood's* against its many detractors, followed shortly by William Blackwood, referred to in this account (as in the *Noctes Ambrosianae*) as Ebony, who protests in the strongest Scotch at the defection of many of his contributors to the side of the new magazine. Various other figures appear although without making long speeches, including, for example, Dr. Maginn himself and the Duke of Wellington. Finally, to the great delight of the ladies, a handsome and unknown young man stands up before the crowd. Identifying himself as Oliver or "honest Noll" Yorke, the young man briefly tells the tragic tale of lost love that motivates his candidacy for the position of editor. "I want employment for my thoughts," Yorke concludes:

> to bring deep sleep to my recollections. I fear not competition. Is there one of the miserable pretenders before me who dare to raise their feeble voices and say they hope to live till a second sun arises, in possession of the world's fair opinion, if they enter into the lists with Noll Yorke? I once more appeal to that fair jury . . . ; I abide by their decision. They are the queens of our creation. I—you—all—are bound to obey their decree.

A "bevy of beauty" instantly surrounds Yorke and leads him to the podium, where the ladies entreat his candidacy. Coleridge then turns to the crowd for their opinion, and:

> Instantly all the people with one voice, shouted—
> "Noll Yorke and Regina for Ever!"
> And again all London echoed with—
> "NOLL YORKE AND REGINA!"
> "NOLL YORKE AND THE QUEEN OF MAGAZINES!"[37]

With that the interested parties, now with Oliver Yorke in charge, depart for dinner at the Freemason's Tavern.

On one level the implication of the "Election of the Editor" would seem to be that some sort of revolution has taken place. As Yorke himself later puts it in the "Symposiac the First":

> [T]he alteration of the face of affairs on the Continent cannot be more aptly compared to anything that I know of, than to the revolutionary appearance

imposed upon the whole periodical world of England by Fraser's Magazine. [*Loud cheers.*] There is what the French would have called a *bouleversement.* The old and worn-out despots are chased away, or their domination totters. A new order of things is prevailing, and the effete editors and curmudgeon contributors are gone to their native abode of darkness, never to emerge.[38]

In their place the reins of power have apparently been taken up by readers, especially of the female variety as embodied by their handsome and unanimously elected representative, Oliver Yorke. At the same time, though, on another level this *bouleversement* is a complete and obvious farce.

This election never took place, and no one thinks that it did. Coleridge, Thomas Moore, the Rev. George Croly, William Blackwood, and other "real" participants in the affair never spoke the lines Maginn gives to them here, nor did those figures who partake of a more ambivalent and more literary reality, for example Mephistopheles or Christopher North. Perhaps Oliver Yorke and his lady readers can be considered to have said and done what is attributed to them here, but only because they are wholly the invention of William Maginn. While there really is a Lincoln's-inn Square, the likes of Sir Morgan O'Doherty and the Duke of Wellington, not to mention Sir Morgan O'Doherty and William Maginn himself, could not interact there. The space of their interaction is instead a virtual Lincoln's-inn Square, a mock public sphere or marketplace as rendered in the pages of *Fraser's Magazine,* and this space is anything but democratic. Despite the claims made by the legend of the "Fraserians" or the story of Noll Yorke and his lady readers, *Fraser's* was instead a space that was ruled for many years entirely and even despotically by William Maginn alone.

Oliver Yorke's commentary in the "Symposiac the First" makes very clear the political dimensions of the Romantic representation of readers and reading. Whether we consider the texts themselves, their authors, or critical commentary then and now, we often find a strong if simplistic sense of some kind of democratic impulse, as if the real readership is growing or changing and authors are entering into true collaborations with their audiences, whether that audience is cast as friends or customers, real or imagined. As Noll Yorke notes, this apparent literary democracy finds its counterpart in political events of the day, including not just the French Revolution, but also, in the Russian context, the 1825 Decembrist Rebellion. Certainly the list of Romantic writers associated with progressive politics is long, even if many, like Schlegel and Wordsworth, later threw in their lot entirely with the establishment while others, like Gogol, were simply misunderstood from the start. *Fraser's* "Election of the Editor" makes the point, however, that democracy in the Romantic context is best understood in ironic terms.

What is especially striking in the example of *Fraser's* is the paradoxical combination of the journal's real and long-standing reputation as a "little literary republic" with the obviously joking pretense of the writer-critic's handing over power to his or her readers, and it is exactly this same paradox that marks the *Library for Reading*. On the one hand the *Library for Reading* famously turned its attention away from the literary elite of the capitals toward a new, much larger, and mostly provincial reading public, as if to give the average reader a voice in the literary world, and Senkovskii was often accused of simply pandering to this new readership. This apparent transfer of power on the outside of the journal may also appear to be matched by a transfer of power on the inside, for example when Brambeus is forced by the Baronessa into an ignominious retreat to Germany, or when Kritikzada fears for her life at the hands of the Sultan. Again, though, as in the case of *Fraser's*, any apparent power sharing on the part of the Baron and Kritikzada is but a veneer adorning what is really a critical coup d'état. Brambeus, after all, openly tells us that what the reader wants is "ready-made pleasures and ready-made thoughts," and that is exactly what we get, as Senkovskii's critical practice in the *Library for Reading* might best be described as an extreme and even contradictory version of reader response.

In his "Prolegomena to a Theory of Reading" (1980) Jonathan Culler asks that a reader-oriented literary criticism explain what he calls "facts about form and meaning," a process that involves making explicit "the special conventions and procedures of interpretation that enable readers to move from the linguistic meaning of sentences to the literary meaning of works."[39] Culler's reader-response critic, then, would identify and analyze the acts of "real" readers but also, through his or her creation of ideal, "hypothetical" readers, teach those "real" readers how to read better. Senkovskii's reader-personae, particularly the Baronessa and the Sultan, provide obvious examples, in fact, too obvious, of Culler's "hypothetical" reader created by the critic to teach "real" readers what and how to read. Senkovskii exceeds Culler's directive by creating his "hypothetical" readers with such artistry that they entirely overwhelm the real ones.

In the pages of Senkovskii's criticism "hypothetical" critics and "hypothetical" readers come to life, each gifted with his or her own idiosyncratic personality and much more alive than the shadowy "real" critic and "real" readers we can only imagine. The "real literary public" we saw described in "Brambeus and the Young Literature" as flitting here and there in the scant hours of free time between morning duties and evening entertainments is the palest of beings next to the three landowners, the Baronessa, and the Sultan, while the "real" literary critic, Senkovskii himself, is drab and dull compared with his exotic fictional doubles. As Brambeus and Kritikzada play the parts of critics while the three landowners, the Baronessa, and Piublik-Sultan-Bagadur play the parts of readers, Senkovskii does not just tell his "real" readers how to read and how not to read but also shows them, his many characters enacting before our eyes the interpretative moves that constitute reading, and as the lines separating "real" and "hypothetical" become increasingly blurred, showing how to read turns into actually doing the reading for us.

Senkovskii does the reading for us because his drama of reading can only be understood one way. Contemporary reader-response theories do not intend to restrict meaning; indeed, just the opposite, for they generally derive the importance of the reader from the existence of gaps within every text—gaps, as Culler tells us, that come from the potential reversibility of every figure, as every figure can be read either referentially or rhetorically, first one and then the other, creating a chain of meaning presumably unique to every reader.[40] Senkovskii's figures, however, are not potentially reversible. Over and over again Senkovskii's joke is to literalize metaphors, turning ideas into passengers needing horses and travel papers, for example, or a sturdy moral defense into a large expanse of flesh, so that his ideas are not potentially reversible but rather in a permanent state of reversion; there is nowhere that we the readers can take those figures that they have not already been. In Senkovskii's criticism real readers are constrained by imaginary ones and our reading preempted by his, as Senkovskii is ultimately no more willing to cede power to readers than he is to writers. We are left with the choice of reading Senkovskii's criticism his way or not reading it at all.

The Romantic Absorption of the Reader

Senkovskii's example demonstrates a sleight of hand at work in many attempts at reader response, Foucault's "What Is an Author?" included, that, in apparently trying to hand power over to readers, instead concentrate it in the hands of the critic as a kind of super-reader. Culler, for example, quietly returns power to the critic when he writes: "Either teachers of literature have brought off an unprecedented confidence trick, or else there is knowledge and skill involved in reading literature: skill which can be imparted."[41] The same movement from controlling text to controlling critic much more dramatically marks Stanley Fish's triumphant claim: "No longer is the critic the humble servant of texts whose glories exist independently of anything he might do; it is what he does, within the constraints embedded in the literary institution, that brings texts into being and makes them available for analysis and appreciation."[42] Whatever might account for this subterfuge as practiced by contemporary reader-response critics, in the case of Senkovskii and the later Romantic periodicals we might try to associate this move once more with the exigencies of the literary marketplace.

The trope of reading that marks all of Romanticism has been loosely associated with the rise of the literary marketplace in a number of different ways. There is a sort of neutral stance which would argue that Romantic writers, for finding themselves apparently newly dependent on an increasingly anonymous reading public, necessarily if unconsciously reflect in their texts their awareness of the fact of writing now not just to friends and acquaintances but also to customers. If real readers of both sorts inspire the fictional ones, then we might argue that the representation of readers and reading in Romantic texts truly does offer an opening in the text for other voices, at least in the sense of Bakhtinian dialogism. The word may still be the writer's, but the writer's very tendency to tell a tale of reading makes evident the extent to which his or her word has been shaped by what Bakhtin calls its blatant orientation "towards a future answer-word."[43]

This awareness of the reader, however, often elides easily into an awareness of the reader's deficiencies, and like Culler, Romantic writers might seek not just to anticipate the real words of real readers but also to mold them. While the Baronessa and the Sultan seem a particularly hapless pair, still, as we heard with the cry of *Vieleserei* in Chapter One, the new readers of an apparently burgeoning literary marketplace in Russia, Great Britain, and elsewhere have generally been credited with a good deal less sophistication than the smaller and more elite reading publics of earlier eras. Accordingly it may be that Romantic writers seek in their representations of reading not to cater to or even simply include their audience, but to model right reading for readers who lack both experience and education, perhaps because they are of a lower class or increasingly female. In this sense the "qualified reader" that Afanas'ev describes may be less the necessary condition for Pushkin's prose than its intended product, and the Baron and Kritikzada only more openly enact a critical shaping of the reader that Belkin left implicit.

While readers ill-equipped to understand the choices before them already make rather poor participants in a literary democracy, this urge toward didacticism may also re-combine with the literary marketplace to produce a still more ominous phenomenon. Despite his emphasis on the democratic potential of the participatory public spheres offered by the media, Raymond Williams in *The Long Revolution* (1961) also acknowledges, in Kristin Leaver's words, that "the media operates within a marketplace that works insistently to construct its audiences as consumers, and that the ideological and economic conditions of production in class society implicitly exclude certain groups from full participation in the public exchange of ideas."[44] The sort of didacticism that the literary journals of the 1830s offer, then, may be intended to shape not just an audience for literature, but specifically an audience for the *Library for Reading* or for *Fraser's*, and that audience creation operates by convincing the reader that he or she is already part of an intimate, special set.

Peter Murphy, following the work done by Jon Klancher, argues that the readers we find in *Blackwood's* ease the reading public's transition to the literary marketplace by reproducing an old way of being that the literary marketplace has replaced. Instead of what Murphy calls the world "full of anonymous faces, large profits and mass markets" that is the new, or at least the perceived reality, all these "dialogues" and "conversations" between writer- and reader-personae offer a fictional rendering of an apparently earlier intimacy and even orality that the marketplace has done away with once and for all.[45] By the same token, the great familiarity with the reader that marks so much of Russian literature in the 1830s, from Pushkin's *Tales* to Gogol's and Odoevskii's, can be seen to artificially reproduce the intimacy that was the hallmark of the Russian literary salons in the 1810s and 1820s, as exemplified once again in the protocols of Arzamas that were never even intended for publication.[46]

In the Russian context, though, it is apparently only in Senkovskii's hands that this familiarity has so obviously been transformed from a democratic gesture into a selling point, a fact that would seem to set his trope of the reader apart from earlier renderings as it separates the workings of the literary marketplace from the more idealistic operations of Romantic aesthetics.

I have already indicated, however, the extent to which Senkovskii's practice of reader creation in fact finds echoes in other periodicals. What I would suggest now is that the coercive elements of that practice also underlie other, apparently more pure representations of the reader in earlier Romantic texts. Certainly a literary marketplace, real or imagined, might conform the rendering of readers and reading to itself in any number of complicated ways, limiting readers' options within the text, for example, while at the same time enfranchising ever new readers. Still, we can account for the multileveled and contradictory nature of Romantic readers without any recourse to the marketplace at all. For any attribution of Senkovskii's particular representation of the reader to his grasping commercialism alone ignores not just the important role readers play in Romantic theory, but the various modes in which they do so.

On the most idealistic level, if Friedrich Schlegel's Romantic work marked by heterogeneity, fragmentariness, and infinite incompletion is still to be *a work*, a whole of its own, it is only because the reader can create that whole through an act of reading that *Athenaeum Fragment* 116 appropriately enough calls "divinatory criticism." As reading is to provide, in Benjamin's words, a method of the work's "consummation," so it is every reader's function to become the "true reader" who, as Novalis writes, "must be the extended author. . . . the higher tribunal who receives the case already worked up in advance by the lower authorities."[47] These quotes would seem to offer the text up to the mercies of real readers who are then co-creators of the work of art together with writers, and the apparent political dimensions of Jena's program are perhaps made most clear in Friedrich's *Critical Fragment* 103, where he calls for the work to be joined by "that free and equal fellowship in which, so the wise men assure us, the citizens of the perfect state will live."[48] These political dimensions partake also of the personal, as an absence of hierarchy is expressed again in the theme of the friendship of writer and reader that runs through all of Jena's published works.[49]

Friedrich Schlegel seemingly reaches out to his real friends in the fundamental *Frühromantik* notions of "sympoetry," for example, and also of *Witz*, that all-important element of the ideal Romantic genre that Friedrich in *Critical Fragment* 9 defines as "absolute social feeling or fragmentary genius." The idea of poetry as an exchange or social act among equals also finds formal expression in the many dialogues and conversations that fill the *Athenaeum*. The *Dialogue on Poetry*, for example, which in its very form embodies the ideas of the symposium and its "fragmentary geniality," also begins with prefatory remarks that prepare the reader for the *Dialogue* by explaining its basic principles. Lest we wonder why Antonio and his friends have gathered together for this conversation, the introduction explains that "[l]ove needs a responding love," and that "for the true poet communication, even with those who only play on the colorful surface, can be beneficial and instructive" for "[h]e is a social being."[50]

Gary Handwerk has argued that this ironic construction of the fragmentary and provisional self only through ongoing dialogue with the other is as much an ethical as an aesthetic act. Romantic irony, in this sense, is not just a way of (de)constructing a literary work, but a particular way of being in the world: as Schlegel puts it with just a touch of sentimentality, "[l]ove needs a responding love." Without in any way questioning Schlegel's commitment to ethical irony, however, I would note that all of Schlegel's dialogic texts, the *Dialogue* included, also openly find that "responding love" largely within themselves, a tendency that on another level (ironically) calls into question Schlegel's in any event brief democratic leanings and, along with them, the meaningfulness of any real audience.

Just as we might account for the prominence of readers and reading in Romantic literature generally by the presence (or absence) of certain kinds of real, historical readers, so we might argue that all the various dialogic and/or epistolary pieces in the *Athenaeum* reflect specifically the real circle at Jena. To do so, however, is to overlook the actual workings of these texts, as the *Dialogue on Poetry* demonstrates. The *Dialogue* contains its own readers who model for us possible responses to the various texts mostly in the pauses between the different presentations, with the important exception of that part of the *Dialogue* that is Antonio's "Letter on the Novel." In the case of the "Letter" at least one reader's response is also anticipated in the piece itself, which Antonio claims to have written originally to Amalia but that he then, with Amalia's permission, reads aloud to the entire group. While he is now reading to the entire group, however, Antonio still addresses Amalia throughout, beginning his presentation, for example, with the words "I must retract, my dear lady, what I seemed to say yesterday in your defense, and say that you are almost completely wrong."[51]

It is no accident that scholars cannot agree on the exact identities of the *Dialogue*'s participants, for in this layering of readers within readers so that Amalia models the group who models the ideal reader Schlegel suggests that his readers are something other than his real friends and equals, and in *Critical Fragment* 112 he reveals his hand in a still more straightforward fashion. "The analytic writer," he explains, "observes the reader as he is; and accordingly he makes his calculations and sets up his machines in order to make the proper impression on him." On the other hand:

> The synthetic writer constructs and creates a reader as he should be; he doesn't imagine him calm and dead, but alive and critical. He allows whatever he has created to take shape gradually before the reader's eyes, or else he tempts him to discover it himself. He doesn't try to make any particular impression on him, but enters with him into the sacred relationship of deepest symphilosophy or sympoetry.[52]

It would seem contradictory that the "deepest symphilosophy or sympoetry" arises not when the analytic writer "observes the reader as he is" but when the synthetic writer "constructs and creates a reader as he should be," but this contradiction, as Schlegel well knows, is fundamental to Romanticism.

In *Critical Fragment* 112 real readers are also ideal readers, the living and critical products of a "synthetic" writer who is him- or herself also an unstable amalgam of life and literature, a revelation that renders extremely problematic the whole notion of collaboration as it undercuts Jena's many expressions of friendship. Certainly Romantic texts ranging from the *Noctes Ambrosianae* to the Russian salon poetry of the 1820s often present themselves as produced by and for a small group of friends or "happy brotherhood," and if these representations of intimacy on some level reflect an earlier reality when readers and writers really did know one another, still *Critical Fragment* 112 suggests that for Schlegel the "deepest symphilosophy or sympoetry" never did depend on the real collaboration of real friends nor even of real people. Senkovskii's later obvious manipulation of his readers may reflect a changed literary world where we are not all friends any more, but then, as *Critical Fragment* 112 reminds us, we never were, and the phoniness of Senkovskii's gestures of intimacy serves also to raise the curtain on an illusion that at least Friedrich Schlegel always knew that he was perpetuating. Schlegel was well aware that while Romanticism ideally offered a democracy of reader and writer, that democracy was always ironically already a critical dictatorship, and in "On Philosophy. To Dorothea" he even casts his critical omnipotence, exactly as Maginn and Senkovskii later would, in the form of a romance with the reader.

Romancing the Reader

If Senkovskii's criticism tends to tell a story of the marriage of critic and reader and all the ladies fall in love with Oliver Yorke, it is because there is a romance to Romanticism, and especially to Romanticism as imagined by Jena. According to *Athenaeum Fragment* 116, Schlegel's "Romantic kind of poetry" is to reconcile every imaginable opposition, from epistemology and ontology to parts and wholes, subject and object, and criticism and poetry, and this aspiration for Romantic genre is notably also an aspiration for Romantic androgyny, as Schlegel frequently sums up the infinite set of apparently equal and opposite pairs by what one critic calls "the prototype of all polarities," the eternal dichotomy of male and female.[53] While Schlegel claims true androgyny when it suits his purposes, he is more often drawn to marriage as the most obvious real-world incarnation of an otherwise irretrievably lost androgynous ideal, and in works like the *Dialogue on Poetry* or his scandalous novel *Lucinde* (1800), the reconciliation of male and female in a romantic relationship often serves him as a kind of shorthand, a concise but infinitely expandable representation of his proposed Romantic genre.[54] In "On Philosophy. To Dorothea," however, the romance that Schlegel then offers to bridge this ultimate opposition turns out to subvert his apparent aim.

"On Philosophy" was published in the *Athenaeum* in 1799 and is couched as an open letter to Schlegel's then mistress and later wife, Dorothea Veit, encouraging her apparently unfeminine interest in philosophy. In fact, Friedrich tells Dorothea, philosophy is precisely what women need in order to lift themselves from their everyday world and realize their true humanity, while poetry is what men need to return them to earth. Fortunately, what one gender lacks is what the other has to give, and Friedrich proposes a romantic relationship whereby he and Dorothea would together make up the ideal "balance in human life [that] can only be obtained through antitheses." As the two will combine to make one whole, however, at the same time through their love for one another they will also better approximate that balance each within him- or herself alone. Friedrich hints at something more like true androgyny when he claims that sexual difference is finally meaningless, a merely "external aspect of human existence" and even an obstacle to the creation of a harmoniously whole human being. "Only a gentle masculinity, only an autonomous femininity are right, true and beautiful," he writes. "And if this is so, one must not further exaggerate the character of the sex in any way . . . but rather seek to soften it by means of powerful countermeasures, so that everyone, in what is proper to him or her, is able to find a space as boundless as possible in which to move freely, according to pleasure and love, in the entire sphere of humanity."[55] According to Friedrich, what Dorothea as a woman needs is to develop the tendency within her own self toward masculine philosophy and abstract thought. She also needs to find a voice, and a written voice in particular.

The association of the feminine with orality that marks all of Schlegel's works is particularly prominent in "On Philosophy," as Friedrich describes Dorothea as one who "disdains everything written and lettered" and who "would probably prefer a conversation" to his letter. Writing, however, is what she will get, both because Friedrich as a man is himself "an author through and through," and because the dawn of eternity glimmers only through the written word. For Friedrich "the silent strokes . . . are a more fitting husk for the deepest, most immediate expression of the spirit than the breath of the lips," because "to live is to write" and the sole destiny of humanity is "to engrave the thoughts of the divinity on the tablet of nature with the stylus of the forming spirit." Dorothea, he says, must take her part in the development of the human race, "be silent less" and, when it comes time to read the divine writing, do her own work rather than "just let others read for her and explain [it] to her."[56]

The didactic tone Friedrich takes with Dorothea here may sound suspiciously Brambeusian, as if the reconciliation of philosophy and poetry, abstract and concrete, written and oral, in short, male and female that Friedrich proposes is not exactly a union of equals. We might also note that although Friedrich claims to want to give Dorothea a written voice, a written voice is what she most pointedly lacks, as while his text is studded with quotes of her imaginary oral responses, the writing remains his alone. Still more striking are his plans for Dorothea's philosophical education. As writing is for Friedrich the ideal mediation for the "deepest and most immediate expression of the spirit," so does he see himself as the ideal mediator for at least certain philosophers, as, despite his recommendation above, what he offers is precisely to read them for her and then explain them to her in a written form all his own.

According to Friedrich, Dorothea is not one to shy away from difficulty. Still, the reduction of an original philosophy to its essential characteristics demands a level of abstraction, a "separation from [her] being," that she as a woman might find difficult. Fortunately, says Friedrich, for certain philosophers he trusts himself to be just such a mediator, and he guarantees to bring her, or indeed anyone who would "form himself through philosophy" a good deal closer to that goal. Friedrich, for example, has long cherished the idea of addressing the imperfections of Kant's presentation. He would only lend a little more order to Kant's writing, with regard to certain repetitions, for example, without in any way detracting from the wit and originality that mark the great man's work. The only freedom he would allow himself, he says, is "approximately that which the ancient critics took with the classical poets" in order to show that Kant, too, is a literary phenomenon and "should be grouped with the classical writers of our nation."[57]

Of course, this sort of mediation is not necessary for every philosopher. Fichte, for example, does a wonderful job of explaining himself all on his own, as "his newest writings are friendly conversations with the reader, in the ingenuous, homely style of a Luther." For Spinoza, while there is the problem of translation, his "hybrid genre somewhere between excerpt, exposition and characteristic" should make his work even more accessible to Dorothea. Still, Schlegel writes, "I would like very much . . . to try to treat in writing for you and also for other dilettantes what I wanted to suggest to you orally . . . to make selections from all of philosophy taken together and to present them coherently and with the greatest popularity."[58] Friedrich has many friends of both sexes who stand in need of such a "philosophy for mankind," a work that would help mankind realize its own humanity, and he imagines creating of them a composite reader, what he calls a *Durchschnitts-Figur*, toward whom he would aim his writing.

In simple terms, what Friedrich is offering now not just to Dorothea but to his male friends as well is a work of criticism very like Senkovskii's later book reviews where the critic arranges and interprets selected passages for the "average" reader. For Schlegel, though, there is nothing simple about criticism, neither in its future nor in its present form. This grandiose philosophical chrestomathy would be for Friedrich the labor of many years, and in the meantime he sets himself the goal of smaller attempts for which he does not know quite the right name. He intends to write something like "soliloquies on matters of concern to all mankind," with "no more analysis than is allowed in a friendly letter," "in the tone of a coherent conversation, something like this writing to [Dorothea]."[59] In fact, what Friedrich is describing is exactly this writing to Dorothea, and it is here that the real import of "On Philosophy. To Dorothea" is finally made clear.

"To achieve the genre I have in mind," writes Friedrich, "one must above all be a human being [Mensch]; and then of course also a philosopher."[60] In other words, to be the mediator that Friedrich claims he is, the critic and author of the sort of work that "On Philosophy" exemplifies, one must already have overcome the dichotomy of male and female so as to be a complete human being in and of oneself, and if Friedrich's claim to *Menschheit* is openly made only on the final page of his essay, in retrospect his pretensions are apparent throughout, in his offer to mediate for male as well as female friends, in the superior tone he takes with Dorothea and above all in the very form of his as yet unnamed genre. It is, after all, a feminine immersion in the everyday that joins with the masculine tendency toward overabstraction in Schlegel's allegorization of his real-life romance. Friedrich can also serve as a mediator for the same reason Fichte does not need one, because his criticism combines masculine writing and feminine orality, both in his theory of "soliloquies" and in the fact of "On Philosophy," an essay written in a conversational tone complete with its addressee's imaginary oral responses.

When man as critic is already complete unto himself, Friedrich and Dorothea's relationship becomes a little redundant, and indeed, an ironic subversion of the dialectic is part of the Romantic agenda all along. On the one hand, Friedrich proposes a union of man and woman both metaphorical and real whereby his and Dorothea's actual relationship becomes symbolically the union of philosophy and poetry, knowing and creating, epistemology and ontology. On the other hand, this vision of harmony is ironically undercut as in every pair of opposites the second element is simply swallowed up by the first. In the one example that stands for all, Friedrich's ease at incorporating into his writing the spoken word and his ability to cast his abstract thought in the concrete terms of a real love affair argue that what he has to give Dorothea is not just himself but himself combined with her already. As critic, Friedrich has already achieved androgyny on his own and now offers only to share it with Dorothea and, indeed, with all his future readers, for once Schlegel has created his *Durchschnitts-Figur*, it is not just that his male writing will include female speech, his abstractions incorporate the everyday, but that his mediation, having by definition absorbed and reworked the writer, will also already contain its own reader, whomever that reader may be.

In Senkovskii's hands, Schlegel's ironically undercut ideal of androgyny loses much of its irony and all of its idealism to become quite openly what on at least one level it always was: a bid for critical power. Like Friedrich, both the Baron in "Brambeus and the Young Literature" and Kritikzada in the "Literary Chronicle" for January 1838 are romantically involved with their readers, the Baronessa and the Sultan respectively, although in their cases only as contained safely within the bounds of holy matrimony. While more conventional, both the Baron and Kritikzada's relationships with their readers are at the same time also entirely redundant, for Senkovskii's writer-critic personae prove in the end to combine male and female each in him- or herself alone, achieving androgyny almost exactly in the terms set forth by Friedrich.

In "On Philosophy" Friedrich associates masculinity with abstract thought and femininity with a concrete level of existence, only to merge the two in the transformation of Schlegel's real-life romance into allegory. Brambeus and Kritikzada, on the other hand, usually work in the opposite direction, as Senkovskii's favorite device is the rendering of the abstract in comically concrete terms, and much of the humor of his work then comes from an oscillation between the two planes, as literary salvoes become a rain of cannonballs or a "real" hernia is cured by a review of a book on the same topic. Friedrich also pointedly associated man with writing and woman with orality only to demonstrate his command of both types of words in the very form of "On Philosophy," and Brambeus and Kritikzada prove equally ambidextrous. As noted in Chapter Two, Brambeus's writing is marked by his consistently chatty tone and by the many interpolated quotations of his own words and those of others, while Kritikzada's "Literary Chronicle" is cast almost entirely in dialogue form.

It is not just that Senkovskii adopts for his critics the combination of writing and orality, abstract and concrete, that Friedrich advocates, however, but that he also makes starkly explicit what Schlegel only suggests. Where Schlegel certainly never uses the word "hermaphrodite," Senkovskii does, and he comically matches his "moral hermaphrodites" of readers with a hermaphroditic critic. Kritikzada does for the gentleman reader what Brambeus does for the lady, and just as the apparent need for marriage in the first place would argue that the Romantic reader is in fact *not* a hermaphrodite, so the actual workings of their marriages most definitely show that the Romantic critic *is*. In Senkovskii's rendering it becomes evident that the function of this relationship is at best to placate the reading public, to give it a false sense of importance, since while the reader cannot create "real literature" on her own, the critic evidently can. His or her power is constrained only by his or her ability to convince his reader-spouse to heed his or her words, an ability, however, that no critic can take for granted.

The threat hanging over Kritikzada's head makes especially clear the point that without a reader to read his or her words the critic is not only powerless, but actually ceases to exist. Still, Kritikzada's marriage to the Sultan, like the Baron's to the Baronessa, does anything but give the reader the upper hand. As critic, Kritikzada is already complete in herself and the marriage she proposes is quite blatantly not the harmonious reconciliation of male and female, but a means of control over the reader; for where Friedrich in "On Philosophy" and Brambeus in "Brambeus and the Young Literature" in their different ways both aspire to mediate between the reader and the text, Kritikzada actually does so. The form of her nightly review of books combines Schlegel's two possible types of mediation, both the "selections from all of philosophy taken together [presented] coherently and with the greatest popularity" and also the smaller pieces "in the tone of a coherent conversation."[61] At the same time, in terms of content it is also a real review of nineteen real new books, from *The Poems of Vladimir Benediktov, Book Two* to *A Stroll with the Children Around St. Petersburg and Its Environs, the Composition of Victor Bur'ianov.*

Kritikzada summarizes the contents of these works and offers her own critical judgments with frequent quotations from the texts under consideration, exactly as Senkovskii himself does in the vast majority of his articles. In fact, the sort of theorization without reference to specific texts offered by "Brambeus and the Young Literature" occurs very rarely in Senkovskii's work, as usually his various personae and opinions appear to frame often quite lengthy quotes and plot summaries, and in this format we find the source of Senkovskii's power. Like Spinoza's philosophy, Senkovskii's criticism in the "Literary Chronicle" combines "extract, exposition and characteristic," and so proves self-sufficient, a mediator that itself needs no mediation because it is both written and oral, abstract and concrete, both male and female.[62]

Simulating Readers

The example of the *Library for Reading* casts into high relief the contra-dictions of Romantic readers and reading. The journal's success and sheer number of contributors suggest that by the time we reach the later liter-ary periodicals, increasing numbers of increasingly diverse real readers have made their presence felt, using their real purchasing power to dictate the form and even content of literature. In this sense the *Library for Reading* represents the furthest extreme of a certain kind of Romanticism, one we associate with real changes in real readers and a democratic trend expressed in literature on many different levels. The Romantic overturning of the hi-erarchy of genres, for example, or the shift to prose form and prosaic con-tent in the writing of poets like Wordsworth and Pushkin, can be and have been read as attempts to stretch the confines of literature in various ways to include more and different sorts of readers, above all of the female and lower-class kinds. But if Romanticism as a *bouleversement* can be an ap-pealingly idealistic image, the particular example of the *Library for Reading* also reminds us of its darker side. Inclusivity can also be read as a kind of "dumbing down" of literature, one dictated not by the writer's disinterested love of humanity but his entirely interested concern for his pocketbook, and it often has, although not usually with regard to the same writers, and once more Balzac can be credited in *Lost Illusions* with the most vivid portrayal of a literature aimed for the lowest common denominator.

Just as the *Library for Reading* offers an extremely crude example of Ro-manticism apparently responding to the needs and desires of "real" readers, however, so it also offers a laughably exaggerated instance of the equally Ro-mantic principle of reader creation and manipulation. With only the barest nod to the ideal of "ethical irony" in the plot device of marriage, Senkovskii uses the image instead to make his intentions with regard to the reader quite clear. We as readers marry this critic only at our peril, for the act of mediation will swallow us up by offering us predigested books, Brambeus's "ready-made pleasures and ready-made thoughts." The reader's marriage to the already androgynous critic promises that he or she will do the reading for us, cutting us out in the form of a *Durchschnitts-Figur* and inserting us into his or her text only to hand us our own selves back. Senkovskii's attitude and purpose may be less than attractive, but we should at least ap-preciate his honesty in letting us know his objectives in no uncertain terms.

Not every writer offers such a clear-eyed view of his or her intentions, and contemporary reader-response critics are far from the worst culprits in this regard. For if Senkovskii casts into question our contemporary critical practices, he is an equally destabilizing presence in his own Romantic context, forcing us to reconsider even that embodiment of Romantic sincerity, Jean-Jacques Rousseau himself.

Looking backwards from the undoubtedly jaundiced viewpoint of the *Library for Reading*, the sort of real response to *Julie* that Darnton documented in the case of the real reader Jean Ranson appears a great deal more artificial. I would even argue that Ranson's supposedly genuine response was in fact carefully constructed by Rousseau, as any real readers of *Julie* only stepped into a role already prepared for them by the text, and first of all by its genre. *Julie* is an epistolary novel, a collection of letters written both by and to the various characters in the book, from St. Preux to Julie, for example, or Julie to Claire, which means that any reader as he or she reads a given letter on some level adopts the imaginary stance or persona of the letter's original addressee; as Monika Greenleaf notes, in the epistolary novel the reader is not only "an external eavesdropper on the entire correspondence" but also "the 'you' to whom each letter is addressed."[63] To the exigencies of his genre Rousseau also adds the two prefaces that are clearly intended to shape an ideal reading of his text, so much so, in fact, that the "sincere" responses of his real readers were obviously prefabricated for them.

The first preface is by and large taken up with the categorization of different kinds of readers, and even as Rousseau's blunt instructions to the various types suggest that every reader belong to one group or another, his highly weighted language pushes us to identify with one group in particular. He explains:

> This book is not meant to circulate in society, and is suitable for very few readers. The style will put off people of taste; the contents will alarm strict people; all the sentiments will be unnatural to those who do not believe in virtue. It is bound to displease the devout, the libertines, the philosophers: it is bound to shock gallant women, and scandalize honest ones. Whom then will it please? Perhaps no one but me: but very certainly it will please no one moderately.
>
> Anyone who is willing to undertake the reading of these letters must summon his patience with respect to language mistakes, trite and bombastic style, banal thoughts expressed in turgid terms; he must tell himself in advance that their writers are not French wits, academicians, philosophers; but provincials,

foreigners, solitary youths, almost children, who in their romantic imaginations mistake the honest ravings of their brains for philosophy.

Rousseau concludes that the book is particularly suited to women and especially "to those who in their dissolute lives have preserved some love for honesty," but not to chaste maidens, and while he sympathizes with the "austere man" who puts the book down in disgust after a few pages, he defies the anger of anyone who reads the entire book in the most personal of terms: "But should anyone, after reading it all the way through, dare censure me for publishing it; let him proclaim it to the world if he pleases, but let him not come tell me: I feel that I could never in my life have any regard for such a man."[64]

Rousseau's ideal reader sounds suspiciously like Rousseau himself or at least like his very close friend, and the terrible price for not reading Rousseau as he wants to be read is to be excluded from that intimate circle. For the vast majority of Rousseau's thousands of readers all over Europe, however, that intimate circle did not exist in any real sense; that Jean Ranson could refer to Rousseau always as "*L'Ami* Jean-Jacques," does not mean that he actually was. What is nonetheless striking and even unique in the reception history of *Julie* as Darnton recounts it is the extraordinarily strong desire of both writer and readers to bridge this gap and take on the roles created for them by the text. But for a great many other post-Schlegelian, more deliberately ironic, and as I have defined it, more Romantic writers and readers, the point is not to elide the difference between ideal and real, but to exploit the tension between the two.

Senkovskii's outrageously overdetermined readers drive home the point that when Pushkin addresses the reader of *Eugene Onegin*, for example, or when Lermontov excoriates the Russian reading public in the "Author's Preface" to *A Hero of Our Time*, it is not that these reader-constructions have no bearing on real readers with bodies in the world, whether we understand those real readers as bound to a particular time and space or simply as you and me. It is rather that they do and they don't. As the writer-critic constantly shifts among different levels of reality, the Romantic overdetermination of the reader ironically ensures that that reader will always elude us, for exactly what reader we are talking about and when and where his or her reading takes place is finally impossible to determine. It is ultimately in this sense that Friedrich Schlegel's reader, like his writer, is a function or aspect of the critic, because as the sign of the reader swings wildly among various and even mutually exclusive significations, it points most insistently to the fact of literature itself.

Jonathan Culler writes more narrowly with regard to a particular type of reader-construction that the poetic device of apostrophe "makes its point by troping not on the meaning of a word but on the circuit or situation of communication itself." "Such apostrophes," he adds, "may complicate or disrupt the circuit of communication, raising questions about who is the addressee, but above all they are embarrassing: embarrassing to me and to you." We are indeed embarrassed by Senkovskii, because his overt personification of the reader reveals the self-sufficiency of the Romantic critical act that can descend to critical solipsism. Culler argues that "[t]o read apostrophe as sign of a fiction which knows its own fictive nature is to stress its optative character, its impossible imperatives: commands which in their explicit impossibility figure events in and of fiction." Reading Romantic readers in the same way leads us, like Culler, to "reflect on the crucial though paradoxical fact that this figure which seems to establish relations between the self and the other can in fact be read as an act of radical interiorization and solipsism."[65]

As Romantic readers, like Romantic writers, are absorbed into the Romantic critic, it finally does not much matter of what sort they are, nor how we approach them. For the ultimate function of the Romantic trope of the reader, I would argue, is not to reflect nor to create a certain kind of readership, nor even a particular relationship between self and other, but rather to draw us into a critical space that is sufficient unto itself, one where words like "real" and "imaginary," "self" and "other," no longer have much meaning. This is once more the space of the simulacrum, the space where Senkovskii and his critical ilk are all-powerful, for it is the place where reader- and writer/critic-personae of all kinds meet to simulate literature, or in other words, to produce literary criticism. Romanticism represents this space in any number of guises, from Ambrose's Tavern and Lincoln's-inn Square to Bulgarin and Grech's "Typographic box," and the *Library for Reading* has its own peculiar variants. There is first of all the complicated space that shaped the *Library for Reading* from the outside, the Russia where Senkovskii lived and worked, and then also the crowded form his journal took on the inside. While Chapter Five will turn to the Russian Empire as Romantic space writ large, the next chapter will explore the smaller Romantic spaces encompassed within the *Library for Reading*, and even within the space suggested by its title alone: the library.

4. The Romantic Library

Senkovskii's Romantic readers and writers meet to simulate literature largely in the pages of the *Library for Reading*, and the intent of this chapter is to explore the idiosyncrasies of that space. Mapping a literary work proves a difficult business, however, and in the case of the *Library for Reading* perhaps especially so. While we can start with the apparently simple matter of a particular spatial arrangement of words on a page, we will quickly find that the *Library for Reading*, like any periodical but especially those of the Romantic variety, has an extremely complicated notion of genre. Romantic space in the *Library for Reading* is also not limited to its pages but rather includes the many neither entirely real nor entirely imaginary spaces to which Senkovskii's work refers, diverse venues such as the literary marketplace, the Orient, and Tver. Fortunately, in fine Romantic fashion, Senkovskii suggests a way of bringing together all these rapidly expanding and different kinds of spaces in his very choice of title: the *Library for Reading*.

The library of the *Library for Reading* is first of all a literary genre. As an "encyclopedic" journal, each issue of the *Library for Reading* gathered within its covers a great variety of printed material, including not just works of literature and of literary criticism but also articles on science, industry, and agriculture. Scholars have attributed the wide range of reading matter to the editor's own late-Enlightenment education and corresponding didactic aims; his contemporaries argued instead that it was Senkovskii's base commercial instincts that prompted him to offer something for every imaginable reader. The diversity that characterized the *Library for Reading*, however, can also be understood in entirely Romantic terms. Romanticism was largely driven by the search for a certain kind of literary genre, one marked by heterogeneity, fragmentariness, and infinite incompletion. This search began in a periodical, the *Athenaeum*, and we might argue that by the 1830s and the proliferation of literary journals not just in Russia but across Western Europe, Romanticism had come full circle, returning to the genre that gave it its original impetus.[1] In the particular case of the *Library for Reading*, not only does its encyclopedic and periodical form realize the ideal genre first expressed and embodied by the *Athenaeum*, but this later literary space also makes explicit a notion of library that lies perhaps hidden in the first. In nineteenth-century Germany, an "athenaeum" was a temple to Athena or by extension a school or an academy. In England and the United States it was also a room or even a shelf of books.[2]

While the library as Jena's Romantic genre is a literary space, Senkovskii's title also points to an actual building: the new lending library that Senkovskii's publisher, A. F. Smirdin, opened in 1831 above his new bookstore on Nevskii Prospect. This very specific and real-world reference has its more symbolic dimensions as well, for as an allusion to the real library for reading located on the second floor of Smirdin's Nevskii address, the *Library for Reading* also implies a larger and less tangible space, that elusive literary marketplace that somehow overlaps with Romanticism. As the bricks-and-mortar juxtaposition of Smirdin's library for reading with his bookstore would indicate, lending libraries were an essential part of an apparently burgeoning literary marketplace across Europe, especially in England, France, and Germany, where they are popularly held to have dictated certain modes of book production while making books available to a broader readership. In Russia the lending libraries were much less important to a literary marketplace that we are not sure even existed. But in the seeming absence of a real literary marketplace, Senkovskii's title takes one last Romantic twist, as the *Library for Reading* only pretends to point to Smirdin's real building while actually replacing it with a reality that never was.

Lending libraries, like the *Athenaeum*, suggest the library as a collection of books. We might more accurately delineate the shared space of the *Library for Reading* and Romanticism if we also expand our concept of the library just a little further. A library more broadly speaking might be a repository of knowledge organized and catalogued into some sort of order, and it might be designed not just for storage, but also for display.[3] The *Library for Reading* is also a library in this sense, for as the frighteningly learned Senkovskii strings together facts on an extraordinarily wide range of topics, he approximates in himself and in his journal the sort of literary cabinet of curiosities that Peter Conrad associates first with *Tristram Shandy*. Conrad notes "a significant critical tradition which treats *Tristram Shandy* as a cabinet or a museum, each thought a curio, each association an arcane exhibit," and he quotes none other than Sir Walter Scott on the novel's tendency to "proliferate" into "a collection."[4] Scott would certainly know a proliferating collection when he saw one, as he himself was a noted collector of antiquities, from the traditional Scottish songs that made up his first published work, *Minstrelsy of the Scottish Border* (1802), to the facts that crowded his *Waverley* novels and the endless artifacts that cluttered his house at Abbotsford. Antiquarianism grounds the writer-as-collector in a particular space of the past; it can also lend itself to a particular kind of performance. In Sterne's work Conrad discerns "virtuosity" in a new sense, not just as "scholarly curatorship" but as "self-exhibiting improvisation," and in this notion of virtuosic performance we find another source of the Romantic display of writer- and reader-personae.

Where Scott's antiquarian "editors" point to his own native soil, however, Senkovskii's personae largely point to a very different but equally Romantic space: the Orient. While perhaps most antiquarians at the time directed their energies toward the amateur exploration of their own corners of Europe, as professor of Oriental languages at the University of St. Petersburg Senkovskii instead had a professional interest in the collecting and arranging of the Middle East. When practiced in that part of the world, antiquarianism becomes Orientalism, as Edward Said has famously described it. The Orient is another much-noted aspect of Romantic space, and one that finds particularly interesting expression in Senkovskii's writing. Senkovskii's Orientalist work encompasses travelogues, actual scholarly work, and stories "from the Arabic," all three aspects culminating in an Eastern-flavored literary criticism that lays bare the device some one hundred and fifty years before Said. The Orientalist purports to mediate between East and West, explaining one to the other from a vantage point somewhere in between, just as the critic claims to mediate between reader and text and reader and writer. Senkovskii, however, openly reveals the uncomfortable fact that the two produce instead what Said calls "highly stylized simulacra," and as Senkovskii's Orientalism blends into his literary criticism, the "Mongol attack" T.-O. supposedly launched on Russian literature becomes the threat of absorbing writer, reader, and text all into the personality of the Orientalist-critic alone.[5]

If the library, like any Romantic space, ultimately only returns us to the slippery realm of Romantic literary criticism, still the roundabout route serves above all to emphasize the political aspects of this apparently literary domain. The last chapter in particular has already questioned the democratic impulses with which Romanticism has long been associated, and the manifestation of Romanticism in the form of the Orientalist library makes clear the extent to which Romantic politics are not only often undemocratic but even explicitly imperialist. Empire, though, if encompassed within the antiquarian and especially the Orientalist libraries, also constitutes a space all its own, and Chapter Five will go on to explore the Romantic spaces that shape the *Library for Reading* not from within but from without: the space of Senkovskii's own centripetal movement from Poland to St. Petersburg, and finally the space of Russia itself.

The Space of the Romantic Genre

Romantic writers and readers meet most obviously in the literature that Romanticism produced. This literature, as we have already seen, is marked by a strong, even all-absorbing critical consciousness, and it also partakes of a particular form. As Friedrich Schlegel famously explained in *Athenaeum Fragment* 116, the sort of literary space Romanticism describes is of quite a special sort, and I quote now both the beginning and the end of this long aphorism:

> Romantic poetry is a progressive, universal poetry. Its aim isn't merely to re-unite all the separate species of poetry and put poetry in touch with philosophy and rhetoric. It tries to and should mix and fuse poetry and prose, inspiration and criticism, the poetry of art and the poetry of nature; and make poetry lively and sociable, and life and society poetical; poeticize wit and fill and saturate the forms of art with every kind of good, solid matter for instruction, and animate them with the pulsations of humor. . . . Other kinds of poetry are finished and are now capable of being fully analyzed. The romantic kind of poetry is still in the state of becoming; that, in fact, is its real essence: that it should forever be becoming and never be perfected. It can be exhausted by no theory and only a divinatory criticism would dare try to characterize its ideal. It alone is infinite, just as it alone is free; and it recognizes as its first commandment

that the will of the poet can tolerate no law above itself. The romantic kind of poetry is the only one that is more than a kind, that is, as it were, poetry itself: for in a certain sense all poetry is or should be romantic.[6]

The beginning of this aphorism insists that the "romantic kind of poetry" should be heterogeneous in form, a mix of all kinds of poetry and of poetry and life, while the end lays claim to its fragmentary nature, "forever becoming and never . . . perfected." A heterogeneous genre is a literary space that apparently includes all other literary and even nonliterary space; a fragmentary genre is not its own space at all.

Either way, Schlegel's Romantic project might sound more like an infinitely expanding library than a single work of literature, and indeed, Jena often presented it as such. Novalis once wrote to Caroline Schlegel of his inclination "to devote [his] whole life to a single novel which should constitute a whole library by itself."[7] In a similar vein, in the unpublished dialogue already quoted in Chapter One, Novalis not only speaks of the business of books but also of the library, as his alter ego B. expresses the desire "to see before [him] a whole collection of books from all arts and fields of knowledge as the work of [his] spirit."[8] To the extent that the Romantic genre ever was realized in a single work, however, it was in a work that itself approximated an ever-expanding library: the *Athenaeum*.

The *Athenaeum* appeared from 1798 to 1800 in three large volumes each consisting of two parts. It is here that Friedrich Schlegel presented his literary ideal, not just in *Fragment* 116 but in other critical texts, including the aforementioned *Dialogue on Poetry* and "On Philosophy. To Dorothea," and also "On Goethe's Wilhelm Meister" (1798), *Ideas* (1800), and "On Incomprehensibility" (1800). Schlegel's writing points always to a fragmentary and heterogeneous literary form that hovers just outside the criticism aimed at producing it, a "romantic kind of poetry" that is infinitely deferred; in this sense Romanticism is a kind of waiting, Blanchot's "work of the absence of work."[9] While acknowledging the empty place that ironically lies at the center of Romanticism, however, we should also note that something of Schlegel's ideal adheres in the very structure of the *Athenaeum* itself. It is not just that the various pieces that made up the *Athenaeum* offer dialogues, generic hybrids like the *Dialogue on Poetry* with its mix of spoken and written forms, and literal fragments as in the collectively produced *Athenaeum Fragments* or Novalis's collection of aphorisms, *Grains of Pollen* (1798). More to the point, the *Athenaeum* was itself the perfect medium for Friedrich

Schlegel's message because a journal, like a library, embodies the same ideals of heterogeneous and fragmentary form.

In the preface to the first issue of the *Athenaeum,* the Schlegel brothers explicitly frame their project with reference to the diverse forms, topics, and opinions they imagine it will encompass in a "fraternization" both metaphorical and literal. With or without explanatory preface, however, any literary journal is a heterogeneous whole made up of a variety of articles on a variety of topics and written by a variety of authors; although, as we have already seen, especially that last point can be complicated in a number of ways. The periodical is also quite literally fragmentary, both in the sense of the various pieces that make up a given issue and in the infinite incompletion that periodicity itself presupposes. While individual issues can be collected, the work that is the whole of the journal only ever hovers just beyond reach.

Romantic works of a more "poetic" sort, from "collected" tales to "found" manuscripts and even verse creations like *Eugene Onegin* or Wordsworth's *Prelude* all, in Handwerk's terms, "use ironic structures to call into doubt the integrity and boundaries of the subject," not just the integrity and boundaries of the reader- and writer-subjects we have already seen, but also, perhaps above all, of the subject-work itself.[10] But despite the complicated edges of these more "poetic" works, it is the later "critical" journals that express Schlegel's ironic ideal most clearly, although of the journals discussed here, perhaps only *Blackwood's* demonstrates any direct connection to the *Athenaeum* project. J. H. Alexander notes in his article "*Blackwood's*: Magazine as Romantic Form" (1984) that John Lockhart had evidently read at least one work by Friedrich Schlegel, as he published an important review of the translation of Schlegel's *Lectures on the History of Literature* published in Edinburgh in 1818. Whether intentionally or not, however, it is Lockhart and his friends who regularly describe *Blackwood's* in terms that sound most like the "Romantic kind of poetry" from *Athenaeum Fragment* 116.

In one issue, for example, we find Odoherty explaining to none other than Byron that readers take up *Blackwood's* "not as a Review, to pick up opinions of new books from it, nor as a periodical, to read themselves asleep upon, but as a classical work, which happens to be continued from month to month;—a real Magazine of mirth, misanthropy, wit, wisdom, folly, fiction, fun, festivity, theology, bruising, and thingumbob."[11] "Thingumbob" is a wonderfully *Blackwood's*ian rendering of the Romantic ideal of heterogeneity, and in a later issue the Ettrick Shepherd is equally at home in his own dialect when he says:

> In the pure air o' the kintra, beuks hae an immortal life. I hae nae great leebrary—feck o't consists o' twenty volumes o' my ain writing; but, oh! man, it is sweet to sit down, on a calm simmer evening, on a bit knowe, by the loch-side, and let ane's mind gang daundering awa down the pages o' some volume o' genius, creating thochts alang with the author, till, at last, you dinna weel ken whilk o' yoou hae made the beuk. That's jus the way I aften read your Magazine, till I could believe that I hae written every article—Noctes and a'.[12]

Blackwood's serves the Ettrick Shepherd in place of the missing "great leebrary," and accordingly as a work of a very special sort, for as the Ettrick Shepherd creates "thochts alang with the author," *Blackwood's*, like the Ettrick Shepherd himself, becomes truly infinite, "forever becoming" and "never perfected." In the letter "To Mr Blackwood" published one issue earlier, Coleridge, himself no stranger to German aesthetics, sets the tone for the Shepherd's musings when he describes the journal as a "Philosophical, Philological, and Aesthetic Miscellany." As Coleridge goes on to explain, "the word miscellany, however, must be taken as involving a predicate in itself, in addition to the three preceding epithets, comprehending, namely, all the ephemeral births of intellectual life, which add to the gaiety and variety of the work, without interfering with its express and regular object.'"[13]

Just as the *Noctes Ambrosianae* reflect a social gathering that could not have actually happened, at least not in that form, so *Fraser's* "symposiacs," the *Son of the Fatherland and Northern Archive's* "Box" and the mock letters and dialogues of the *Library for Reading* serve not to reflect reality but, as Lacoue-Labarthe and Nancy explain with regard the *Athenaeum*, to "put [*Witz*] to work in the work."[14] Like *Blackwood's*, these journals also all share an ironic view of identity formation that allows them to fragment their real friends and enemies, readers and contributors, into a sometimes wildly heterogeneous set of distinct personalities. Finally, in their clear dependence on the heterogeneity and fragmentariness inherent in any periodical form, these works also strikingly echo both the *Athenaeum* and the ideal Romantic literary space that it exemplifies. If these literary journals all reflect the fragmentariness that any periodical implies, however, the *Library for Reading* offers the most extreme example of Romantic heterogeneity.

With its seven regular sections comprising not only Russian Literature, Foreign Literature, Criticism, and the Literary Chronicle but also Arts and

Sciences, Industry and Agriculture, and Miscellaneous, the *Library for Reading* ranged far afield in its attempt to "mix and fuse poetry and prose, inspiration and criticism, the poetry of art and the poetry of nature." As Grits et al. point out, however, the new journal's "encyclopedism" was apparent not just in the contrast of topics and styles that the reader would find as he or she moved from Foreign Literature, for example, to Industry and Agriculture, but also within each of the separate sections, including Russian Literature.[15] Indeed, where most of the journals of the day tended to publish literary works by a given circle or faction, Senkovskii's intent was to publish the entire spectrum of Russian writers, and the first issue listed as current or future contributors everyone who was anyone in the Russian literary world.[16] For Belinskii this eclecticism pointed straight to the provinces, as he scornfully wrote in 1836:

> Imagine the family of the steppe landowner, a family reading everything that it comes upon from cover to cover. [On receipt of *The Library for Reading*] [t]he daughter reads Ershov, Gogniev, and Strugovshchikov's poetry and Zagoskin, Ushakov, Panaev, Kalashnikov, and Masal'skii's stories; the son, as the member of a new generation, reads Timofeev's poetry and Baron Brambeus's stories; the papa reads articles about the two- and three-field systems and about various means of improving the land, while the mama—about a new means of curing tuberculosis and dyeing thread.[17]

For us, however, Senkovskii's excessive heterogeneity can point to yet another sort of space, not to the provinces nor even to the Romantic genre, but to another sort of Romantic library: the lending library.

The Lending Library and the Literary Marketplace

The apparent redundancy of the name the *Library for Reading* quickly drew the scorn of Senkovskii's enemies. On hearing of the plans for the projected journal, Viazemskii wrote to a friend in some disgust: "The *Library for Reading!* What else would a library be for? Nashchekin says: 'After that one could say: a carriage for riding.'"[18] In their haste to mock Senkovskii, however, Viazemskii and his friends indulge in a willful misunderstanding. As the sort of literary genre described above, a library obviously is for reading, and to that extent we can appreciate their witticism. But as Viazemskii et al. knew well, Senkovskii's title much more evidently pointed to the library as an actual building or institution, and here their joke completely misses its mark.

For in the early nineteenth century relatively few such libraries actually were "for reading," either in name or in fact. Aside from the private collections amassed by wealthy bibliophiles, St. Petersburg boasted by this time a number of noted libraries, including the enormous holdings in the Hermitage and collections of various sizes attached to institutions like the Academy of Sciences and the Sukhoputnyi military school. Still, access to these various collections was extremely restricted, so much so that when Vasilii Sopikov, librarian of the newly established Imperial Public Library, wanted to consult the library at the Academy of Sciences, he had to obtain special permission through sponsors and then even after lengthy negotiations was only allowed in the library two times per week.[19] Starting in 1814 the Imperial Public Library itself was a significant exception, as it was officially open three days a week to "Any reader who observes the rules of decorum . . . of whatever title or rank he may be."[20] In the country as a whole, despite an imperial decree in 1830, public libraries only began to take hold in the second half of the century, and in the meantime libraries designated specifically "for reading" were of an entirely different sort. Exactly like Senkovskii's journal, real "libraries for reading" were lending libraries, that is, commercial enterprises usually affiliated with a bookseller's.

Lending libraries began to appear in Russia in the last third of the eighteenth century. True to form, libraries for reading were initially to be found on the premises of the foreign booksellers in St. Petersburg; for example, the bookseller K. I. Dalgren, who opened one of the first fee-based lending libraries in St. Petersburg in 1783. The lending pattern seems to have been roughly the same. Subscribers who paid a certain sum of money in advance plus a deposit to guarantee return of the item borrowed could then choose a text in accordance with the prices listed in the catalogue of the establishment. Miranda Beaven Remnek suggests that foreign bookstore owners were influenced to open lending libraries by the example of the foreign reading societies, including the German Reading Society founded in St. Petersburg in 1777 and also the French Reading Society started in 1780. While *Books in Russia and the Soviet Union* is undoubtedly correct in the claim that the foreign booksellers in St. Petersburg "recognized in [the reading societies] a means of attracting more patrons and increasing profits," it is also true that by the 1770s this same innovation was already well established in the booksellers' native countries.[21] The variously named *Lesekabinetten,* *Lektürkabinetten,* and *Leih-* or *Lesebibliotheken* began to appear in German bookstores as early as 1767, and approximately the same time in France. While John Lough notes an isolated mention of a Grenoble bookseller who rented novels to his customers in the 1650s, the earliest Parisian *cabinets de lecture* he lists again date from the 1760s and 1770s.[22] As usual, however, real credit for this advance in the marketing of books should go to the British.

According to Guinevere L. Griest in her *Mudie's Circulating Library and the Victorian Novel* (1970), the circulating-library movement grew out of two responses to a growing reading public, first the "booksellers' custom of charging a small fee to customers who read books in the shop" and second "the example given by the flourishing social and literary clubs."[23] One of the earliest of the lending libraries seemed to have been opened about 1725 by Allen Ramsey in connection with his Edinburgh bookstore, and by around 1742 the Rev. Samuel Fancourt had opened one of the first circulating subscription libraries in London. By the early nineteenth century the lending libraries were already operating hand-in-glove with the book industry, so much so that many scholars attribute the increasing popularity of gothic and sentimental novels to the circulating libraries William Lane opened in 1791 in conjunction with his Minerva Press. Still, the growth of the British book industry in the first third of the nineteenth century was not steady, and after surviving the vicissitudes of the Napoleonic wars, many of the libraries closed in 1825 in response to an economic crash. It is accordingly not until the 1850s that we see the rise of the most influential of the British lending libraries, Mudie's.

Charles Edward Mudie was born in London to Scottish parents in 1818 and began to lend books from his stationer's shop in 1842. By 1852 he had moved his thriving library business to a larger location, and in 1860 he moved again, this time, as a contemporary noted, "with festivities attended by 'nearly all the best names in literature and the trade.'"[24] Mudie's was by that time a massive operation, as the library not only served clients in London but also shipped books to every corner of the British Empire, and in 1864 Mudie reorganized his business into a limited liability company with half the needed money invested by a group of London publishers. According to Griest, the most significant consequence of this refinancing was the absolute dominance of the three-volume or "three-decker" novel in England in the latter half of the nineteenth century.

In the eighteenth century, novels had come in various lengths, anywhere from two to seven volumes. It was then first Sir Walter Scott in the *Waverley* novels who set the fashion for the three-decker, a fashion that the lending libraries had every reason to support. The lending libraries in Great Britain as elsewhere provided access to books to a reading public that lacked not only entrée to any other sorts of libraries but also the means to purchase its own copies. In this sense the lending libraries have been seen as forces of democracy, what Harry Earl Whitmore calls "blockade runners" boldly slipping through the economic obstacles separating the reader and the printed page.[25] At the same time, the lending libraries actually created economic obstacles of their own as they worked to keep this new reading public by artificially maintaining the high cost of books.

In France, for example, the lending libraries encouraged the publication of volumes sometimes called "editions de cabinet de lecture"; according to Whitmore: "These books were generally published in octavo, usually with several volumes to the title, and contained excessive white space and even blank pages."[26] In Great Britain the collusion of the lending libraries and the publishers produced the mandatory three-decker through the end of the nineteenth century. As Griest notes, the libraries' needs shaped not only publishers' habits but even readers' tastes, and she illustrates her point with an episode recalled by Nathaniel Hawthorne's son Julian. So closely was the three-decker associated with "good literature," she writes, that Wilkie Collins on meeting Julian praised especially the second and third volumes of Hawthorne's *The Scarlet Letter* when the novel in fact came out only in one: "'Even the second volume, where most novelists weaken, is fine, and the third fulfills the splendid promise of the first,' said Collins, nor would he believe Julian's protests that it was only one until he found it on his bookshelf. 'You are right. One volume and not over 70,000 words in all! It is incomprehensible!'"[27] If short prose was problematic, poetry suffered even more under this regime, as again Balzac's *Lost Illusions* reminds us. Lucien de Rubempré, himself an early habitué of the *cabinets de lecture*, finds that his sonnets are worth more to the booksellers unpublished. Dauriat is happy to buy Lucien's manuscript for 3,000 francs and along with it the budding journalist's good will. But publishing it is another matter entirely, as Dauriat sees no possibility of a book of poetry returning any further investment.

In Russia it is hard to claim that the libraries for reading had anything like that sort of influence on an admittedly much more fledgling publishing industry. It is probably safe to say that anyone who had anything to do with books in Russia operated in a much more volatile environment, both economically and politically, than his or her counterparts in Western Europe, and in Russia the affiliation of lending libraries with the book industry proceeded only in fits and starts. Shortly after the foreign booksellers introduce the practice, we find Russian booksellers following suit. A. A. Zaitseva notes that the first "Russian Establishment for Reading" was opened in St. Petersburg in 1784 by Matvei Ovchinnikov. Ovchinnikov lent books for twelve rubles a year, or for one ruble and twenty-five kopeks a month, or overnight for five kopeks. In the wake of the French Revolution and also Paul's ascension to the Russian throne in 1796, a wave of reaction closed a number of lending libraries, and the business resumed only with the progressive policies that marked the start of Alexander's reign in 1801. Shortly thereafter, as in Western Europe, the Napoleonic wars presented a number of economic obstacles to the growth of the book industry, although Napoleon was also responsible for perhaps the most important advance in the Russian library for reading. It was Napoleon's imminent invasion of Moscow in 1812 that sent A. F. Smirdin fleeing to St. Petersburg, where he first met the bookseller V. A. Plavil'shchikov. In 1817 Smirdin returned to St. Petersburg to take up employment as Plavil'shchikov's chief shop assistant, and upon his employer's death in 1823 he acquired, along with a press and the largest bookstore in St. Petersburg, one of the most significant private book collections in Russia at the time.

Plavil'shchikov had first opened his library to the public together with his bookstore in 1815. He had only begun collecting books the previous year, and in 1815 his library consisted of a mere 1,800 titles. Within two years, however, a newly published catalogue of the collection listed some 3,000 titles, and by his death in 1823 an updated version listed more than 7,000. On taking possession of the library, Smirdin immediately began to add to it, and by 1832 he listed 12,035 titles in his collection.[28] He also instituted a set fee for its use. Contrary to what seems to have been standard practice at the time, Plavil'shchikov had apparently usually refrained from charging a fee for the use of his library.[29] Smirdin set what Grits et al. consider to have been the fairly expensive rate of thirty rubles for a year, twenty rubles for six months, twelve rubles for three months, and five rubles for one month. Customers who wanted to take out the latest magazines as well as books needed to add an additional twenty, twelve, seven, or three rubles, respectively.

As already noted, by 1832 the success of both the store and the library was such that Smirdin was able to transfer the entire enterprise to a fashionable and extremely expensive location on Nevskii Prospect. Just as we saw in the case of Charles Mudie's relocation, Smirdin's move some thirty years earlier was a major literary event, one marked by announcements in the papers, a dinner party attended by all the lights of the St. Petersburg literary world, and the publication of the collection *Housewarming*. While stories have also been told of other and even earlier Russian bookstore-cum-libraries serving as a "literary-professional salon,"[30] it is nonetheless Smirdin's establishment that was immortalized as the first or best of its kind, perhaps above all by the covers of the two volumes of Smirdin's own commemorative anthology.

The cover of the first volume of *Housewarming* presented an engraving of the actual celebratory dinner amidst the bookshelves with various of the guests recognizably represented. At the head of the table we find the fabulist Krylov with Smirdin standing behind him to his right; sitting next to Krylov on his right is the poet Khvostov and, next to Khvostov, Pushkin with his unmistakable sideburns. Standing to give the toast is our friend Grech, and seated to his left Shakhovskoi and then Bulgarin. The cover of the second volume shows the interior of the store, with Pushkin and Viazemskii in animated conversation in the right foreground, Smirdin in back behind the counter chatting with Senkovskii, and to the left Smirdin's chief assistant loaded down with books.[31] Smirdin's "literary club" was also commemorated in words, perhaps most notably in Pushkin's apparently expromptu verse:

If ever you come to Smirdin's
You won't buy anything,
Either you'll find Senkovskii
Or you'll tread on Bulgarin.

This silly ditty is recorded in a number of memoirs at the time and reproduced, it would seem, by every scholar of the period, sometimes in the alternative form:

If you go into Smirdin's
You won't find anything there,
You won't buy anything there,
You'll only knock into Senkovskii.[32]

Despite their popularity with later literary scholars, however, the relationship of these more or less artistic renderings to the historical reality of

Smirdin's library for reading is a little unsteady. The picture of literary amity offered by the engravings, for example, is not very convincing, and the actual tenor of the relationships between these Russian men of letters might be more accurately represented by Pushkin's vaguely insulting verse. Still, given the strong anti-Senkovskiian bent that characterizes most readings of the Russian literary world in the 1830s, we might do better to reserve judgment on the truth value of Pushkin's poem as well; certainly one can only wonder if Pushkin really intended his jingle for posterity. Still more difficult to sort out than the actual atmosphere of Smirdin's "true book club," however, is the relationship of that "club" to the literary marketplace.[33]

Belinskii's 1834 announcement of the "Smirdin period" in Russian literature is only the first attempt to mark a sharp divide in Russian letters right around the start of the 1830s. These accounts often focus on Smirdin's practice of paying his authors more for the privilege of publishing their works, of charging his customers less to purchase these books and, as Beaven Remnek notes, considerably more to borrow them. Whether historians then or now tell a tale of Smirdin's commercial advances in his real library for reading (or one of Senkovskii's money-grubbing tactics in his periodical one), of Pushkin's literary professionalism, of the struggle of the literary aristocrats with the literary proletariat, or of the demise of poetry, the notion of a distinct and commercially oriented change in the literary way of doing things remains. Certainly it may be only that, a notion, especially when offered up not as Smirdin's real library for reading but as Senkovskii's literary representation of the same. It is precisely because the *Library for Reading* renders the literary marketplace in particularly ambiguous form, however, that Senkovskii's magazine offers such an ideal example of this particular Romantic space.

After all, no literary marketplace is a real space in the sense that, say, the local farmers' market is, as Smirdin and his colleagues and competitors did not actually set up booths adjacent to one another in a city square and meet face to face with their customers. It is instead always a virtual space and, in the context of Romanticism, a virtual space twice over. As I have argued, the literary marketplace not just in Russia but also in France, Germany, and even Great Britain matters at least as much as an idea as it does as an actual source of income—and perhaps more. Just where the idea stops and the reality begins, however, is impossible to determine and ultimately irrelevant, as is any sort of functioning of cause and effect. All we can say with any sort of assurance is that, whatever the actual contours of the literary marketplace in the 1830s, it is simulated in a particularly virulent form in the *Library for Reading*, which then opens out into Russian literature and European literature a commercial space that may have existed in Russia or perhaps in Western Europe or perhaps nowhere outside its own pages. It is at least striking that here it is Smirdin's party that preceded Mudie's, as if the imitation heralded the original.

In its reference to Smirdin's real building, Senkovskii's title once and for all sums up the entirely ambiguous relationship of Romanticism to the literary marketplace. His title, however, also does more than that, for as a reference to the library more generally, Senkovskii taps into yet another Romantic space. The library in the Romantic context is not just an engine of a would-be literary marketplace, but also a space for the collection and display of books and learning in a broader sense—an endeavor not entirely separate from the workings of the literary marketplace, as for example it was Senkovskii's famous erudition that served as one of the selling points of his "encyclopedic" journal. This second sort of library nonetheless takes us into other, apparently further reaches of Romanticism. The "literary cabinet of curiosities" brings us back to the writer as collector, and in Senkovskii's case, to the writer as collector of not just stories but also objects from a particular place: the Orient.

The Antiquarian Library

In *Shandyism: The Character of Romantic Irony* Peter Conrad describes the space of *Tristram Shandy* as a "palace of thought":

> In the first place, it is an image of [Tristram's] mind, a minute chamber which unfolds into a world. But the random accumulation of the mind's contents suggests, to romantic commentators, another kind of space: Locke called the mind of man at birth an "empty cabinet," gradually filled up, and there is a significant critical tradition which treats *Tristram Shandy* as a cabinet or a museum, each thought a curio, each association an arcane exhibit.

According to Conrad, starting from the moment of its publication there was an old way of perceiving the "curio cabinet" space of *Tristram Shandy* and a new one:

For Voltaire, Tristram is an antiquarian, storing up pedantic oddities in the lumber-room of his head; for the romantics, he is an imaginary architect, whose chimerical structure has the intricacy but also the insubstantiality of memory and desire. For Voltaire, he is the older kind of virtuoso, collecting objects of vertu; for romantics, he is the new virtuoso, who does not collect remarkable objects but is himself a remarkable subject, and who plays upon the instrument of his sensibility with the same uncanny dexterity the musical virtuoso employs on the keyboard or his violin strings.[34]

Conrad's description exactly suits the third library I find in the *Library for Reading*, with one important exception. Where Conrad traces a transition to a Romantic sort of reading as Tristram "passes from magpie collector to mesmeric performer," I would argue that the Romantic "curio cabinet," for both readers and writers, is best characterized instead by a tension between the two poles.

Readers have long noted what we might call Senkovskii's Voltairean side. Senkovskii was a professional scholar with the kind of vast expertise more typical of his time than of our own, and he deliberately used the *Library for Reading* to display his erudition. For Pedrotti, Senkovskii's aspirations to encyclopedic learning, his didacticism, and his penchant for satire all mark him as an heir to the Enlightenment, particularly as it was developed at his alma mater, the University of Wilno, well into the nineteenth century. Senkovskii graduated from the University of Wilno in 1819, exactly the same year as Adam Mickiewicz. The publication only three years later of Mickiewicz's *Ballads and Romances* (1822) is usually taken as another of those sharp dividing lines separating different eras of literary history, in this case Polish neo-Classicism and Romanticism. Despite the revolution in Polish letters that *Ballads and Romances* announces, however, Czesław Miłosz writes that "Mickiewicz and his friends were, stylistically and spiritually, the direct descendants of the eighteenth century."[35] The same is all the more true for Senkovskii.

Senkovskii was not a friend of Mickiewicz's, but he was his classmate and he knew many of the same professors in Wilno, including the philologist Gottfried Groddeck, the rationalist mathematician and astronomer Jan Śniadecki, the historian Joachim Lelewel, and the university librarian Kazimierz Kontrym. But where Mickiewicz helped form the semi-clandestine student group the Philomaths, Senkovskii was invited in 1818 to join the somewhat more official and certainly more conservative Brotherhood of Scamps. The Brotherhood was made up mostly of university professors in various fields, including the sciences, along with a smattering of writers, doctors, lawyers, and even government ministers, many of them Masons and all imbued with decidedly neo-Classicist ideals. The group took for its motto the well-known "*ridendo castigare mores,*" a principle carried out largely by the periodical *Sidewalk News* first published by Kontrym in 1816 and then, under the aegis of the Brotherhood, weekly until 1822.

As Pedrotti notes, the influence of the Brotherhood of Scamps on Senkovskii's later work is clear. His constant recourse to satire, at least sometimes with didactic aims, owes a great deal to the style of the *Sidewalk News*, as the sheer amount of information he conveyed through the *Library for Reading* testifies to his ambitions to truly enlighten the Russian reading public. The table of contents for any of the issues of the *Library for Reading* offers articles on an astonishing array of topics, most of them written by Senkovskii himself. In the field of literature his areas of expertise included his own belletristic contributions and reviews of the latest Russian literature as well as articles on everything from Scandinavian sagas and Arabic poetry before Mohammed to the current state of literature in France, England, and Germany. Senkovskii, however, in no way restricted himself to the literary realm, and was also the author of articles on papermaking, galvanism, the future of European railroads, and the science of sound, to mention only a very few. He also reviewed books on every imaginable topic, including works on beekeeping, homeopathy, a history of financial institutions in Russia, and even, writing as Dr. Karl von Bitterwasser, on the use of mineral waters.[36]

Still, despite his close ties to a mostly older, more "Voltairean" generation, Senkovskii was far from immune to the Romanticism that so infected his classmate Mickiewicz. The alias Dr. Karl von Bitterwasser is fully in keeping with the sort of Addison-and-Steele, "Mr. Spectator" style of writing practiced by the *Sidewalk News* and also by the Russian satirical journals of the eighteenth century. Senkovskii's more flamboyant personae, however, are not. Mr. Spectator presented himself as just that, a spectator who observes the world but does not participate in it, and as Michael G. Ketcham points out, Mr. Spectator's impartial view of the world was intended to serve as a more or less transparent window onto his creators.[37] In contrast, the weight of the personalities of Brambeus, Tiutiun'dzhiu-Oglu, Kritikzada et al. detaches the personae from the person behind them, in the process transforming Senkovskii's Voltairean display of erudition into something very different. In Conrad's terms, "scholarly curatorship" becomes "self-exhibiting improvisation," and it is exactly this oscillation between the two poles that marked the writing of Friedrich Schlegel as well.[38]

As Lacoue-Labarthe and Nancy write, Schlegel "made virtuosity his vocation," and again this virtuosity partook of both Conrad's "Voltairean" and his more "romantic" sorts.[39] While Schlegel never did achieve the appointment at the university that he sought, like Senkovskii he was a noted philologist and author not just of literary-philosophical pieces, but also of more scholarly works such as *On the Study of Greek Poetry* (1797) and *On the Language and Wisdom of India* (1808). It was once upon a time his more scholarly pieces that were his claim to fame. Now the Schlegel we know best is not of the sort that Conrad calls the "pedantic connoisseur" but is instead the "visionary architect, suspending delicate, elaborate structures of imaginative association in the air," the "hedonist" who "exists self-indulgently taking liberties with artistic shape and moral precept, and [who] incites a rebellion of form against content."[40] In short, we know him as Romantic ironist, as in Schlegel's own definition: "Irony is the clear consciousness of eternal agility, of an infinitely teeming chaos."[41]

The *Athenaeum*, like the *Library for Reading*, ironically enacts encounters between writer and reader, speaker and audience, self and other that are in some sense neither real nor true.[42] In Schlegel's hands this admittedly artificial play of multivoicedness serves to demonstrate the higher truths of our own fundamental duality as both self and other and of the possibility of constructing our own heterogeneous identities only through one another; in Senkovskii's case we may question whether Romantic irony has not lost what Handwerk terms its "ethical" edge. Still in both cases this fragmentation of the writer's voice offers a kind of virtuosic performance that stands in tension with the more scholarly and erudite collection of objects of vertu. Perhaps the best evidence that Romanticism alone encompasses both Conrad's kinds of virtuosity, however, comes not from Schlegel at the beginning of Romanticism nor even Senkovskii at its end, but from a figure operating right in its middle: Sir Walter Scott.

In his own play of personae, Scott, too, is the "new virtuoso," one who does not collect remarkable objects but is himself a remarkable subject. He is also, in his own words, a "virtuoso" of another kind, as Scott was an antiquarian, in fact the antiquarian *par excellence*.[43] Many of our writers-as-collectors collected not just other people's stories but also history and historical artifacts. Pushkin, for example, filled notebooks not just with the historical research he did for his novel *The Captain's Daughter* (1835) but also with brief historical anecdotes from his own time and times recently past; Gogol mined the existing literature on Ukraine and even wrote home for ethnographic details to infuse his *Evenings on a Farm Near Dikan'ka* (1831).[44] If both writers sought to fill their writings with the scraps of other times and places, however, it was because Scott had done so first.

Scott certainly did not invent the practice of antiquarianism, which can be characterized as a material kind of erudition that takes up physical as well as literary space in a particularly cluttered kind of way. As Philippa Levine writes, the "most singular characteristic" of antiquarianism "was its promiscuous mix of sources, its use of both literary and material evidence."[45] Over the course of the nineteenth century, antiquarianism would break up into the separate and increasingly professionalized disciplines of history, anthropology, archeology, and philology. In Scott's day, all four were thrown into the pot together and stirred by a motley and largely amateur group of librarians, museum curators, writers, scholars, and collectors. It is Scott, however, who offers the most famous instance of an antiquarian who parlayed his hobby into a career and a way of life.

From early adulthood Scott collected with what his biographer John Sutherland calls "kleptomaniac intensity," making annual summer raids into the Scottish countryside. According to Sutherland his "booty" was often historical artifacts, for example an old Border war horn. Although not yet himself a writer, Scott also took these early opportunities to find the "originals" for his later novelistic heroes, as Dandie Dinmont in *Guy Mannering*, for example, "was supposedly inspired by Willie Eliot, an upland sheep-farmer, at Millburnholm."[46] Most significant, however, was that Scott returned from these trips with the material that would feed into his first foray into literature, *Minstrelsy of the Scottish Border* (1802).

In *Minstrelsy*, Scott published a collection of songs that were not only not written but often not even collected by him. While the title page bears his name alone, as Sutherland perhaps a little too charitably notes, Scott's "great trick as a ballad collector was his ability to foster collaboration," and the many publicly unacknowledged contributors to the book included fellow antiquarians like Richard Heber, paid student assistants like John Leydon, and local informants such as our old friend James Hogg, a.k.a. the Ettrick Shepherd. The collecting of collections then becomes a theme of his later novels,. not just in the frames offered by antiquarian editor-personae like Jedediah Cleishbotham in the *Tales of My Landlord* or Dr. Jonas Dryasdust in *Ivanhoe* (1820), but often in the texts themselves. Most notably, the third of the *Waverley* novels is *The Antiquary* (1816), which, like Dr. Dryasdust, mocks its own antiquarian origin. This theme is then rematerialized in the Black reprints of the *Waverley* novels in the later nineteenth century with what Sutherland calls "their multitudinous marginal, terminal, and intra-textual embellishments":

> On one page there will be a reproduction of a coin from the reign of Richard; on another page, a depiction of Bruce's dagger runs down the margin; a bracket from the column-work of Melrose Abbey or some appropriate medal will fill up a convenient white space left at the end of a chapter; a whole page will be given to a facsimile of some ancient document.[47]

In Scott's own lifetime, however, the most tangible manifestation of his collecting mania was his house at Abbotsford.

The image of literature as living space is Scott's own, as in *Shandyism* Conrad quotes the Scottish laird's reaction to Sterne's novel. According to Scott, *Tristram Shandy* "resembles the irregularities of a Gothic room, built by some fanciful collector, to contain the miscellaneous remnants of antiquity which his pains have accumulated, and bearing as little proportion in its parts, as there is connection between the pieces of rusty armour with which it is decorated." Scott's comparison leads him even to describe Sterne's well-known plagiarisms as but "the lucky finds of the antiquarian assembling round him his odd dusty tidbits of learning."[48] The transformation of plagiarism into the "lucky finds of the antiquarian" might seem to more effectively describe Scott's own appropriations in *Minstrelsy of the Scottish Border*. We realize the special applicability of this quote to Scott's own life and work, however, when we consider that it was famously the great success of his antiquarian-inspired literature that enabled him to pay for Abbotsford, the (pseudo)historical house he built to display his ever-increasing collection of (pseudo)historical artifacts. As John Sutherland writes:

> The final result was a miracle of eclecticism: combining Scottish Picturesque, Scots-Jacobean, English manor house, with Scottish Castle and monastic styles. Inside, Scott's imagination ran wild. Suits of armour and old weaponry (guns, pistols, targes, claymores, bugles, horns) covered the walls. He had a library-study, with secret recessed compartments. . . . His "curio room" was dominated by Rob Roy's long-barrelled gun, pouch and dirk. Scott collected or commis-

sioned paintings to celebrate his family history and lore. Heraldic devices were posted up in the main hall. . . . And yet, for all the spurious antiquity, Abbotsford had queerly futuristic touches—such things as gaslighting, a pneumatic bell system and water closets.[49]

Scott not only needed a great deal of money to build this "miracle of eclecticism" but also to fill it, and even on the verge of bankruptcy he was still buying antique armor in London showrooms. The answer, of course, was to write more novels, and as the literary marketplace feeds his antiquarian obsessions and vice-versa, the spaces of the lending library and of the literary cabinet of curiosities converge.

We have already made the connection between collecting and commodification in Kevin McLaughlin's reading of Dickens and Balzac as highly commercially successful writer-collectors, and the same association holds for collections of a more material type. Antiquarianism both depended on money and produced it. Levine describes the "notorious" Sir Thomas Phillipps with his collection estimated "at some 60,000 manuscripts and 50,000 printed books and pamphlets, the cost of which had been between £200,000 and £250,000" as a "collector run amok" but also notes the "large and valuable nature of many of these collections." Like Phillips's, Thomas Layton's collection of "11,000 books, 3,000 prints and maps, 3,000 coins, tokens and medals, 9,000 pottery and glass vessels and tiles and 2,600 [assorted] antiquities" was both an investment in the future and a trophy symbolizing large wealth already gained.[50] As Yoon Sun Lee notes in "A Divided Inheritance: Scott's Antiquarian Novel and the British Nation," Scott, too, was well aware of the value the antiquarian marketplace could lend the otherwise worthless detritus of the past, especially in *The Antiquary*.[51]

Early on in *The Antiquary* the narrator explains that our antiquarian hero Mr. Oldbuck took "a pleasure in the personal labour of forming his library" and so "saved his purse at the extent of his time and toil," a practice that Oldbuck himself then describes in his own words. As Oldbuck waxes eloquent on the pleasures of antiquarianism to his new friend Mr. Lovel:

> How often have I stood haggling upon a halfpenny, lest, by a too ready acquiescence in the dealer's first price, he should be led to suspect the value I set upon the article!—how have I trembled, lest some passing stranger should chop in between me and the prize, and regarded each poor student of divinity that stopped to turn over the books at the stall, as a rival amateur, or prowling bookseller in disguise!—And then, Mr Lovel, the sly satisfaction with which

one pays the consideration and pockets the article, affecting a cold indifference while our hand is trembling with pleasure!—Then to dazzle the eyes of our wealthier and emulous rivals by showing them such treasures as this (displaying a little black smoked book about the size of a primmer)—to enjoy their surprise and envy, shrouding meanwhile under a veil of mysterious consciousness our own superior knowledge and dexterity—these, my young friend, these are the white moments of life, that repay the toil, and pains, and sedulous attention, which our profession, above all others, so peculiarly demands!

Oldbuck's favorite story, finally, is the tale of how Davy Wilson, "commonly called Snuffy Davy, from his inveterate addiction to black rappee," paid twopence for a rare edition of Caxton's "Game of Chess, 1474" and then sold it for twenty pounds together with twenty pounds worth of books. Oldbuck recounts how the work was then sold and resold again until "this inestimable treasure blazed forth in its full value, and was purchased by royalty itself, for one hundred and seventy pounds!" As Oldbuck gleefully concludes, "Could a copy now occur, Lord only knows what would be its ransom; and yet it was originally secured, by skill and research, for the easy equivalent of twopence sterling. Happy, thrice happy, Snuffy Davy! and blessed were the times when thy industry could be so rewarded!"[52]

Clearly the antiquarian library, like the lending library, is a space shaped to some extent by commercial interests; it also is one that partakes of a particular political dimension. Antiquarians are by nature fundamentally conservative, at least in the sense that their mission is conservationist. Certainly Scott was a Tory and a stout unionist in largely Whig and often separatist Scotland, and while Scott's cultural allegiance to what Lee calls a "triumphal British nation" has been questioned, it is still safe to say that any centrifugal force he represents is at best partial. Just as the lending library disseminates books more widely only ideally to consolidate the book business within its own doors, so the antiquarian often reconstructs the past of a peripheral part of the empire only to better integrate himself into its center. This tendency is especially marked in Scott with his repackaging of the Scottish past for a largely English audience, and also in Gogol, with his fictionalized Ukraine served up to the St. Petersburg literary elite. Still, the political dimensions of Romantic antiquarian space become most apparent when the antiquarian turns his attention away from the obscure corners of Europe and to Asia. In this case, however, we no longer call the practice antiquarianism, but Orientalism.

The Orientalist Library

Where Scott began as an antiquarian, Senkovskii began as professor of Oriental languages at the University of St. Petersburg. Only twenty-two at the time of his appointment, Senkovskii seemed well on his way to a brilliant academic career. Yet from very early on his more popular literary aspirations were also evident, first with his publication of travel accounts and then with the stories "from the Arabic" that he published in the almanac *Polar Star* in 1823 and 1824 to great acclaim. Pushkin himself so appreciated the stories in the *Polar Star* that he wrote the editor Bestuzhev, "The Arabic tale is lovely; I advise you to hold on to that Senkovskii."[53] This sort of easy movement between a scholarly and a more literary East was not atypical, as most nineteenth-century Orientalists, like their antiquarian kin, switched and swapped genres and disciplines with abandon. As Said writes, "A nineteenth-century Orientalist was . . . either a scholar (a Sinologist, an Islamicist, an Indo-Europeanist) or a gifted enthusiast (Hugo in *Les Orientales*, Goethe in the *Westoestlicher Diwan*), or both (Richard Burton, Edward Lane, Friedrich Schlegel)."[54]

Said has famously argued that the intent of all this genre swapping was anything but the revelation of what we might call a real part of the globe. Nineteenth-century Orientalists were first of all much more interested in an ancient East than in the East in its current form. As Said notes, when Friedrich Schlegel famously claimed in the *Athenaeum* that "It is in the Orient that we must search for the highest Romanticism," "he meant the Orient of the *Sakuntala*, the Zend-Avesta, and the Upanishads." "Nowhere," Said complains, "does Schlegel talk about the living, contemporary Orient." More important, Said has also argued that Orientalism is less about the East than about its representation specifically by and for Europeans. Accordingly we find ourselves once more back at the antiquarian curio cabinet, but now with an even greater emphasis on the display or even the performance of knowledge. Said explains:

> Under the general heading of knowledge of the Orient, and within the umbrella of Western hegemony over the Orient during the period from the end of the eighteenth century, there emerged a complex Orient suitable for study in the academy, for display in the museum, for reconstruction in the colonial office, for theoretical illustration in anthropological, biological, linguistic, racial, and historical theses about mankind and the universe, for instances of

economic and sociological theories of development, revolution, cultural personality, national or religious character."[55]

This form of "specialized knowledge," in Said's view, does not and cannot
reproduce the entirety of the East. Just as Abbotsford in its selection and
arrangement of an eclectic set of artifacts of sometimes questionable authenticity re-creates mostly the Scottish part of Britain literally in bits and
pieces, so Orientalist space displays an East made up of fragments, and in
this act of partial and even artificial reconstruction, the Orientalist, like the
antiquarian, plays a central role.

"Since the Orient cannot be known without his mediation," Said writes,
it is the job of the Orientalist to pick and choose among various pieces of
the East. His or her task is not just to select only certain texts and not others,
for example, but even to select only excerpts from certain texts that he or she
then combines into didactic forms such as anthologies and chrestomathies,
in effect textbooks "in which a relatively small set of powerful examples
delivers the Orient to the student."[56] As Said's "mediator," the Orientalist
is then exactly the Romantic literary critic, the writer as collector or editor
who purports to only present selections of a text or texts to his or her audience when what he or she really offers is his or her own persona holding
together a simulation of the whole. What the Orientalist as opposed to the
literary-critical or even the antiquarian library makes particularly evident,
however, are the possible ideological implications of the act of collection
and presentation.

Orientalism in Said's reading is another weapon in the European imperialist arsenal, a means of establishing and maintaining Western hegemony
over the East, and it may be that the hegemony attempted by Romantic literary criticism has equally imperialist ambitions. If the example of
Senkovskii and the *Library for Reading* suggests a connection between the
Romantic-critical and imperialist projects, however, it does so in a way that
Said's work does not quite anticipate. Said's West is something of a mono-
lith, and his analysis leaves no room for an Orientalizing power as uncertain
of its place between East and West as Russia, nor for the particular example
of a Polish Orientalist who threw in his lot with the Russian Empire.[57] Despite its uniqueness, the Senkovskiian experience in St. Petersburg also suggests that what Said lacks is an appreciation of irony. Where Said's writers
and scholars seem largely unaware that they have produced anything other
than the real East, Senkovskii is a past master at simulation, and it is a mea-

sure if not of his Romantic irony, then of his contempt for his audience that he so openly reveals what he clearly knows.

ORIENTALIST TRAVELER

On graduating from the University of Wilno in 1819 with a speciality in Oriental languages, the young Senkovskii immediately set off for the Middle East with the avowed intention of exploring the historical ties between Turkey and Poland. It seems likely that Senkovskii's research was also intended to serve practical political ends, as the Poles who initially financed his trip were clearly interested in resurrecting those ties at the expense of the Russian Empire.[58] Senkovskii's own political aims, however, were perhaps a little different from those of his mentors. On first arriving in Turkey, Senkovskii immediately had himself put on the payroll of the Russian mission, essentially supplementing his funds by offering to spy for Russia. More important, after two years spent largely in Syria, Senkovskii disappointed his original sponsors by returning not to Wilno nor even to Warsaw but to St. Petersburg.

Senkovskii apparently attempted to bring back to Europe a very special artifact, the famous zodiac carved in stone that decorated the ceiling of the temple of Dendur. According to his first biographer, P. Savel'ev, with the help of his Maltese servant Senkovskii managed to cut the zodiac from its resting place and load it into a boat destined for Alexandria, only to give up his enterprise in the face of the Greek revolution and the corresponding restrictions imposed on Christians by the Ottoman Empire. Despite this disappointment, what Senkovskii did succeed in bringing back to Europe was a knowledge of the Islamic East and a fluency in Arabic apparently unprecedented, at least in Russia. Senkovskii immediately parlayed his linguistic achievements into two prestigious posts, the first as a translator at the Ministry of Foreign Affairs and the second as professor of Oriental languages at the recently reorganized University of St. Petersburg.[59]

It was clearly Senkovskii's grasp of the living language that mattered most to his future employers, although they were hardly in a position to gauge the extent of his knowledge. In recommending Senkovskii for the post at the Ministry of Foreign Affairs, Russian Academician Christian-Martin von Frahn, himself professor of Oriental languages, could finally only recuse himself, writing in conclusion: "As for the spoken language, in which Mr.

Senkovskii is especially strong, I cannot even begin to compare myself with him, since I have studied this language only from books, manuscripts and monuments. And I sincerely regret that, since I am no valid judge in this matter, I am unable to render sufficient praise to this remarkable young man."[60] If it was Senkovskii's actual experience in the East that launched his Orientalist career, still the Orientalist writings he produced in the course of that career did not actually traffic in any sort of real East. Nor, still more strikingly, did they pretend to do so.

The space of Senkovskii's early travelogues is already complicated, and the issue as always is Senkovskii's unstable identity. On his return from the Middle East in 1822 Senkovskii almost immediately published four brief accounts of his travels, "A Brief Outline of a Trip to Nubia and Upper Ethiopia," "A Visit to the Pyramids," "An Account of Letters from Cairo from 11/22 December 1820," and "The Return Trip from Egypt by Way of the Archipelago and Part of Asia Minor." That these are accounts of Senkovskii's trip should perhaps be qualified: while "A Visit to the Pyramids" is subtitled "From the Travel Notes of Iosif Senkovskii," and "The Return Trip" is subtitled "An Excerpt from the Daily Travel Notes of I. Senkovskii," the other two pieces appeared anonymously. In calling himself "Iosif" or simply "I. Senkovskii," the Polish József-Julian Sękowski began the process of Russianization that would eventually result in the name by which he is known in Russian literary history, Osip Ivanovich Senkovskii. If the progressive Russianization of Senkovskii's name already suggests a certain instability in at least his literary identity, his early use of anonymity offers a destabilization of another kind. In presenting anonymously what are apparently the facts of his own life, Senkovskii undermines the association of the experiences recorded in these texts with any real body in the world, when it was exactly that association on which his own authority as an Orientalist nonetheless apparently depended. This practice becomes still more problematic when Senkovskii returns to the genre in the early 1830s, now as editor of the *Library for Reading*. While his more belletristic "Abu Simbel. Nubian Scenes" (1835), for example, is again published anonymously, his "Reminiscences of Syria" (1834) appear pseudonymously, not by Iosif Senkovskii, but by one Osip Morozov.

Senkovskii's claim as Orientalist travel writer is always that it is he alone who offers his readers the truth about the East.[61] The other European travelers he meets in his narratives, all of whom are hard at work at their own travel books, are as ignorant as the natives are indifferent, and their encounters usually result in mutual incomprehension. The fault most often seems to lie with the superficial view of the East adopted by the average European. Still, the attempts of the Europeans to penetrate a bit deeper into the Orient are even less successful. In "A Visit to the Pyramids," Senkovskii notes that a statue of a sphinx found in an extremely deep well was unfortunately broken in the process of pulling it out. He is even drier in his description of the fate of a particularly lovely catacomb. A plan was afoot to take the catacomb entirely to pieces and reassemble it in Paris where, Senkovskii says, it would have given the Europeans a much better understanding of ancient Egyptian art than any book or drawing could. "Later I learned," Senkovskii continues, "that during the process of taking down the plaster . . . they broke it into pieces, and after completely destroying the beautiful catacomb abandoned their enterprise."[62]

It is not surprising that Senkovskii thinks poorly of the writing produced by such ignorant and even destructive research, and his criticism is usually sweeping. In "A Visit to the Pyramids" he explains that while "[t]here is nothing to add to the already well-known descriptions of the interior arrangements of the pyramids . . . there is a great deal in them that is necessary to abridge." In fact, Senkovskii tells us:

> Inside [the Pyramids] there is nothing beautiful or striking, and nothing reminds one of the external grandeur of these buildings. . . . Only one extremely tall staircase faced in pink granite is worthy of notice; everything else does little to satisfy the curiosity of those who, having read the magnificent descriptions of these monuments, think to find in them something extraordinary.[63]

By 1835 and "Abu Simbel," other writers have apparently switched from exaggerated praise to the same sort of exposé style Senkovskii himself practices, and now he must turn to debunking the debunkers with the claim that the real evil of "unbridled Pindarism or the desire to keep one's readers in uninterrupted astonishment" is the recent appearance of travel books that "to the dismay of the enthusiasts . . . mercilessly abuse everything Egyptian, both the shabby and the truly grand."[64]

Senkovskii's complaints are also often directed at one writer in particular, the famous Baron Dominique Vivant Denon who memorialized Napoleon's invasion of Egypt in his *Travels in Upper and Lower Egypt* (1802). In "Abu Simbel" Senkovskii can understand Denon's exaggerations because, unlike

later commentators, Denon "found himself under the influence of the un-
expectedness of the discovery, the newness of the subject, lack of time, and
the military glory that posed all the questions"; in "A Visit to the Pyramids"
he is less forgiving. Here Senkovskii attacks travel writing in general and
Denon in particular when he writes:

> It's too bad that you don't find in nature a single one of those lovely phrases
> that jingle so pleasantly in the descriptions of travel. "The mountains that sur-
> round them (says M. Denon of the pyramids in his *Voyage*) are not as large and
> not so well preserved." For the truth of that description there is nothing lack-
> ing in nature except the mountains: the Libyan range at that point represents
> the very smallest rise on the surface of the earth, while in the surroundings
> there are no mountains at all.[65]

There is also a more subtle dismissal of Denon in the first part of Osip
Morozov's "Reminiscences of Syria," "The Solar Eclipse."

"The Solar Eclipse" begins with a wonderfully entertaining account of
Osip Morozov's adventures learning Arabic mainly in a Maronite monastery
in Syria, adventures that Senkovskii's first biographer, P. Savel'ev, does not
hesitate to attribute to Senkovskii himself. Morozov/Senkovskii describes
how he dragged himself over mountaintops in his desire to learn Arabic,
"the sound of which, like the silvery voice of a bell enclosed in a human
breast in the lips of a Druze or a Beduin, had captivated [his] ear with
its novelty and driven [him] to despair with its inimitability." Indeed, he
writes, "it not infrequently happened that I myself was forced to smile at
my own linguistic vanity when the chameleons that ran gaily along the cliffs
stopped alongside me, opened their mouths wide and stood amazed at the
piercing quality of the guttural sounds that I with such effort extracted from
the depths of my lungs."[66] By dint of studying so hard that he becomes
desperately ill, Morozov/Senkovskii eventually achieves his goal, and is even
locally renowned for his linguistic abilities, so much so that the Arabs come
to treat him as something of an oracle of wisdom; for example, on the occasion of the eclipse when Sheikh Beshara comes to "Khavadzha Yusuf" to
learn "what it means."

Morozov/Senkovskii describes the planetary system at some length
only to overhear the Arabs laughingly dismiss his explanation as they leave
the monastery, still convinced that the eclipse is an ill omen. At the time
Morozov/Senkovskii sees the Sheikh and his friends as blockheads, but
by the end of the year events conspire to cast their stance in a very dif-

ferent light. With the start of the Greek revolution the Turks institute oppressive measures against the Christian minority, worst of all in Syria, and many of the Maronites flee to Egypt where Morozov/Senkovskii once more encounters his friends. In reply to their question "Well, Khavadzha Yusuf! . . . What about that eclipse? Do you remember how you argued then?" he only reached into his pocket "and pulled out a modest alm for bread for people who not long before had entertained [him] lavishly in their own homes."[67]

Senkovskii's two explanations for the eclipse, one presented as based on European science and the other on Arab superstition, echoes a story Denon tells about thunder, but with a rather different conclusion. According to Denon, thunder occurs so rarely in Egypt that even "thinking people" do not attempt to attribute it to a physical cause, and he gives the example of a "person in the law" who explains to General Desaix that thunder is the work of a tiny angel roaring against the wickedness of men. When General Desaix tries to explain thunder in terms of science, Denon says, the old man finds this explanation "so inferior to his own that he even did not take the trouble to listen to it," and here Denon's story abruptly ends.[68] Morozov/Senkovskii, however, offers a certain vindication of the Arab view, not just in the reencounter in Egypt but in the final explicit statement of his moral: "I, for my experience, derived from the event unfolding before me only that benefit that I was an eyewitness to the process by which nature and fate create for us delusions and keep tribes in ignorance."[69]

His disputes with contemporary commentators suggest that Senkovskii saw current writing on the East as offering an alternative reality, a more or less purely literary construction that exaggerates or detracts, misunderstands or even destroys the actual Middle East. The suggestion seems to be, too, that Senkovskii's own Orientalist writing is less literary and more "real," perhaps above all in "Reminiscences of Syria" where the locals rather pointedly become real people and even real friends. Still, if Senkovskii wants his readers to understand "Reminiscences of Syria" as the real reminiscences of a real place, one can only wonder why he does not sign the piece with his real name. Senkovskii may well have assumed the sort of easy equation of Morozov with himself that Savel'ev, for example, was later to make. While in some respects Osip Morozov is Osip Ivanovich Senkovskii, in other respects he is not, and in the confusion between the two Senkovskii deliberately subverts his own apparent Orientalist aims.

There is a certain irony in the fact that as typical travelers to the Orient Senkovskii's narrators almost always take a moment to inscribe their names. In "A Visit to the Pyramids" the narrator notes that the walls of one of the interior rooms, while never well polished, were now covered with inscriptions, as various travelers "had thought to attain immortality by tracing their names with a pencil on the walls," while in "The Return Trip" Greek monks keep a book in which all the visitors to their monastery from its earliest days write their names.[70] In "Abu Simbel" the travelers carve their names on the eye socket of one of the statues standing guard outside the temple. That name might be Senkovskii, but it might not, and the meaning lent by this ambiguity to the almost obligatory practice of inscribing one's name on the Orient is made clear by a comparison with Chateaubriand.

Said finds special significance in the fact that in his *Journey from Paris to Jerusalem and from Jerusalem to Paris* (1810–11), Chateaubriand tells us that although unable to actually visit the pyramids himself, he nonetheless sent an emissary to inscribe his (Chateaubriand's) name there. According to Said, when Chateaubriand then ends his travelogue with a reference to the metaphorical monument that is his writing and that is also inscribed with his name: "We will have understood that his egoistic Oriental memoirs supply us with a constantly demonstrated, indefatigably performed experience of self. Writing was an act of life for Chateaubriand, for whom nothing, not even a distant piece of stone, must remain scriptively untouched by him if he was to stay alive.[71] To make this statement appropriate for Senkovskii, however, we would have to change singular to plural: his memoirs offer an indefatigably performed experience of selves, as Senkovskii plunders East for "East" not so much to keep himself alive, as to bring to life an ever-expanding set of Senkovskii simulacra.

Said's Orientalist presumably fails to see that he has inserted himself between his reader and the East. Senkovskii's excessive play of personae, on the other hand, would suggest that Senkovskii is well aware that as Orientalist he has absorbed the entire interaction into himself. This open absorption of the East into the Orientalist self exactly prefigures the functioning of Senkovskii's later literary criticism, as does Senkovskii's work in a perhaps still more unexpected genre, not a travel account but a more scholarly piece: the review of noted Viennese scholar J. Hammer's *On Russian Origins* (1827), which, as Kaverin tells us, "once and for all strengthened Senkovskii's position among linguists and linguistics of his day."[72]

ORIENTALIST SCHOLAR

Much of Senkovskii's scholarly work both in the 1820s and even later was entirely conventional in form and included translations of primary texts, histories of various Eastern peoples, dictionaries, and encyclopedia entries. Among this collection, his review of *On Russian Origins* stands out. It first appeared in Russian in 1827 in Bulgarin's *Northern Bee* as the "Letter of Tiutiun'dzhiu-Oglu-Mustafa-Aga, actual Turkish philosopher, to one of the publishers of the *Northern Bee*," and it was republished in an amplified version in French in 1828, first as a separate brochure and then in the *Bulletin du Nord* under the title "Letter of Tutundju-Oglou-Moustafa-Aga, actual Turkish philosopher, to M. Thaddée Bulgarin, editor of the *Northern Bee*; translated from the Russian and published with a knowledgeable commentary by Koutlouk-Fouladi, former ambassador to the court of Boukhara at Khiva (ancient Germania), currently merchant of preserved apricots in Samarkand and man of letters."

The "Letter" begins with Tiutiun'dzhiu-Oglu-Mustafa-Aga's explanation of how Hammer's book came into his possession, a story that necessitates a certain amount of background information. Tiutiun'dzhiu-Oglu is now a soap merchant in Gostinnyi dvor, but he comes from a long line of Turkish tobacco merchants in Jaffa (his name means "tobacconist's son") that met a sad end. The governor of their part of Palestine, unwilling to burden his subjects with taxes, had found two ways to make money: he would either buy all the silk and cotton in his district at prices set by himself and then sell it at market rate to the Franks or, if the Franks were not buying silk, he would send the Arabs into the desert to gather alkali and make enormous amounts of soap that he would then "give" to his richest subjects in exchange for a substantial amount of money. When Tiutiun'dzhiu-Oglu's father was presented with such a gift, however, he refused to pay the requisite sum, and accordingly the Pasha had him killed and confiscated his entire estate except for the soap. Tiutiun'dzhiu-Oglu was left with no other means of supporting himself, and since no one needed more soap in Palestine, he made his way eventually to St. Petersburg where, last Thursday, he went to a typography to purchase scrap sheets of paper to make wrappers for his wares. To his great pleasure he found that the paper he had been sold was printed with something in Arabic, Persian, Turkish, and French. On returning to his shop he put these sheets of paper in order and discovered that "in the form of scrap paper they had sold me a composition under the title, *Sur les origines russes, extraits de manuscrits orientaux par Mr. J. de Hammer, St. Pétersbourg, 1827.*"[73]

Unfortunately, Tiutiun'dzhiu-Oglu found himself perplexed as to the nature of this work. At first he thought that the book was intended as a continuation of the *Arabian Nights* as he was otherwise unable to account for a number of apparently fantastic claims its author makes; for example, that Mohammed mentions the Russians in the Koran, that the Russian people used to live in Bukhara, and that the Don Cossacks already existed in the tenth century. As he read further, however, he realized that *On Russian Origins* was meant as true history and that the source of Hammer's extraordinary claims was not his imagination but his absolutely idiotic mistranslations and misreadings of texts. "It is in vain that you so often attack our Prophet in your *Northern Bee*," Tiutiun'dzhiu-Oglu tells Bulgarin, for "he was an intelligent man and himself stated positively in the Alcoran: 'O orthodox people! If you fall into the temptation of translating books, then you should first of all gain a fundamental knowledge of the language from which you wish to translate.'" "I've been told," he adds, "that one of your literary men once rendered into Russian the name Chadyr-Dag, la montagne de la tente, as *auntie's mountain*. But what will you think when I tell you that you can find two or three such felicitous translations on almost every page of the learned Viennese Orientalist's small book?"[74]

The rest of the letter then details Hammer's many mistakes, including wrong etymologies, misreadings, and misspellings. When he comes across the Arabic word *ikhtiar*, for example, which Tiutiun'dzhiu-Oglu defines as "free will, proposal, opinion," Hammer thinks it is a proper name, so that instead of translating "in the opinion of Ibn-Djerir" he invents an entirely new character, "Ikhtiar-Ibn-Djerir," who has no opinion at all. Hammer has a similar problem with the participle he transliterates as *mounféschan*, "spreading" or "growing," so that his translation, rather than describing how the territory of the Allains expanded toward the north, instead creates a mysterious northern people, the *Mounfésha*, prompting Tiutiun'dzhiu-Oglu to ask: "How do you like this sort of geography? This *Mounfésha* is matchless, a nation of grammatical origin!" Hammer creates another country, the previously unknown "Land of *Birket*" when he confuses the person Bérgué-Khan with the Arabic word for pond or lake, and indeed Tiutiun'dzhiu-Oglu gives an entire list of peoples and places "formed from the pen of Hammer in the same way" and summarizes: "Hammer reads Oriental manuscripts poorly, he doesn't know medieval Asian geography or the meaning of a number of the most simple and widely used expressions, and so it appeared to him that Oriental Writers speak about Russians and Slavs in places where there is not one word about them." Finishing his criticism with a series of side-by-side translations in French, Hammer's and his own, Tiutiun'dzhiu-Oglu concludes, "with this sort of criticism you could prove not only that the Russians come from Bukhara, but that they come from the moon."[75]

Senkovskii's attack on Hammer's work may well be justified and indeed, given its reception in Europe, it probably was. Still, the greatest irony of the "Letter" is the extent to which the criticism Senkovskii levels at Hammer applies to the "Letter" itself, starting with the problem of genre. After all, while his readers might not take seriously Tiutiun'dzhiu-Oglu's claim to have confused *On Russian Origins* with the *Arabian Nights*, they might be forgiven for operating under a similar misapprehension themselves with regard the "Letter." More important, however, just as in his travelogues Senkovskii criticized other travelogues for inventing an imaginary East, so in his scholarship does he condemn Hammer for inventing peoples and places from language when again what he himself is doing is not so very different.

The very vehemence of his attack on Hammer suggests the primacy Senkovskii always gives language, as do his concluding remarks about the Indo-European hypothesis. In the last part of his letter Tiutiun'dzhiu-Oglu ridicules the notion, as he puts it, that "certain German Ulems have invented some sort of Indo-Germanic nation and argue in all sincerity that they arrived in Bonn and Berlin straight from Calcutta and Seringapatam."[76] Tiutiun'dzhiu-Oglu mocks the absence of any historical evidence that would support the existence of this people, nor does he offer any that would contradict it. Instead, the argument takes place on the level of language alone, as where the German "Ulems" contrived this story of Indian origin to account for the similarity of a hundred or so German words with Sanskrit, Tiutiun'dzhiu-Oglu claims that in fact these words are much closer to Persian dialects that had doubtlessly spread to Europe in ancient times.

Senkovskii may disagree with Hammer's position but he, too, is willing to derive a particular tribe, what he calls "the original Europeans," from language alone, and in this attachment to language we are reminded of Osip Morozov who nearly died in the effort to master the Arabic that had "captivated [his] ear with its novelty." Senkovskii's only argument would seem to be that whereas Hammer creates an imaginary East because his language is wrong, he himself reveals the real East because his language is right. But he does not reveal the real East, and I say that not just because modern scholars would probably agree with the "Indo-Germanists" but also because the real problem, again exactly as in "Reminiscences of Syria," is the use of a persona. For Tiutiun'dzhiu-Oglu is not real, nor is the East from which he comes, and Senkovskii never pretends that they are.

The criticism of Hammer is entirely serious, but Tiutiun'dzhiu-Oglu is a colossal joke, from his opening cry "My most honored, most magnanimous, most generous Sultan, Publisher Effendi! May God provide you with every kind of good thing and forgive you all your sins, your errors and misprints!" to his concluding words: "Now having wound the thread of my story into a ball of eloquence I must cut it off with the scissors of silence. Farewell! May God preserve you in perfect health and not allow your compositions to be turned into scrap paper." As for his East, sometimes it would seem that this East is really West, for example when Tiutiun'dzhiu-Oglu explains the Pasha's system of forcing his subjects to buy his soap and then adds: "I have been told that somewhere in Frankistan there is a land in which the land-owners in the same way give out vodka to their serfs: *nihil novi sub sole.*" Sometimes it would seem that Tiutiun'dzhiu-Oglu's Jaffa has nothing to do with any real place on earth; for example, when Tiutiun'dzhiu-Oglu warns that he has forgotten much of what he used to know about Oriental history and literature while working in Gostinnyi dvor, a place where "as you know, scholarly knowledge in this sphere is limited to *The Story about the famous Vizir Martsimilis and the Hishpanish King Brambeus,* who was married to *the beautiful Ryntsevena, Queen of the Kundish Kingdom.*"[77]

The trick of the "Letter" and the source of its undeniable power is that Senkovskii grounds Tiutiun'dzhiu-Oglu's authority in his status as an "actual Turkish philosopher" while at the same time rendering that "actuality" absurd, trapping his reader in what is the quintessential operation of the simulacrum. In other words, in Senkovskii's Orient we find ourselves in a realm that operates exactly like his later literary criticism, as Senkovskii himself makes clear. Tiutiun'dzhiu-Oglu's comparison of his "real" story to the fairytale of the *Hishpanish King Brambeus* begs the question of what exactly the difference between the two heroes is, and the answer is that they are really very much alike. A king in Senkovskii's favorite Turkish "Tale of Frantsyl the Venetian," Brambeus reappears as a baron and as the author of a number of works in Smirdin's collection *Housewarming* and then as the leading literary critic of the *Library for Reading*, which happens to be where Tiutiun'dzhiu-Oglu, too, later publishes two book reviews.[78] What Senkovskii openly found in his Orientalism, both in the form of travel books and serious scholarship, was not the East but rather a realm of circulating signs that he could control. It is exactly the same space that he would find in the later literary criticism that he wrote for the *Library for Reading*.

ORIENTALIST LITERARY CRITIC

Senkovskii's frequent recourse to Orientalist personae makes the extent to which his Orientalism led directly into the *Library for Reading* a little hard to miss, and in his ponderous way even his archenemy S. P. Shevyrev made the connection. When Shevyrev fiercely attacked Senkovskii's principle of combining personal criticism with personae in his lead-off article in the newly founded *Moscow Observer*, "On Criticism Generally and Here in Russia," he took what he perhaps thought was a clever tack, casting his criticism almost entirely in terms of T.-O.'s apparently Asian origin. Given its impressive readership, Shevyrev writes, the *Library for Reading* can only be considered the "all-Russian criterium" for Russian literature. All the more terrible, then, that this standard is set by someone who not only hides his real name but even calls himself by a pseudonym that Shevyrev can only describe as "Turkish, Manchurian, or Tatar (given my ignorance of eastern languages I can't determine which), but certainly Asian." The "Asian" pseudonym reflects not just the critic's Oriental lack of openness but also his Oriental despotism, as Shevyrev asks in some despair:

> Has not a new Tatar invasion befallen our Literature? Is not the *Library for Reading*'s Criticism a new Golden Horde, to which all our writers must travel as tributaries in order to seek out the mercy of this literary Mamai, this Tiutiun'dzhiu-oglu?
> The idea involuntary comes to mind when you read the edicts of this Khan and see with what despotism he lavishes fury on one, mercy on another, and with what decisiveness he pronounces his sentences![79]

But the problem with Shevyrev's clever rhetoric is that the joke is already Senkovskii's, and his slings and arrows just glance off a *Library for Reading* that, as always, has already made that reading for us. Senkovskii was not an Oriental but an Orientalist, and moreover one who knew very well the game he was playing, as he draws on typically Orientalist imagery only to create an entirely mocking pretense of otherness, above all in his parody of the *Arabian Nights*, the "Literary Chronicle" for January 1838.

Like T.-O.'s review of "Mazepa" that so infuriated Shevyrev, the "Literary Chronicle" tells a tale of critical tyranny. Certainly it begins with an exaggerated emphasis on the critic's precarious position, ever at the mercy of a capricious Piublik-Sultan-Bagadur. What the "Literary Chronicle" then offers, besides Senkovskii's opinions on nineteen new books, is the story of Kritikzada's gradual establishment of complete control over her husband and so over all of literature. If Senkovskii's goal of creating a "literature" that he as critic controls and even creates might seem a little dastardly, his aim, despite Shevyrev's claims, was hardly un-Russian or even un-European. What is truly astonishing and perhaps even unique, however, is the brazenness with which he announces his intent.

Literary criticism in general professes only to mediate between reader and text and reader and writer, just as Orientalism claims to mediate between East and West. But Senkovskii's critic, exactly like his Orientalist, almost disdainfully flaunts his intention to do much more. In the "Literary Chronicle" as indeed in all of Senkovskii's criticism, the critic does not explain the writer but quite openly replaces him or her, on one level suggesting that literature is the creation of the critic and the reader alone. On another level, as the Sultan-reader is in turn also the creation of the critic, this relationship of two reduces still further to a relationship of one: that of the critic to him- or herself, endlessly spinning out his or her own existence. In the final analysis Senkovskii's criticism presents itself as not in between but everywhere, filling every corner of a kingdom where the critic rules supreme.

Outside the Library Walls

We might argue that this kingdom exists only in writing, in a sort of fantasyland like the Baghdad where, as Brambeus sums up in his story "The Happy Man" (1834), Haroun-Al-Rashid "in a word . . . did everything he could to amaze people, to make merry at the expense of history, to confuse his contemporaries, and to make for posterity the reading of *A Thousand and One Nights* pleasant and engaging, even in the German translation of Mr. Hammer."[80] In this sense, the Orientalist library returns us to the space of Romantic literary criticism that we never really left. Scott's antiquarian Scotland, like Gogol's Ukraine, is largely the product of his own writing, and even the lending library is more of a literary space than Smirdin's actual building would suggest; while Smirdin's library extended in three dimensions, still the notion of the "library for reading" pointed most significantly for Senkovskii to a literary marketplace that may have had little real existence outside the two dimensions of the printed page. By the time we reach the Orientalist library, this eternal return to literary criticism may have taken its toll. Whatever claims we may make about the meaning of the Romantic project, this pull ever into an ir- or a-reality may seem to diminish the importance of Romanticism altogether.

Yet the real effect of Said's *Orientalism* is not to cut the ties that would bind our signs of place to any real location in the world, but instead to show those ties to operate in a much more complicated fashion than we may have thought. It would certainly be easy to dismiss Romantic space as imaginary, but also inaccurate, and it is finally in this last sense that Senkovskii's Orientalism and his Romantic literary criticism approach one another. Like the Orientalist texts that purport to represent the East only to replace it, Romantic literary criticism, too, is an apparently literary phenomenon that nonetheless derives from and gives shape to real places in the world, and even to real places of a certain sort. If the *Library for Reading* looks like a library from the inside, whether of the *Athenaeum*, lending, antiquarian, or Orientalist varieties, it is shaped on the outside by the place where the real Senkovskii lived and worked. This place is Russia, but Russia in a very specific guise. Especially given the imperialist overtones the antiquarian and Orientalist libraries lend an already less than democratic Romantic project, my reader will perhaps not be surprised to learn that the Russia that matters most for the *Library for Reading* is Russia in its imperial aspect.

While nation is the political state more commonly associated with Romanticism, there is hardly one to be found among the leading Romantic players. The British combine England with Ireland, Scotland, and Wales as well as increasingly far-flung possessions, particularly India, while the French under Napoleon strive to create an empire also in various parts of the world, including across much of Europe. The Germans when not being absorbed into the French Empire were fragmented into as many as two hundred and thirty-four separate units. If Russia with its despotic rule looms as only the most imperial of nineteenth-century empires, still it may be just this quality that marks the Russian Empire as especially Romantic. Empire again, if perversely, expresses the paradoxical combination of heterogeneity and fragmentariness into one ever-expanding whole that the library also embodies. Empire is also the necessary environment for a play of periphery and center that characterizes the life and work of a great many Romantic writers, Senkovskii included, who only ever wielded mainstream power from a position on the peripheries. It is this Romantic space outside the *Library for Reading*, one that lends a certain form to Senkovskii's journal even as the library shapes it from within, that the next and last chapter will explore.

5.   Romantic Empire

The Romantic library is already quite a large and multifaceted space. Still, the many complicated encounters of Senkovskii's Romantic readers and writers exceed its walls, spilling out into a place we might call Russia. We can only be a little tentative in that designation, despite the apparent reality of the place where Senkovskii and his 5,000–7,000 subscribers actually existed in material form. Russia has of course long served the West, in Brambeus's words, as a kind of terra incognita.[1] In Senkovskii's own day, it was famously also something of a terra incognita to itself. The process of identity formation that marked Romanticism in Russia as elsewhere was not just a matter of the identity of individual writers and readers but finally also of the nation, and it was a process in which Russia was especially deeply engaged. If the isolation of national originality was the apparent goal, however, Romanticism's means often took it to very different ends, never more so than in the place where Senkovskii lived and worked. As Monika Greenleaf and Stephen Moeller-Sally argue, scholars have begun "to detect a collaboration, rather than opposition, between Russian 'translation and imitation,' on the one hand, and 'self-fashioning and national identity' on the other."[2] We can also understand this distinctively Russian syncretism in more broadly Romantic terms.

The extreme point toward which Romanticism always tended is expressed perhaps most vividly and even mockingly in a text that lies just outside the borders of the *Library for Reading*: the lecture Senkovskii gave upon resigning from the university in 1847, "On the Antiquity of the Name Russian." By 1847 Senkovskii's literary career was considerably diminished, although not yet at an end. In 1844, ten years after the first issue of the

Library for Reading, an already weak Senkovskii took his first long break from the magazine and spent the summer in Revel (Tallinn). In 1848 he fell seriously ill with cholera, and the tightening-up of censorship restrictions in the wake of events in Western Europe also put a damper on his literary work, so that while Senkovskii was still listed as editor until 1856, by the end of the 1840s active control of the journal had already passed to his one-time assistant, A.-V. V. Starchevskii. In the meantime it had also long been Senkovskii's habit to excuse himself from any academic duties, usually on account of severe migraines. It was only in 1847, however, that he formally retired from his professorship, marking the event with a perfectly outra-geous "farewell dissertation."

The occasion of Senkovskii's lecture was not just his retirement but also the closing of the academic year. Since in 1847 Senkovskii's scholarly and lit-erary reputations were still at their height, "On the Antiquity of the Name Russian" attracted a large audience, including high-level officials from the university and also the Ministry of Education. To the surprise of this distin-guished audience, however, Senkovskii did not appear himself to deliver his own speech. Once more claiming ill health, Senkovskii sent in his place an adjunct professor, V. F. Dittel'. As Dittel' began to read Senkovskii's text, the public's surprise turned to bafflement. Utilizing exactly the sort of pseudo-philological approach that he was long known for condemning, Senkovskii's lecture drew on patently absurd etymological derivations to make the claim that the Russians were the most ancient of all peoples and also the most widespread. According to Senkovskii, the Russians were the most important of the Scythian tribes that, he said, had settled all of Europe, including Scandinavia, and also the larger part of Asia, and he alluded to manuscripts that offered the most convincing evidence for his assertions and could be found locked up in one of the towers of the Alhambra. As Dittel' read on to the claim that all of ancient history was actually an account of the Slavs and that the chroniclers had simply confused geographic names, bafflement began to give way to something else. When Dittel', still reading with what one auditor called "imperturbable German phlegm," reached the part where Senkovskii alleged that the campaign of Cyrus had actually taken place in Belorussia, with the main battle fought near the town of Orsza, offering as evidence the fact that Napoleon himself in 1812 had described Orsza as a town of great strategic importance, the hall could no longer contain itself and howled with laughter.[3]

As the most dignified of the dignitaries left the room and the poor adjutant read on, Senkovskii deliberately sent his own Orientalist career up in flames. His so-called academic lecture informally also marked an end to the *Library for Reading*. Certainly the journal continued under Starchevskii's guidance and then under new owners beginning in 1856. Still, with Senkovskii's gradual relinquishing of control, the *Library for Reading* as a Romantic site where reader- and writer-personae met to simulate literature and various kinds of realities—from the literary marketplace to the antiquarian and Orientalist libraries—no longer existed, and his farewell lecture punctuates its end in more than one way. The lecture in its utter dismissiveness first of all indicates the extent to which Senkovskii's attention had already increasingly been devoted to other pursuits, including a failed investment in a tobacco factory (shades of Tiutiun'dzhiu-Oglu?) and in a never-to-be-perfected orchestrion, a mechanical device intended to replicate the sounds of an entire orchestra. The lecture also sums up once and for all much of the Romantic project as exemplified in the *Library for Reading*.

In "On the Antiquity of the Name Russian" Senkovskii's words once more are presented as not entirely his own, as they derive from evidently spurious manuscripts said to be locked up in the Alhambra and are also placed in the mouth of a surrogate, his unfortunate German adjunct, and this layering of personalities and personae has its usual destabilizing effect. While the adjunct professor continued reading even after the departure of the most important audience members, the rest of the lecture went unheard as those remaining heatedly discussed the question of whether Senkovskii should be punished for offering such an insult to his colleagues, or whether the esteemed professor actually believed that Cyrus had fought at Orsza.[4] In the very confusion of listeners who are both mocked and amused and also invited to investigate matters themselves, we are reminded again of the power that a Romantic troping of audience lends the writer, as Senkovskii's foray into the antiquarian depths of pseudo-philology also returns us to the space of the Romantic library. The lecture also introduces us to one last feature of Romanticism, the Romantic concept of the space that lay outside the literature Romanticism produced.

Romanticism is well known for its engagement with questions of what we might call national space. Romantic national space is not usually conceived in the form of Russia, however, and certainly not in the form of the absurdly large Russia of Senkovskii's lecture. Germany tends instead to get a good deal of attention—for example, in Friedrich Schlegel's claims of an Indo-Germanic language—as do the Romance languages and literatures to Friedrich's south who seemingly lent their very name to the movement; the shores of Albion are also a perennial favorite, at least with the English Romantics and their historians. The problems posed by Senkovskii's Russia are moreover compounded by the fact that it was not really his Russia at all. The much-touted rise of Romantic nationalism has often lent itself to an understanding of the ideal Romantic space as homogeneous, whole, authentic, and complete, one nation clearly demarcated from another. As a Polish émigré in the Russian Empire, Senkovskii necessarily lived in space that can only be described as none of the above.

Senkovskii's troubled position vis-à-vis the space from which he wrote, however, turns out to be not particularly unique among Romantic writers. As Senkovskii moved from the periphery of the Russian Empire to its center while nonetheless remaining always an outsider, so many of the other writers discussed here followed much the same path, including not just Senkovskii's compatriot Bulgarin but also Gogol, Scott, Maginn, and the *Blackwood's* people. These writers were anything but politically radical, and they by and large strove to put their outsider status to entirely conservative ends. Still, their very presence in a national literature destabilizes any idea of nationhood, reminding us once more of the underlying irony of Romantic identity formation. Rather than marked by homogeneity, wholeness, authenticity, and completion, Romantic space without as within, just like Romantic writers and readers, is more often imagined in heterogeneous, fragmentary, inauthentic, and incomplete terms. We might finally also understand better the principles of European Romanticism if we cast that space exactly in Senkovskiian terms, not as nation but as empire, and even as the Russian Empire in particular.

While by the early nineteenth century France's imperial ambitions were fluctuating and Germany had yet to really recover hers, Russia, like Great Britain, was already a fully fledged imperial power, with her borders expanded on the West to include Poland, Finland, and the Baltic states and on the East Siberia, Central Asia, and the Caucasus. Senkovskii's parodic absorption in "On the Antiquity of the Name Russian" of a large chunk of the world and of world history into an original Russian space and time reflects the fact of this Russian Empire. It also reflects and even highlights particular aspects of Romantic theory. Once in Russia the Romantic ideal of heterogeneous and fragmentary space tends to look distinctly imperial.[5] Perhaps still more important, in the Russian context it also becomes apparent that so-called Romantic national originality was only ever constructed through a principle of imitation.[6]

After all, while other imperial centers like London or Paris were sure they were centers, St. Petersburg as an imperial center famously always knew that it was also a periphery, a distant satellite revolving around yet another cultural center located in various and shifting points further west. This realization of an apparently second-tier, imitative, and inauthentic status can provoke anxiety, and in Senkovskii's day it often did. Senkovskii's infinitely expanding Russia, however, mocks that anxiety as it suggests another and more ironic approach to the conceptualization of Russia and also of Russia's place in European Romanticism. The quintessentially Russian question of identity, originality, and authenticity is also a more broadly Romantic one, and it may be that no answer was ever possible nor even always intended. Certainly if authenticity always eludes us in the *Library for Reading*, it is not because Senkovskii has somehow failed, but because as an outsider, Senkovskii was also the quintessentially Romantic insider, his carefully constructed marginality pointing ultimately not to his own insignificance nor even to the peripheral status of Russia, but to one last feature of Romanticism: the ironically empty space at its center.

Periphery and Center

A play of periphery and center defines Senkovskii's life and work in complicated and even contradictory ways. Senkovskii's tendency was always to use various kinds of marginality in order to better ingratiate himself with the center, an oscillation between in- and outside that is most evident in two features of his biography in particular: his Orientalist career and his status as a Pole in St. Petersburg. These two features are apparently interrelated, since Senkovskii's Orientalist ambitions may well have been thwarted precisely by his expatriate existence. Whether separately or together, these two aspects of Senkovskii's life operated in markedly similar and also, I would argue, Romantic terms. In her reading of "The Fountain of Bakhchisarai," Katya Hokanson, like Iurii Lotman, writes of the "three corners" of the world not just of Pushkin's poem, but of the Russian national literature that the poem seeks to create: "the Crimea/Caucasus (south), Poland (west) and Russia (north)."[7] Senkovskii's own existence as a Polish Orientalist in Russia maps onto almost identical coordinates. Moreover, his self-willed exile, exactly like his Orientalism, suggests the profound engagement with spatial differences and deterritorializations of all kinds that characterize European Romanticism as a whole to a striking degree, most especially in its later manifestations.

As an Orientalist, Senkovskii lent himself to a manipulation of difference that, in broad terms, was intended to produce the hegemony of one side over the other, West over East and Russia over its eastern (and southern) acquisitions and neighbors. At the same time, however, another and more limited kind of power play is more immediately evident, as it was clearly Senkovskii's hope that his striking qualifications as an Orientalist would propel a young émigré from an undistinguished background to a higher-level position in the Russian government. Senkovskii's academic career quickly took off, and by the end of the 1820s he had been made the recipient of a number of honors, including an honorary doctorate at Krakow University and membership in the Asian Society based in London. The diplomatic career he sought, however, did not materialize, and while Senkovskii himself apparently blamed his lack of success on the personal dislike felt for him by Count S. S. Uvarov, later Minister of Education, in retrospect a more obvious explanation strikes us. No matter how clever Senkovskii was at wielding the tools of Orientalism, still he was a Pole, and in St. Petersburg especially in the 1820s and 1830s, a Pole was inevitably suspect.

In moving from Wilno to St. Petersburg Senkovskii had not actually changed governments, since starting in 1772 increasingly large parts of what was once the Polish-Lithuanian Commonwealth had been incorporated into the Russian Empire. In the early nineteenth century, though, partitioned Poland was a relatively new and highly contested acquisition. During the Time of Troubles in the seventeenth century, the Polish-Lithuanian Commonwealth had advanced as far as Moscow, and while they had failed to take the city, still the Poles gained a good amount of previously Russian territory; in the episode of the False Dmitrii, they also came very close to establishing their own puppet government in Moscow. By the late eighteenth century the tables had turned, however, and a weakened Poland faced serious encroachments from its more powerful neighbors, not just Russia but also Prussia and Austro-Hungary.

The Poles rose up against the Russians first in 1794 in response to the second Partition of Poland. The result of that rebellion was the massacre of the inhabitants of the Warsaw suburb of Praga by Russian soldiers under General Suvorov and, in 1795, the total dismemberment of the Polish state in the third Partition. The Poles would stage a military uprising against the Russians again in 1830, and yet again in 1863. In between these armed insurrections the Polish question remained very much on the mind of the Russians, especially as the Napoleonic wars brought in their wake first the Duchy of Warsaw in 1807 and then the Congress Kingdom in 1815, that strange and doomed entity where Alexander I, an autocrat at home, dabbled in poorly understood notions of constitutional monarchy. Poland remained an issue in Senkovskii's day not just because of its constantly changing status but also because Poland represented something of an anomaly in the Russian Empire, we might even say a special thorn in its side.

The peculiar position Poland occupied derived only in part from the Poles' resistance to inclusion in the Russian Empire. Other peoples resisted, too, and perhaps more successfully, for example the Chechen and Dagestani mountain peoples who under Shamil fought the Russians for nearly twenty-five years, surrendering only in 1859. Poland's special place was also not dependent on the fact that in an earlier period it had been Poland on the brink of colonizing Russia; again, the Mongols were much more successful in that regard. It is nonetheless the Poles in this period who are the beneficiaries of a special kind of attention, and who seem also to provoke a particular kind of fear. Above all, it was only the Poles who were deemed worthy of Alexander I's post-Napoleonic flirtation with constitutional monarchy, and in Senkovskii's day it was also this move that did much to raise Russian hackles.

In his magisterial study *The Russian Empire* (2001), Andreas Kappeler gives Alexander's constitutional rule of Poland special weight. While subject peoples to the West, in particular the Finns, not infrequently enjoyed greater rights than those to the East or even in Russia proper, still, Kappeler writes: "Never before had a Russian ruler allowed himself to be bound by an oath sworn to his subjects, and never before had he guaranteed a constitution." Accordingly, he argues: "The Kingdom of Poland, a constitutional monarchy with a liberal political, judicial, and social order, was a foreign body in the Russian empire."[8] Russians in Senkovskii's day felt much the same, although they tended to express their opinion in considerably stronger terms.

In his 1819 "Opinion of a Russian Citizen" Karamzin spoke for the conservative majority when he advised against giving the Poles any special freedoms, warning the Tsar that "the Poles will never be to us either sincere brothers or faithful allies. . . . If you make them stronger, they will want to become independent and their first step towards independence will be separation from Russia," when "[t]he Poles, legally established as a distinct and sovereign nation, would be more dangerous to us than the Poles as subjects of Russia."[9] What the liberals apparently saw as Alexander's favoritism did the Polish cause even less good among more left-leaning Russians. The future Decembrist Sergei Trubetskoi, for example, was angry enough to send an inflammatory letter home from the Vienna Congress claiming that Alexander's real intent was to unite the Russian Polish provinces to the more limited territory of the Congress Kingdom and then to move the imperial capital from St. Petersburg to Warsaw.[10] In preparation for their rebellion, the Decembrists did make contact with the underground Polish National Patriotic Society in hopes that they could be counted on to neutralize Grand Duke Constantine, heir apparent to the Russian throne and at the time commander-in-chief of the Polish army. Their program for their own liberation, however, included at best a Poland still tightly linked to Russia "by a close military alliance and an identical internal military order."[11]

After Nicholas I's ascension to the throne had quashed any hopes of Polish as well as Russian democracy, the lack of sympathy felt by even the more progressive factions of Russian society for their neighbors' plight is remarkable, particularly at the time of the Polish uprising in 1830. By and large the Russian response to this insurrection was one of righteous indignation, perhaps best exemplified by Pushkin's 1831 poem, "To the Slanderers of Russia."[12] While himself familiar with the desire to break free from the shackles of Russian autocracy, Pushkin describes the Polish uprising as nothing more than a "family quarrel," "an old domestic fight" of "Slavs amongst themselves." In his first stanza Pushkin pointedly asks, "Who will be left standing in this unequal fight: / The strutting Pole or the true Russian? / Will the Slavic streams flow together into the Russian sea? / Or will it dry up? That is the question."[13] As Pushkin elides pan-Slavism into what can only be called pan-Russianism, his presentation of the Polish rebellion, particularly in light of his well-known sympathy for the Decembrists, strikes us today as fairly staggeringly one-sided.[14]

Despite the evident hostility to "the strutting Pole," there was no question of offering special freedoms to any other peoples subject to the Russian

Empire, and it is here that we reach the crux of the problem. As Kappeler notes, Alexander's motivations in his special treatment of Poland remain a little unclear. To the extent that Alexander understood the implications of his actions, he was certainly interested in placating other European powers and also in co-opting the Polish nobility; Poland was also intended, like Finland, to serve as a model for possible reforms of Russia itself.[15] Still, if a constitutional monarchy could be seen as even remotely possible for Poland, it was ultimately because Poland, as opposed, for example, to Chechnia or Dagestan, was not to the East of Russia, but to its West, occupying a position of apparent cultural superiority that has long given rise to sentiments of admiration, resentment, identification, and revulsion. While any number of examples could be adduced—from the Polish maiden who seduces Andrii away from the Cossack cause in Gogol's "Taras Bul'ba" (1835) to the Polish court that welcomes Kurbskii in Eisenstein's "Ivan the Terrible" (1946)—in Senkovskii's day the strange mix of pro- and anti-Polish sentiments is perhaps most strikingly expressed in the person of Grand Duke Constantine.

Constantine bizarrely combined a desire to impose by force his ideal of military order on the often recalcitrant Polish army with a striking and long-standing interest in the Polish ladies. Constantine's first recorded infatuation was with the Polish Princess Helena Lubomirska in 1800, followed shortly by involvements with "not one, but two shining stars of the Russian salons," the princesses Zoneta and Maria Czertwertynski, the latter then for many years after her marriage to the Russian D. L. Naryshkin the mistress of Constantine's brother, Alexander I.[16] While Polish army officers responded to Constantine's harsh discipline with an alarmingly high suicide rate, Constantine's apparently more tender attentions to Polish women reached their culmination only with his second marriage, to the Polish Joanna Grudzinska in 1820.[17] It was also this marriage that perhaps not coincidentally dashed any hopes Constantine might have had of someday inheriting the Russian throne, as Alexander gave permission for the morganatic marriage only on the condition that Constantine surrender in writing his rights of inheritance to his younger brother Nicholas. By the 1830 uprising Constantine's loyalties were so confused that he not only apparently commented on how valiantly his Polish troops were fighting the Russians, but also died mysteriously in the midst of the insurrection with the words: "Tell the Tsar, I am dying, I beg him to forgive the Poles."[18]

From the point of view of the Russian elite, the issue was not merely the admiration and support the Poles as Westerners could gain from among the Russian ruling family. Still more galling was that which they received from their fellow Europeans. Western Europe hardly paid much attention to Russia's long struggle with Shamil, let alone protested his defeat, nor did Russian incursions into Siberia or Central Asia provoke much of a response. The bloody suppression of the Polish rebellion of 1830, however, was another matter entirely, and the "slanderers of Russia" to whom Pushkin addressed his poem were largely the French. While the government remained neutral, the French press came out strongly on the side of the Poles, prompting a swift reaction from the erstwhile Francophile Russian elite. In "To the Slanderers of Russia" Pushkin wonders if Europe hates Russia because Russia alone stood up to Napoleon, "and with our blood redeemed / the freedom, honor and peace of Europe?" In any event, Pushkin is ready for the western Europeans: "You are threatening in words—try deeds!" Did they think that:

> The old bogatyr, resting on his bed
> Is lacking the strength to fix on his bayonet of Ismail?
> Or the word of the Russian tsar is already powerless?
> Or it is something new for us to fight with Europe?
> Or the Russian has grown unaccustomed to victory?
> Or there are few of us?

As the actual armed struggle with the Poles recedes entirely into the background of the poem, Pushkin instead invites Europe to send its armies back to Russia once more. This new battle, while hypothetical, clearly matters much more to Pushkin than the real "family quarrel" with the Poles. As he finishes:

> So then send to us, O orators,
> Your embittered sons:
> There is a place for them in the fields of Russia,
> Amidst graves not alien to them.[19]

In this charged atmosphere it is easy to see how Senkovskii's loyalty might be in question. Senkovskii's position was also complicated by his ongoing ties to Poles of a more dissident nature back home, in particular Joachim Lelewel, Senkovskii's professor of history at the University of Wilno who was not only dismissed from his chair at the university in 1824 for his association with underground student organizations, but also took a leading role in the 1830 uprising. It is important to note, however, that Senkovskii's

"Polish-ness" did not always operate only to his disadvantage in Russia, as one episode in particular would suggest. The play of difference in which Senkovskii engaged as a Pole in Russia was extremely complicated, and I should acknowledge that in the end he pleased no one. While Russians certainly in his own day could hardly forgive his long-standing friendship with Lelewel, Poles have most often also regarded him as a traitor to their cause, above all on the occasion of his official representation of the Russian government in the 1826 inspection of the Belorussian school district.[20] Yet what strikes me as important in the story of the inspection is less the light it sheds on where Senkovskii's loyalties truly lay than in how it reveals Senkovskii trying to turn even his Polish difference to his own advantage.

The inspection of the Belorussian school district was originally proposed by Prince N. N. Khovanskii in 1824 as a measure for the "eradication of Polonism." In 1826 the Belorussian school district operated under the auspices of Senkovskii's alma mater, the same University of Wilno that had already suffered a purge of its more pro-Polish elements only a few years earlier, including Lelewel, a fact that makes the choice of Senkovskii for this mission a little odd. Indeed one critic wrote to the Minister of Education to vigorously protest his appointment on the grounds that Senkovskii "was by birth precisely a Pole, educated at the University of Wilno, and at this University only very recently." Given that Senkovskii's Polish connections were hardly unknown to the Ministry, it may be that he was chosen not despite his background, but because of it. If so, the inspection posed a special challenge. As Kaverin puts it, Senkovskii's choice was either "to defend the Belorussian schools at clear risk to his own career in the civil service, or to seriously indict the university with which, despite all quarrels, he was closely tied."[21] According to Kaverin, he did neither.

Senkovskii instead made every effort to place the blame for any anti-Russian sentiment on the monastic orders that ran the local Catholic schools, such that his final report proposed the elimination of religious schools and their replacement with secular institutions modeled on the schools in the Wilno district. Senkovskii's antimonastic bent, as Kaverin points out, was nothing he learned in Russia but rather an important element of his Polish Enlightenment education. In other words, Senkovskii was just pretending to function as a Russian government official when he was really only ever a member of the Brotherhood of Scamps. As Kaverin concludes: "[While] the ideological struggle of the Polish liberals fundamentally differed from the methods by which Senkovskii acted during his inspection, still all the same one cannot deny his cleverness. To realize the aims of Polish patriotic societies by means of the Russian government, all the while not forgetting about his own civil service career,—that thought could arise only in his head."[22] Despite his relatively warm defense, Kaverin himself acknowledges that the actual strength of Senkovskii's attachment to Poland, or lack thereof, in this particular episode as elsewhere, is ultimately quite difficult to discern. What Kaverin's analysis does suggest, however, is that Senkovskii's difference as a Pole, while perhaps hindering his government career as an Orientalist, nonetheless opened other doors.

The inspection of the Belorussian school district in the end did Senkovskii no harm, nor did it advance his government career in any way. Had he displeased his masters, it would only have been because Senkovskii was not just a Pole only recently arrived in Russia but even a Pole who had studied in Wilno. Had he succeeded, it would have been not just because his loyalties were evidently in the right place, but also because his Polish birth actually lent him a certain expertise very much like that which he wielded in his academic career. In other words, it may well have been Senkovskii's Polish-ness that did in his career at the Foreign Ministry. When his aspirations turn instead to the Ministry of Education, however, we see Senkovskii attempting to manipulate difference in exactly the same way. As an Orientalist Senkovskii was an expert on the Eastern margins of the Russian Empire, and as a Pole at least a would-be expert on its Western edge. Either way his modus operandi was to use a position on the peripheries to better ingratiate himself with the center, and to a great extent it is this same play of periphery and center that enabled the careers of many of the Romantic writers discussed here, above all Senkovskii's fellow Pole, Bulgarin.

Senkovskii's compatriot Tadeusz Bułharyn, a.k.a. Faddei Bulgarin, lived most of his life outside of Poland, not only using his other-ness to play one side off against the other (most notably in the Napoleonic wars), but also consistently cultivating high-ranking officials, both in the Russian military and in the civil administration, who happened also to be of foreign background. Bulgarin also used his own Polishness as a springboard into Russian literature, beginning his literary career in St. Petersburg with the publication in Grech's *Son of the Fatherland* in 1820 of "A Short Survey of Polish Literature." Especially given that Bulgarin's education was almost entirely Russian, Frank Mocha suspects that the piece was at least partly plagiarized.[23] Despite its questionable provenance, however, Mocha describes the multipart article as "pivotal," not least because its publication in *Son of the Fatherland*, at the time a liberal organ and the unofficial journal of the Free Society of Lovers of Russian Literature, "meant Bulgarin's acceptance in the ranks of Russian writers."[24]

Bulgarin's early associations among Russian writers were in fact largely with writers who were also future Decembrists, and these close connections led to his arrest in the wake of the failed revolt. These same connections no doubt also made his immediate offer to serve the Empire especially attractive, and from 1826 Bulgarin acted as a sort of consultant on literary affairs to the Third Section. While Bulgarin has gone down in Russian literary history as the quintessential stool pigeon, rewarded by the Emperor for his efforts by permission to publish political news in his *Northern Bee*, A. I. Reitblat has argued that Bulgarin was especially active only until his move to his estate in Derpt (Tartu) in 1831 and even then was never entirely trusted. Among the various Russians of foreign background who made up Nicholas's security network, Bulgarin was close only with his first contact at the Third Section, Maksimilian Iakovlevich von Fok, director of the Special Chancellery of the Ministry of Internal Affairs. Bulgarin had little to do with von Fok's boss, Count Benckendorff, and while he went back to more active reporting after his return to St. Petersburg in 1837, the new director of the Special Chancellery, L. V. Dubel't, made him at times very uncomfortable. Bulgarin evidently took to the spying business, as he did to service with the Russian army, from expediency rather than conviction, as his own life reads like the picaresque novels he himself wrote. As Reitblat notes, Bulgarin crossed geographical and social spaces with the greatest of ease, from Poland to Russia, Germany, France, and Spain, and from officer to prisoner, legal petitioner, writer, and publisher.[25] Bulgarin's chief characteristic was his impressive ability to adapt to new circumstances. Never, though, was Bulgarin exactly at home.

If Bulgarin, like Senkovskii, casts the Romantic play of periphery and center in an unsavory light, not every practitioner of this sort of Romantic irony descended to actual double-dealing, and most also steered a little more clear of politics. It was also not necessary to be a Pole, nor to take up one's expatriate existence in Russia. Just as Bulgarin in a more literary mode traded on his Polishness as a sort of (borrowed) literary exoticism, so Gogol used his well-researched Ukrainian-ness in much the same way, first gaining acclaim in the Russian literary world with his representation of Ukrainian local color in *Evenings on a Farm Near Dikan'ka*. In Great Britain, William Maginn of *Fraser's* was famous for an encyclopedic breadth of knowledge and a command of languages that rivaled Senkovskii's; as Sir Morgan Odoherty claimed in his imaginary conversation with Byron, "There is no language on the face of the earth I could not learn in three days,—except Sanscrit, which took me a week."[26] As a cosmopolitan Maginn was also, however, an Irishman, and one who began his literary career with *Blackwood's* as their heavily Irish-inflected correspondent from Cork and then only later took up residence in London. As for the *Blackwood's* people themselves, they were all Scots, from the proprietor William Blackwood to the editors John Wilson and John Lockhart and the writer James Hogg, otherwise known as the Ettrick Shepherd. The best example of a use of the peripheries in order to ingratiate oneself with the center, however, comes from a Scot who almost never left Edinburgh: Sir Walter himself.

While Scott's antiquarian efforts, both in his collections of objects and in his writing, did not focus exclusively on Scotland, they certainly tended to do so. *Ivanhoe* offers a well-known exception, but still most of Scott's literary creations, from *Minstrelsy of the Scottish Border* to *Waverley* itself, *The Antiquary*, *Guy Mannering*, and all the *Tales of My Landlord* served up a romanticized Scotland for a British reading public still largely made up of the English. Scott no doubt found the history of his native land uniquely interesting. Commercial considerations also clearly drove his literary representation of Scotland, as the English appetite for tales of Rob Roy, the Scottish Highlands, Scottish bandits, and the like, once aroused, made his sale of the Scottish past highly profitable. Scott's political motivations, however, have remained a little more open to question.

In "A Divided Inheritance: Scott's Antiquarian Novel and the British Nation," Yoon Sun Lee questions the traditional assumption of Scott's English allegiance, arguing that Scott's antiquarian mode of reconstructing history in *The Antiquary* stands in sharp contrast to the dominant rhetoric of British nationalism at the time. According to Lee, the threat of French invasion, especially in 1803, when *The Antiquary* is set, gave rise to an image of the British nation as timeless and priceless, and to British patriotism as a kind of constant, an ever-present means of connecting past eras of British greatness with the present. Although the novel actually deals with the threat of invasion, Lee argues that Scott in his very choice of subject matter emphasizes not historical continuity, but its opposite. The antiquarian reconstructs only what has been lost, and in turn, it is only what has been lost that accrues value; the more rare the item, the more money it is worth, as the antiquarian marketplace puts a price on the past and indeed a higher price the more fragmentary that past may be. In Lee's argument, then, *The Antiquary* offers another example of the sort of irony that we have seen mark *The Heart of Midlothian* as well. Just as Cleishbotham in the preface to *The Heart of Midlothian* both asserts and undermines his own authority as narrator, so Scott in *The Antiquary* both affirms and subverts the idea of the British nation and the historical enterprise that would create it.

Still, the past that is reconstructed in *The Antiquary*, as in most of Scott's work, is not the British nor even the English but specifically the Scottish past, a fact that may tilt Scott's political stance just a little toward one side. Lee quotes from Scott's essay "Border Antiquities" (1806) where "Scott notes that the antiquary's field of activity comes into existence only upon the demise of a living political, cultural or ideological formation." Scott's point is that the border between England and Scotland has become fruitful for the antiquary only inasmuch as it has ceased to be a border. "The frontier regions of great kingdoms," Scott writes, because they are often violently contested sites, "are unavoidably deficient in subjects for the antiquary." "The case becomes different," he adds, "when, losing by conquest or by union their character as frontier, scenes once the theater of constant battle, inroad, defence and retaliation, have been for two hundred years converted into the abode of peace and tranquility."[27] Lee understands Scott here to be emphasizing the role of the antiquary in stitching together the seams of an obviously torn British national past. I would argue instead that what Scott's essay suggests is how the antiquarian project (like the Orientalist one) marks and also perpetuates the creation of empire.

The Scottish union with England made Scott's antiquarianism possible because it is only relative peace that can both preserve relics of the past for Scott to find and ensure an English audience for his anthologizing of the Scottish past. The demise that enables Scott's great success is that of an independent Scotland, and that Scott was well aware that his interests, commercial and otherwise, lay with the creation of the British Empire is most evident from an episode fairly late in his career, when Scott organized the first and only visit of King George IV to Edinburgh in 1822. The visit was problematic, as the greater part of Scott's fellow countrymen were far from sharing his admiration for the English king. In response, John Sutherland explains, "Scott's strategy was to drown out critics by a deafening barrage of pomp and reach over the heads of the Whig middle classes to the populace," embarking on what Sutherland, after Lockhart, calls "an orgy of Celtification":

> a shameless parade of kilts, bagpipes, sporrans, claymores, and the panoply of Old Gael, all of dubious accuracy but picturesque enough to establish the image of Scotland in the non-Scottish mind for all time. He invented "traditions" as freely as anything in the plots of his novels (one of these inventions, that the Company of Archers were the "ancient bodyguard of the Kings of Scotland," inspired his next novel, *Quentin Durward.*) Underlying everything Scott invented for the occasion was the grand fiction that the Scots are a nation of Highlanders. The " *Waverley* and *Rob Roy* animus" and an "air of ridicule and caricature" permeated the whole of what Lockhart contemptuously called "Sir Walter's Celtified pageantry."[28]

If Lockhart did not like Scott's offering up of a simulated Scotland to the British Empire, however, he also lent himself to it, as *Blackwood's* devoted the September 1822 issue to the trip, albeit in a typically *Blackwood's*ian fashion.

The issue begins with a verse dedication to the King, written in red ink and purportedly by Christopher North. The *Noctes Ambrosianae* then starts in Ambrose's tavern and soon shifts to the Royal Yacht docked in Newhaven, where North actually tries out the King's bed, prompting the following exchange:

> MR NORTH (*from within his Majesty's bed-room*). Come hither, my dear boys, and behold your father reposing on the bed of royalty!
> *They all rush in.*
> MR BULLER. Behold him lying alive in state! Let us kneel down by the bed-side.
> *They all kneel down.*
> OMNES. Hail, King of Editors! Long mayest thou reign over us, thy faithful subjects.
> *Salve, Pater!*[29]

The evening then concludes with a visit to the cottage of some simple Scottish folk where the Ambrosians join in the dancing as Christopher North makes a speech on the greatness of England and of the King. As one scholar has argued with regard to Scott, *Blackwood's* accomplishment, too, is "to anaesthetize Scotland against real nationalism by providing it with a fantasy surrogate"; nor do Lockhart and his friends, again like Scott, let slip an opportunity to make a little money.[30] Where Scott took the King to a staged version of his own, although as yet unacknowledged *Rob Roy*, the *Blackwood's* people transform allegiance to the English king into allegiance to Christopher North and by extension into subscriptions to their own magazine.

Scott's self-serving rapprochement with empire, like Bulgarin's, may make him appear a less than attractive figure; we may prefer our Romantic heroes to be of a more principled sort. We have already seen, however, that they are not, as the slippery space that these writers occupy is an exact corollary to their slippery identities. In his own discussion of Romantic authorship David Glenn Kropf borrows from Deleuze and Guattari the notion of "milieu" that he defines as "a specific place that is bordered by other places," much like a periphery or like expatriation.[31] As an "in-between" space a "milieu" lends itself to the construction of a highly subversive kind of shifting identity, and indeed, Kropf compares the play of authorship in Pushkin, Scott, and Hoffman to the seductions of the libertine who with apparent insincerity creates himself anew for every new woman.[32] The libertine, however, is also the virtuoso, and there is something deeply appealing in the knowing wink of *The Antiquary*, for example, or in North's exploits on board His Majesty's yacht. The extreme examples I give of various sorts of movement from periphery to center, even Bulgarin's, gain their value finally not just because they are often very funny, but because in their very exaggeration they make clear a more fundamental tendency of Romantic space.

In an article on Nabokov written in 1970 George Steiner describes a particular view of Romanticism when he writes: "Romantic theory argues that, of all men, the writer most obviously incarnates the genius, *Geist*, quiddity of his native speech. Each language crystallizes, as it were, the inner history, the specific world-view of the *Volk* or nation." In contrast to this ideal Romantic writer, Steiner offers Nabokov, an exile who, Steiner writes, "moved into successive languages like a traveling potentate. Banished from Fialta, he has built for himself a house of words. To be specific: the multi-lingual, cross-linguistic situation is both the matter and form of Nabokov's work."[33] Without in any way diminishing Nabokov's achievement, still I would argue that his literary space has in some ways been anticipated, and by the very Romantics to whom Steiner contrasts him.

Certainly Romanticism is marked by the idea of what we might call the national poet, be he Pushkin or Goethe or Shakespeare. But at the same time, Romantic writers of all kinds experience exiles, expatriations, and "multi-lingual, cross-linguistic situations" to an astonishing degree. There are the involuntary exiles, both internal and external, like Pushkin, Lermontov, Mickiewicz, and Hugo, and the exiles by choice, including Gogol and Heine. There are also those whose fates fall somewhere in between, for example the scandal-ridden Shelley and Byron.[34] There are writers who express their consciousness of their multilingual environment in dialect-laden texts like Gogol's Ukrainian stories or Scott's *Waverley* novels; there are also Orientalizers who litter their texts with non-Western words, for example Goethe in *West-östlicher Diwan* (1819) or Hugo in *Les Orientales* (1829). Last but not least, there are the representatives of the later Romantic periodical, Maginn and the *Blackwood's* people, Bulgarin, and above all Senkovskii, whose other-ness became their ticket to success.

Romanticism operates in a space like that which Wordsworth called "here, nowhere, there, and everywhere at once."[35] As Romanticism simulates not just readers and writers but also literature itself, it takes place everywhere and nowhere, while the oscillations of Romantic irony send it back and forth also between periphery and center. In many ways like the "minor literatures" that Deleuze and Guattari define in their *Kafka: Toward a Minor Literature* (1975), Romanticism is "affected with a high coefficient of deterritorialization."[36] What is peculiar to Romanticism, however, is that while minor, the literature is also major—and not merely because Romantic literature was usually tied to the literary establishment and was often highly commercially successful. It is also notable that while Romanticism draws on and from the peripheries, it expresses itself by and large not in Gaelic, Sanskrit, or Ukrainian, but in English, German, and Russian. As polymath and polylinguist, Orientalist and expatriate Pole, and eternal outsider who, as the editor of the *Library for Reading*, was also the quintessential literary insider, Senkovskii sums up in his own life and work the particular idiosyncrasy of Romantic space that confuses and conflates margins and mainstreams. He finally does so also from a point on the globe that has its own complicated sense of major and minor, periphery, and center: Russia.

Russian Space: Russia as Tver

Russia makes its appearance in the pages of the *Library for Reading* along with the Orient and the literary marketplace and, it might seem, in much the same form. Like Ambrose's Tavern in *Blackwood's* or Lincoln's-inn

Square in *Fraser's*, Russia as Senkovskii represents it in his writing has apparently at best a tenuous relationship to what we might take to be its reality. But in this case initial impressions may be deceiving. Brambeus's Russia in fact operates a bit differently from North's Ambrose's Tavern or Yorke's Lincoln's-inn Square, and the difference lies in the larger geographic and also cultural spaces to which these literary representations purport to point. For while North and Yorke were simulating ostensibly real places, Brambeus was instead simulating a place that knew itself to be a simulacrum already.

The *Library for Reading* makes the point of Russia's problematic status especially clear in the "First Letter of the Three Landowners from Tver to Baron Brambeus." As noted in Chapter Three, the "Letter" claims to emanate from Tver, a town midway along the highway from Moscow to St. Petersburg, "at the very crossroads of the ideas traveling there and back." Their central location is intended to lend the letter writers a certain authority, so much so that the three landowners can assure Brambeus that "[w]hen we say—Tver province, we mean by that all intelligent provinces, all of Russia."[37] At the same time, as the landowners themselves acknowledge, their quintessentially average address suggests that Tver may be nothing more than an abstraction, the imaginary home of a Russian Everyman who does not really exist. When the landowners turn to their account of how a distinguished British visitor to the Russian capital once doubted the very existence of Tver, however, the issue of ir- or a-reality goes well beyond the problem of average or composite figures.

According to the three landowners, on reading the St. Petersburg papers the Marquis of Londonderry noted with surprise:

> if it was needed in St. Petersburg to toss out a little word in favor of a book that was then being published, or in favor of a company, whose stocks were doing poorly, or in favor of a soap, that someone wanted to invent,—then in the local papers would immediately appear wonderful little articles "from Tver"; if an author, after his book had already appeared and subjected itself to the well-earned reproach of criticism, needed to say that the criticism lies and that his book is superlative, the author sits down and writes praise to himself and to his book "from Tver"; if it was needed to berate someone or something without ruining the awful sentence by signing one's own name, the abuse would then ring out "from Tver" or "from Tver province."

Lord Londonderry so admired the wisdom of this distant place that seemed to know what was going on in St. Petersburg better than its own residents did themselves that he could hardly believe that Tver really existed. The three landowners claim that the Marquis changed his mind when he visited Tver and "[o]n entering the first mail staging-post, assured himself that the abuse that he had read in [the St. Petersburg] papers indeed came from here."[38] Yet the comical end to their story does little to reassure their own readers, who knew quite well that Lord Londonderry was in fact entirely right to question the existence of the Tver that so often appeared in the St. Petersburg press.

What George Gutsche has called the pose of the "offended provincial" was a well-known trope, one adopted perhaps most famously by Pushkin in his *Contemporary*.[39] The first issue of Pushkin's journal in 1836 included Gogol's article "On the Movement of Journalistic Literature in 1834 and 1835." Despite the generality of his title, Gogol's piece was in fact an aggressively polemical attack directed specifically against Senkovskii. Perhaps out of a desire to appease the powerful Senkovskii, or perhaps out of a more programmatic desire to distance himself as editor from the contents of his journal, Pushkin then inserted into the third issue a measured criticism of Gogol's article. Rather than writing in his own person as editor of the *Contemporary*, however, Pushkin chose instead to publish as a certain "A. B., from Tver." As Gutsche notes, while A. B. disagrees with or at least obviates most of Gogol's criticisms of the *Library for Reading*, he notably lets one stand. Like Gogol, A. B. does not see why Senkovskii is so insistent about eliminating the pronouns *sei* and *onyi* from the written language.

The three silly landowners with their ardent defense of Brambeus's "teaching about language" even at the expense of Brambeus's own existence are evidently then largely a response to this other letter writer who, as Senkovskii knew well, was not from Tver either. If we follow the landowners' logic to the end, we find that Senkovskii's intent in the "Letter" was also to target another sort of simulation. Despite the landowners' protests, Tver remains a blank space for anyone's opinion on anything, not just in the St. Petersburg papers that formed the English Marquis's reading, but most especially in their own letter. As they themselves are obviously the creation of Brambeus, so also is the landowners' Tver but an empty vessel, in this case for Brambeus's opinions on the development of the Russian literary language. More important, as the landowners themselves have cast Tver as the embodiment of Russia, the joke on one becomes a joke on the other. Russia in turn becomes just a stop on the highway, and as Russia like Tver plays host to various ideas just passing through, it, too, apparently lacks any identity or even reality of its own. In this sense Russia-as-Tver looks a good deal like the Russia of Senkovskii's 1847 lecture that, rather than offering up anything uniquely its own, instead swallows up other people's history to fill its fundamental emptiness. It is also a Russia that has long had a place outside the confines of the *Library for Reading*.

The question of Russian identity that Senkovskii parodies both in the "First Letter of the Three Landowners from Tver" and again in his 1847 lecture has a very real and also very well-documented existence in Russian culture dating at least from the time of Peter the Great. This question became especially urgent in the Russia of the early nineteenth century, precisely in and around the time of the *Library for Reading*, largely under the pressure of Romantic ideas of authenticity and originality as they have often been understood. In the literary sphere a thoroughly Romantic debate about the merits and possibilities of Russian Romanticism ensued, as Romanticism seemed to demand an original expression of one's self when Romanticism itself was a set of ideas Russia had borrowed from the West. In the political sphere both Romantic and Russian concerns culminated in Nicholas I's wonderfully bizarre policy of Official Nationality, first announced in 1834, the very year that the *Library for Reading* began its publication. In both literary and political terms, a consciousness of Russia as a sort of disparate collection of fragments taken from elsewhere has seemed at odds with a Romantic ideal of the integrity of the self. Yet when Romanticism is seen instead to lend itself to a partial, incomplete, and even inauthentic self, as for example in the Romantic writers and readers that filled the *Library for Reading*, this view of Russia can only take on a different aspect. Russia, like the *Library for Reading*, then no longer looks antithetical to Romanticism, but would seem instead to offer only its most extreme expression.

Russian Space: Nicholas I's Russia

It is no easy task to define national space, particularly when the boundaries in question ever expand to encompass a great many different ethnic and linguistic groups, not to mention clearly non-Russian (because Western European) influences. In the early nineteenth century Russia was deeply engaged in this sort of self-scrutiny, all the way up to the highest levels of Nicholas

I's court. Because Nicholas was easily the most powerful proponent of a vision of Russian nationality in Senkovskii's day, his vision is fundamental to our sense of the Romantic space that shaped the *Library for Reading* from the outside. As Richard Wortman argues in his *Scenarios of Power: Myth and Ceremony in Russian Monarchy* (1995), however, the sources of Nicholas's particular approach to the problem of Russian nationality were in some respects peculiar to the Russian monarchy alone. Wortman's claim is that what marked the Russian monarchy from the first tales of the Varangian princes who came to rule over Rus' was an imperial myth that "took the form of an ongoing dramatization of the ruler's foreignness." Wortman writes: "The devices of identification with foreign sources of power were varied—tales of foreign origin, analogies with or imitation of foreign rulers." In all cases, however, "the source of sacrality was distant from Russian whether it was beyond the sea, whence the original Viking princes came, or located in the image of Byzantium, France, or Germany."[40]

The key word above is "myth," as Wortman makes it quite clear that these concepts of "Russianness" or "foreignness" had little to do with anyone's actual bloodlines. After Peter, Wortman argues, "[t]he Russian court was to become a semblance of the West; but it had to be a semblance, Russians acting as Europeans, performing the metaphor and behaving 'like foreigners.'" Catherine the Great (1729–1796), for example, although herself a German, presented her deposed husband as a "foreigner," while she herself as a "Russian" nonetheless ably adopted the mask of an enlightened Western European monarch. Her son Paul I (1754–1801), on the other hand, while by birth and upbringing a good deal more Russian than his mother, nonetheless managed in his brief reign to impress the nobility with a "foreignness" of the wrong kind, not only too Prussian but even suggesting a sort of Turkish despotism. Wortman acknowledges that a monarch clothed in borrowed plumes is not a uniquely Russian phenomenon, and he makes the comparison in particular with Polynesian practice. Still, he claims, "[t]he distinguishing feature of Russian symbolic development was the continuous and imperative nature of such borrowing, even after the empire had become a great and influential power."[41] This notably Russian practice of simulation only reached its most paradoxical heights in the reign of Nicholas I (1796–1855).

Nicholas I's reign almost exactly spans the period of Senkovskii's journalistic activity, as he ascended the throne in the wake of the Decembrist revolt in 1825 and died with the Crimean War not quite lost in 1855. Nicholas's challenge as a Russian monarch in the age of Romanticism was quite particular and also quite convoluted. By 1825 the ideal state in Western Europe had taken on ever more democratic attributes, a fact that made it increasingly difficult for a Russian monarch to present himself as both foreign and yet also as an autocrat. At the same time, the sort of cosmopolitanism that Nicholas's older brother Alexander had displayed particularly with regard to Poland had by 1830 clearly undermined the western borders of the Empire. Nicholas finally had to reckon with what Wortman calls the "spread of nationalism in Europe and the idealist notion that each nation had its particular identity or spirit that distinguished it from others."[42] As the expatriate experience of so many Romantic writers noted above would suggest, the unequivocal association of the "spread of nationalism" with Romanticism is more than a little problematic. Still, a complicated notion of nationhood was certainly afoot at least starting with Herder, and Nicholas sought to confront it while at the same time addressing also the other two issues. What he produced in response to these challenges was the strange policy of what eventually became termed Official Nationality [*Narodnost*].[43]

In the program Nicholas developed together with Count S. S. Uvarov, once a minor writer and member of Arzamas and now his Minister of Education, Russian nationality was defined as deriving from three fundamental principles: Orthodoxy, Autocracy, and Nationality. While orthodoxy and autocracy may seem to be typically Russian institutions, as Nicholas Riasanovsky notes: "'Nationality' was at the time and has since remained the most obscure, puzzling, and debatable member of the official trinity."[44] Indeed, it might seem that to define Russian nationality as the expression of Russian nationality is to say nothing at all. As Wortman explains it, however, what Nicholas did is define Russian nationality in terms of a quintessentially Russian love of and willing submission to the Orthodox Church and above all a Westernized, foreign monarch. In his words: "The doctrine of official nationalism propagated the notion that it was the Westernized ruler and state, adored by the common people, that constituted the distinguishing feature of Russia's existence."[45]

Nicholas's presentation of Russia as a people united by their adoration of a Westernized monarch allowed him to continue as a "foreign" autocrat in a time when autocracy had become a pointedly Russian institution. His definition also has the interesting effect of allowing for a nationality that is both one's own and at the same time someone else's too, rather like Senkovskii's magically shrinking and expanding history of the world in his 1847 lecture. In its flexibility this doctrine particularly well serves an entity that was in fact not a nation but an empire, or perhaps, as it was rather insistently and at the same time paradoxically defined already by the end of Catherine's reign, "not only an empire, but the most imperial of nations, comprising more peoples than any other."[46]

Nicholas's doctrine of Official Nationality was an active policy pursued in a number of fields, including the arts and most notably architecture. Peter the Great had famously used architecture to reinvent Russia as a simulacrum of various Western European cultures, above all in St. Petersburg, Peter's carefully planned capital city that was designed, in the words of the noted eighteenth-century Italian connoisseur of art, Count Francesco Algarotti, in "a kind of bastard architecture, one which partakes of the Italian, the French and the Dutch."[47] Nicholas in his own time was also necessarily interested in a "European" touch, for example in the Alexandrine column he dedicated in 1834 in memory of his brother and predecessor on the throne. The Alexandrine column was designed by a French architect after the Vendôme Column in Paris and Trajan's Column in Rome, but taller than either, and this kind of mixing and matching combined with an increase in size characterized many of the projects Nicholas planned. His own palace compound at a redesigned Peterhof included buildings in a variety of styles for various members of the imperial family. As Wortman notes, the grand duchess Olga received a Roman house, and the grand duke Alexander a two-story palace with a French mansard roof, while for the Empress herself there was an oversized Gothic cottage (known in Russian as the *Kottedzh*) designed to showcase the royal family's exemplary domesticity. Perhaps most telling, however, are the churches produced during Nicholas's reign.

In his attempt to invent an ideally Russian national style of architecture Nicholas depended on one architect in particular, K. A. Thon (1794–1881), who in turn drew his prototype for national churches from what he called the "Byzantine style." Whatever the term "Byzantine" meant for Thon, in practice his style drew on both the Russian past and Western European culture; for example, in the case of his St. Catherine's church in St. Petersburg. In the design of this church, according to Wortman: "The juxtaposition of Western and Russian forms created an association, dispelled the sense of dissonance between them, and, within the official ideology, gave the Western cultural form a Russian character."[48] In other words, a West that never was incorporated into the projection of a Russia that never was, either, and it is the same tactic of simulation that marks the most famous of Thon's projects, the church of Christ the Savior in Moscow.

For Christ the Savior Thon essentially took the typical design of older Russian churches and enlarged it to massive proportions; he also added purely decorative details that might have been lacking in his originals; for example, four false cupolas. As Wortman notes, the "artificiality [of these cupolas] suggests the impulse to imitate one's own past, just as architects imitated Roman, medieval, and Renaissance models." To the extent that Thon "improved" on his originals, however, he did not so much imitate as reinvent the Russian past in a significantly more capacious form. Indeed, as in the case of St. Catherine's, under Thon's supervision the quintessentially Russian grew so large as to even absorb parts of Western Europe into itself. Thon's pointedly eclectic and also very large designs once more make the point, as Wortman writes, that "[f]or Nicholas, there was no contradiction between national and universal."[49]

The space of Russia as represented in the pages of the *Library for Reading* has long been associated with what have been held to be Senkovskii's conservative or even reactionary politics, and in his *Nicholas I and Official Nationality in Russian, 1825–1855* (1959) Nicholas Riasanovsky has only scorn for what he sees as Senkovskii's crude attempts to curry favor by promoting the tenets of Official Nationality. I would argue instead that Senkovskii's vision of an all-encompassing and yet fundamentally empty Russian nation owes as much to Romanticism as it does to self-serving careerism, or at least that in this case the two are hardly distinguishable. As both Riasanovsky and Wortman note, among the various sources Nicholas drew on to create both his policy of Official Nationality and also its many odd but highly tangible outgrowths, from the Alexandrine column to the church of Christ the Savior, the most immediate is the field in which his Minister of Education, the former Arzamassian S. S. Uvarov, excelled: Russian Romantic literature.

As scholars have noted, the literary debate on Russian nationalism culminates in the early recognition of Pushkin as the quintessentially Russian poet in terms that exactly anticipate Nicholas's later conflation of national and universal. Russian Romanticism not only precedes Nicholas, however, but perhaps even articulates what would become his notion of Russianness a little more strongly. For it is in the sphere of literature that Russia's bent for imitation had long been most readily apparent, and it is in the literary context that Russians formulate their claim to originality most clearly, not by repudiating the fact of imitation, but by transforming it into a uniquely Russian ability to appropriate and absorb. What is especially fascinating about the literary debate is that while it makes pointed reference to specifically Russian history and geography, there is nonetheless little originally Russian about it, neither in the actual raising and framing of the question of Russian nationality, nor in the final answer that Pushkin is held to offer. Instead the literary discussion of Russian *narodnost'* offers only perhaps the most extreme expression of a larger Romantic debate on national originality that itself rejects and yet ultimately advocates a principle of imitation.

Russian Space: Russia in Russian Literature

The early nineteenth-century attempt to define Russia and the characteristically Russian was first and foremost a literary endeavor. Indeed, the very term that Nicholas would so enthusiastically adopt, "nationality" or *narodnost'*, is generally held to have been invented by Viazemskii in 1819 in a letter to his friend A. I. Turgenev. "You cannot recognize a Russian poet by his physiognomy" Viazemskii complained:

> The matter is not about merit, but about imprint; not about smooth-spokenness, but about pronunciation; not about the harmony of movement, but about the *narodnost'* of a few native manners. Why not translate *nationalité— narodnost*? After all, the Poles said: narodowość! The Poles are not as fastidious as we are, and words which do not come voluntarily over to them, they drag over by the hair, and the matter is done. Excellent![50]

If Viazemskii deserves credit for coining the term, still the concept of *narodnost'* enjoyed a complicated life of its own in the context of Russian Romanticism both before and after 1819. As Boris Tomashevskii notes, Viazemskii's letter marks only approximately the moment when Russian literature started to self-consciously draw on Western European terminology in order to articulate an already long-held sense of inadequacy. The problem that Russian writers faced, in an echo of the political situation Wortman describes, was how to determine the most proper and most productive relationship between Russian literature and its Western counterparts.

In the 1810s the debate had divided perhaps more neatly into two sides, the "archaists" (in Tynianov's famous phrase) under Admiral Shishkov, who argued for a sort of Church Slavonicization of Russian literature, and the "innovators" headed by Karamzin, who argued instead for its Europeanization. With the introduction of the term *narodnost'* in the 1820s, however, the literary scene splintered into more and smaller factions. For everyone, as for Viazemskii, the issue seemed to be a lack of individuality or originality in Russian literature and a corresponding propensity to imitate. What various Russian writers understood as imitative, however, and where or how they would locate individuality and originality in Russian literature varied considerably. The essential ingredient of *narodnost'* turns out to have consisted of a number of different components, all weighted differently by different writers.

The imitation that national originality was to replace first meant the translation, adaptation, or writing "in the style" of other, usually Western European writers, a great deal of which went on both before and after 1819. The 1820s would come to be dominated by the young Pushkin. Before he quite took center stage, however, that place was occupied by two poets of a slightly older generation, V. A. Zhukovskii (1783–1852) and K. N. Batiushkov (1787–1855), who were both also well known as translators.[51] Zhukovskii was renowned for his translations from the English and the German and especially for his Russian versions of the Romantic ballads of Schiller and Bürger, and Batiushkov for his renderings of the Greek anthology and also of the French poet Parny. By the early 1820s, both poets as translators were also under attack. In 1822, according to Tynianov, Pushkin was already "infuriate[d]" by Zhukovskii. "It's time for him to have his own imagination and inventions that he himself owns [*krepostnye*]," Pushkin wrote privately, and also: "God grant that he start to create."[52] More public criticism was offered by V. K. Kiukhel'beker (1797–1846), Pushkin's friend from school and later Decembrist, who in his much-discussed article "On the Trend of Our Poetry, particularly Lyric, in the Past Decade" (1824) dismissively wrote that "Zhukovskii was the first among us to begin imitating the latest Germans, above all Schiller," while "[h]is contemporary Batiushkov took for his model two pygmies of French literature: Parny and Millevoye." Despite his scathing reference to French "pygmies," Kiukhel'beker was especially exasperated with Zhukovskii's imitations of the Germans when the Germans, according to Kiukhel'beker, were themselves only still imitators of the French, Roman,

Greek, and even the Italian and the Spanish. It is past time to throw off the chains of German literature, he says: "No one translates translators except for our dozens of translators."[53]

Kiukhel'beker's derision notwithstanding, there was in fact little consensus even in the 1820s on the place, or lack thereof, of translation in Russian literature.[54] Writers of all stripes eagerly awaited N. I. Gnedich's translation of the *Iliad* in 1829, and Viazemskii's own translation of *Adolphe* published in 1831 was considered at least among his friends as a real milestone in Russian literature precisely for its effect on the Russian language. As Pushkin himself wrote in 1830: "It is interesting to see how the experienced and lively pen of Pr. Viazemskii has overcome the difficulty of a metaphysical language, always harmonious and fashionable, often inspired. In this regard his translation will be a genuine creation and an important event in the history of our literature."[55] If producing a translation was not necessarily a guarantee of a lack of genuine creativity, writing something original was also not necessarily productive of *narodnost'*.

As Lauren Leighton notes in his essay "*Narodnost'* as a Concept of Russian Romanticism" (1975), for a number of writers, largely future Decembrists as for example K. F. Ryleev (1795–1826) and especially Kiukhel'beker, *narodnost'* lay in subject matter, and their ideal was a Russian literature that re-created the Russian past in themes taken from Russian history. For others, as Pushkin's comments on Viazemskii's *Adolphe* would suggest, *narodnost'* had to do with the locating of a true and essentially Russian literary language. The difficulty here as it was most often described was that the Russian elite had so contaminated their Russian with the early and sustained exposure to foreign languages that a literary language of their own eluded them. A. A. Bestuzhev in his "Glance at Russian Literature Over the Course of 1823" (1824) especially blamed the Napoleonic wars for this state of affairs, claiming that an initial patriotic fashion for all things Russian quickly faded as "the troops returned with laurels on their brow but with French phrases on their lips" and "a hidden passion for Gallicisms captured all of society more strongly than ever"; the result, he claims, was "the complete cooling of the better parts of society to their native language and to the poets who were beginning to arise at that time and, finally, the complete paralysis of literature in the last year."[56]

Pushkin clearly shared the Decembrists' interest in history, and like Bestuzhev, he acknowledged language as an ongoing problem for Russian literature, particularly in a draft of a reply to Bestuzhev's "Glance" where he complained that the first obstacle to the development of Russian literature was the "general use of the French language and the disdaining of Russian." As Pushkin put it: "Excepting those who are engaged with poetry, the Russian language cannot be for anyone sufficiently attractive; we have neither literature nor books; from early childhood we gleaned all our knowledge and all our concepts from foreign books, we became accustomed to think in a language not our own."[57] Despite his evident concern with both issues, for Pushkin *narodnost'* lay neither in choice of subject matter nor in language but in something still more intangible. In an unfinished article in 1825 he wrote instead that:

> *narodnost'* in a writer is a quality that can only be fully appreciated by his fellow countrymen—for others it either doesn't exist or is even considered a fault. . . . Climate, the form of government, faith give each people [narod] a particular physiognomy that is more or less reflected in the mirror of poetry. There is a way of thought and of feeling, a mass of customs, beliefs and habits that belong exclusively to any people."[58]

This notion of the need for literature to reflect the specific people that produced it underlies all definitions of *narodnost'*, including those that Pushkin criticized. For a significant number of the participants in this debate, however, at issue was less an embrace of the uniquely Russian than a repudiation of the hitherto dominant school of (French) Neo-Classicism.

The Romantic repudiation of Neo-Classicism is again a rejection of imitation, but now in terms that have little to do with Russia's particular lack of its own literature or even its own literary language. Not just in Russia but across Europe Neo-Classicism was a movement predicated on the value of the imitation of classical texts taken as a universal standard of beauty, and most notably Viazemskii in his preface to Pushkin's "The Fountain of Bakhchisarai" opposes his idea of *narodnost'* not to the borrowing of texts, topics, nor even language, but to the borrowing of prefabricated literary forms. His preface is cast in the form of a dialogue between the "Publisher" of the poem and a "Classicist." Where the Classicist refers to the poetics of Aristotle and Horace, the Publisher in what he himself recognizes as a rambling (and therefore Romantic) argument will admit no rules at all, and while he defends what he argues is a long-standing Russian tendency to adopt German ways, he rails against the Neo-Classicist insistence on a strict imitation of the ancients. In fact, he argues: "Homer, Horace, and Aeschylus have a great deal more affinity and correlation with the heads of the romantic school than with their cold, slavish followers, who endeavor to be Greeks and Romans after the fact. Could it be that Homer created the 'Iliad' in advance of Aristotle and Longinus and in accordance with some sort of *classical conscience* then not yet invented?"[59] N. N. Nadezhdin, on the other hand, famously notes the paradox in Viazemskii's reasoning and takes the Romantic insistence on originality one step further. In his dissertation, "On the Origins, Nature and Fate of the Poetry Called Romantic" (1830), Nadezhdin defines true Romantic poetry as a product of the (largely German) Middle Ages, and accordingly every bit as alien to contemporary Russia as Classical literature. What passes for Romantic poetry in his own day, then, and most especially in Russia, is only an imitation and therefore fundamentally un-Romantic.

Nadezhdin believes that the truly Russian can be found, but only if Russian writers cure themselves from the plague of pseudo-Romanticism by an immersion in the study of ancient texts. For other Russian Romantics the obstacle to achieving *narodnost'* is not the absence of certain kinds of literature, whether Classical or Romantic, but the overwhelming presence of literature's evil twin: criticism. Belinskii sounds this note most memorably in his "Literary Reveries" with his repeated cry: "We have no literature!"; but the notion that in Russia criticism has somehow preceded and perhaps even forestalled poetry is widespread throughout the 1820s. The poet D. M. Venevitinov (1805–1827), for example, bemoaned "that very swiftness with which Russia has assumed an outward appearance of educatedness and erected a sham edifice of literature without any foundation, without any exertion of its own inner powers." It is not just that Russia has only ever borrowed ideas from other nations, however, but that its overproduction of criticism serves to conceal that fact. As Venevitinov writes, the literary journals "served as nourishment for our ignorance by occupying the intellect with intellectual play, by convincing us, as it were, that we have equaled the enlightenment of other peoples."[60] In his "Glance at Russian Literature During 1824 and the Beginning of 1825" Bestuzhev writes that everywhere criticism only follows poetry. The unique exception is Russia, "for with us the age of analysis precedes the age of creation; we have criticism but no literature; we have become sated without ever tasting, in childhood we have become peevish old men!"[61]

Here we find ourselves on the territory that Senkovskii and the *Library for Reading* would later occupy entirely, as Russian nationality takes the shape of an empty form awaiting content, criticism without the actual poetry. This notion of Russia as a blank space was widely promoted by the plenitude of criticism that homeopathic critics nonetheless continued to turn out. To the extent that Russian critics in the 1820s and 1830s actually attempted to fill this blank space, however, they did so largely with Pushkin's poetry, and then exactly in the terms that Nicholas would later adopt.[62] As Russian Romantic writers isolate that elusive *narodnost'* in Pushkin's poetry they do not deny the imitation and even absence that has marked Russian literature to date, but they recast it, transforming imitation into imperialistic appropriation and a uniquely Russian capacity to absorb.

As Katya Hokanson has shown in her article "Literary Imperialism, Narodnost' and Pushkin's Invention of the Caucasus" (1994), the literary conflation of the national and the universal is first apparent in the critical debate that surrounds Pushkin's first real claim to fame, the three so-called "Southern poems" that he published between 1821 and 1824. Especially for Viazemskii and also for the poet and critic O. M. Somov (1793–1833), these three poems in particular bear the mark of national originality, a claim that might strike us at first as a little surprising. For the "Southern poems" are just that, Southern, and also largely Eastern: the first, "The Prisoner of the Caucasus" (1821), is set in the Caucasus; the second, "The Fountain of Bakhchisarai" (1823), in the Crimea; and the third and last, "Gypsies" (1824), in Bessarabia. Both Viazemskii in a number of pieces, including the preface to "The Fountain of Bakhchisarai," and also Somov in his 1823 article, "On Romantic Poetry," nonetheless make a point of Pushkin's *narodnost'*, and they do so first of all by making the space of Russian nationality commensurate with the space of Russian imperialism, appropriating for Russian literature a nationality that might more properly be considered someone else's.

Somov's formulation of this notion is especially pointed. Pushkin, he writes, "has embraced the whole space of his native land and in the wayward play of his muse shows to us the cold shores of the Baltic—and then suddenly sets up his tent under the burning sky of the Caucasus or frolics in the flowering valleys of Kiev." The "whole space of [Pushkin's] native land" is apparently quite large, and indeed, Somov is explicit as to the extent to which Russian national literature coincides with the borders of the empire.

The potential that Pushkin has only begun to realize still remains for future Russian writers, as Somov muses: "[H]ow many different peoples merge under the one name of Russians or depend on Russia, not separating themselves from her either by the space of foreign lands or by distant seas! How many different aspects, mores, and habits are presented to the searching gaze in the combined space of Russia alone!"[63]

"Combined space" may seem an unusual euphemism for "empire," but empire is evidently what Somov has in mind, as he goes on to list the Ukrainians and Cossacks, the "fiery" Poles and Lithuanians, the peoples of Finnish and Scandinavian descent, the denizens of ancient Kolkhida, descendants of those who witnessed the exile of Ovid, the Tatars, the diverse tribes of Siberia, the rebellious Caucasians and the Northern Laplanders and Samoeds. Indeed, for an apparently unreflective Somov, Pushkin exactly and paradoxically expresses what Harsha Ram in "Russian Poetry and the Imperial Sublime" (1998) calls "the mutually implicating spaces of nation and empire."[64]

While largely operating on the same conflation of Russian nation and Russian Empire, Viazemskii is even willing to stretch Pushkin's nationality a bit further. In all his articles on the Southern poems Viazemskii repeatedly acknowledges the influence of Byron on Pushkin's nonetheless national genius. With regard to the first, "The Prisoner of the Caucasus," Viazemskii feels bound to admit a "certain resemblance" between the hero and Byron's Childe Harold, although he insists that this instance of borrowing in no way diminishes the literary worth of Pushkin's creation. In reference to the third and last, "Gypsies," Viazemskii still notes the influence of Byron, writing that "if it weren't for Byron there would be no poem 'Gypsies.'" Nonetheless, this time the poem has not "the slightest imitation in it."[65] What Viazemskii seems to be suggesting is that by "Gypsies" Pushkin has made a borrowed Byron his own in a move like that which the future Slavophile I. V. Kireevskii describes in his 1828 article "A Few Words on the Character of Pushkin's Poetry." For Kireevskii, Pushkin has achieved true Russianness in a process of dialectical assimilation. The thesis was Pushkin's earliest phase, what Kireevskii calls the "period of the Italo-French school," and the antithesis, the period of the "echo of Byron's lyre." For Kireevskii, Pushkin is now in the third and last phase, one that has presumably encompassed the other two into itself: "the period of Russo-Pushkin poetry."[66]

Like Thon's church of St. Catherine's that is designed to give a "Western cultural form a Russian character," Pushkin's poetry apparently reaches westward even beyond the borders of the Russian Empire to create something truly national in a kind of all-absorbingness that then becomes the marker for all of Russian literature. For if Pushkin is to be the national poet it must be because he exhibits in the highest and most compressed form the essential characteristic of Russian literature, and in an 1846 essay, "In What, Finally, Lies the Essence of Russian Poetry and in What Its Particularity," Gogol defines this characteristic precisely as an ability to assimilate foreign borrowings. While Pushkin understandably remains his ideal Russian poet, Gogol manages here even to recuperate Zhukovskii, comparing him to a jeweler who does not discover the diamond, but knows how to set it to its best advantage. Such a poet could only appear among the Russian people, Gogol writes, "in whom the genius of receptivity is so strong."[67]

As Hokanson argues, Gogol makes especially clear the means by which especially in the case of Pushkin but also in Russian literature as a whole "foreign subjects and influences could be adopted, embraced, *colonized*, while the essential Russianness of the whole could be preserved."[68] Hokanson ends her article with a culmination of this theme in Dostoevsky's famous Pushkin speech of 1880, which again suggested that the future of Russian literature lay in Russian writers' unique ability, in her words, to "'authentically represent' the other in works of literature."[69] It is perhaps Pushkin himself who makes this point most strikingly, however, and not in his criticism but in an actual poem.

In his 1836 translation of Horace's *Exegi monumentum* that had already been rendered into Russian in 1747 by Lomonosov and in 1795 by Derzhavin, Pushkin explicitly casts his accomplishment as both Russian and imperial:

Word about me will go throughout all of great Rus',
And every people existing in it will call me,
The proud grandson of the Slavs, the Finn, and the now wild
Tungus, and the friend of the steppe the Kalmyk.[70]

Rus' is the name of what Kappeler calls "the first polity of the Eastern Slavs," a quasi-mythical "original Russian state" that in fact included a substantial number of non-Russians.[71] In popular consciousness, though, Rus' is the essence of Russia, and Pushkin then entirely deliberately stretches its borders to encompass the still-expanding Russian Empire of the nineteenth century, once more conflating Russianness with a kind of universality exactly as Nicholas I did in his official presentation of Russian nationality. The only difference is that Pushkin's empire is just a little larger.

As the poem begins:

> I have raised a monument to myself not made by hand
> The people's [narodnaia] path to it will not be overgrown,
> It has raised itself higher by its unsubmissive head,
> Than the Alexandrine column.[72]

When we recall that the Alexandrine column, according to Nicholas's design, both imitates and also surpasses the Vendôme Column in Paris and Trajan's Column in Rome, the full dimensions of Pushkin's claim become clear. Such is Pushkin's genius that the Russian edifice of his poetry not only contains all the peoples of the Russian Empire, but stands taller even than the Empire itself and also the cultures of Western Europe that that Empire has already shown itself to have absorbed. In Ram's words, in Pushkin's hands a truly all-encompassing imperial authority is "wrested from the sovereign and usurped by the poet."[73]

If Pushkin in 1836 was able already to look backwards to find a unique poetic self arising from layers of translation and a uniquely Russian literature that challenges the authority of the Russian monarchy even as it encompasses within itself both East and West, his sublime self-confidence was not widely shared. Even Nicholas's belief in himself became a little patchy by the Crimean War, while the debate on Russian nationality as a whole was characterized by a great deal of anxiety. This anxiety assumed that other peoples know who they are, that their national form comes already equipped with a national content, and indeed, that the latter precedes the former just as poetry precedes the criticism that would describe it. Sure that their inner lack was theirs alone, Russian Romantics could only express their originality as uniquely imitative; yet even here they were hardly original. The whole question of national identity, while certainly grounded in the exigencies of the Russian past, was also one that Russian Romantics derived mainly from their avid reading of the works of Western European Romantics, especially Mme. de Staël's *De l'Allemagne* (1813). What the Russians seem to have missed in their reading, however, is the unsteadiness of national identity that Romanticism actually offers. This unsure identity is the natural corollary of the unsteadiness of writer- and reader-identities argued earlier, as what Russian Romantics in fact borrowed from the West was not only the question of national identity but also its apparently paradoxical answer.

Romantic Space

As central as the debate on Russian nationality is to Russian literature and Russian politics, in the nineteenth century it was also largely a foreign transplant. This point is evident already in Viazemskii's introduction of his famous term *narodnost'* as a translation of the French *nationalité* by way of the Polish *narodowość*, and the influence of German and Germanophile writers is also readily apparent. Lauren Leighton is succinct: "The concept of national originality belongs predominantly to Friedrich Schlegel, who based his own theory on previous German philosophers, particularly Herder and Fichte. The concept was also developed significantly by August Schlegel, and it was made widely popular by Madame de Staël."[74]

An appreciation of the different characteristics that mark different peoples in different places and times is now so commonplace that a rehearsal of the emphasis on the diverse and indigenous that the Schlegels promoted especially in the post-*Athenaeum* surveys like Friedrich's *Lectures on the History of Literature, Ancient and Modern* (1815) would not be terribly revealing. What remains far more interesting are the points when this concept of national originality, well before it comes to Russia, already incorporates within itself the universal and even a principle of imitation. While, as Leighton notes, Fichte is also significant here, perhaps most especially as expressed in his *Addresses to the German Nation* (1807), the most important and most striking conflation of national and universal, original and imitation was accomplished by that advocate of Romantic nationality who was also easily the most influential: August Wilhelm Schlegel's hoped-for lover and long-time employer, Baroness Anne Louise Germaine Necker Holstein-Staël.[75]

It is Staël's *De l'Allemagne* (1813) that ignited the discussion of Romantic nationalism all over Europe. The enormous influence of her work can be gauged by the fact that *De l'Allemagne* has been variously credited with introducing the actual terms "Romantic" and "nationality" to the French and English languages; the Russian debate on *narodnost'* was also carried out entirely under de Staël's auspices.[76] The great irony, however, is that the main purveyor of a concept of what Deidre Shauna Lynch calls "a reterritorializing of literature, a canonizing of that writing that was homegrown" so manifestly lacked a native land of her own. Born in Paris to Swiss protestant parents, Staël married a Swede and then proceeded to bear "five children (four out of wedlock) by four different fathers of three different nationalities."[77] Exiled by Napoleon first from Paris and then from France, Staël variously lived on her Swiss estate at Coppet, visited Germany, and barely ahead of Napoleon's armies, traveled to Russia, then to Sweden, and finally England.

Exactly like Senkovskii, Staël is defined always by her other-ness in space, and if Staël in her very person would appear thus to contravene her own theories, the promotion of nationalism by someone less than national herself is also one of the primary features of Staël's 1807 novel, *Corinne, or Italy*, whose half-English, half-Italian protagonist has been dubbed "a national heroine without a nation."[78] Staël is finally important to us, however, because both in *De l'Allemagne* and in the preface to her 1802 novel *Delphine* she also paradoxically promotes an originality that can only be achieved by way of imitation. This point is perhaps obvious in the overall polemical thrust of *De l'Allemagne*, which is to urge the French to stop imitating the ancients and write original works like the Germans instead. Certainly it was readily apparent to Viazemskii, who in his preface to "The Fountain of Bakhchisarai" embraces exactly this contradiction when his "Publisher" attacks the neo-Classicist imitation of the ancients while yet vigorously defending the Romantic imitation of the Germans. Staël in her own presentation in *De l'Allemagne*, however, tends to obfuscate what is nonetheless her fundamental point.

In her famous chapter "Classical and Romantic Poetry" Staël insists that "the question for us is not between classical and romantic poetry, but between the imitation of the one and the inspiration of the other." She also explains that "[f]or the moderns the poetry of the Ancients is a transplanted literature: the romantic or chivalric literature is with us indigenous, and it is our religion and our institutions that have made it blossom."[79] As John Clairborne Isbell notes, the difference between "imitation" and "inspiration" is not at all clear. "Us" and "our" are also confusing terms in a book written to introduce first the French and then all of Europe to a hitherto little-known German literature.

Staël's notion that German literature is indigenous to all Europeans may derive from Jena's understanding of "German" as pointing simply toward the best in humanity. Novalis, for example, in a letter to August Wilhelm Schlegel described "German nature" as "cosmopolitanism mixed with the strongest individuality," while in *Athenaeum Fragment* 291 he wrote: "There are Germans everywhere. Germanism is confined to a particular state as little as Romanism, Hellenism, or Britannism, are; these are universal characteristics of humanity that have only on occasion achieved perfect universality. Germanism is genuine popularity and therefore an ideal."[80] This simultaneous specificity and universality of the German nation is the exact counterpart to the "Romantic kind of poetry" in Friedrich's *Athenaeum Fragment* 116 that combines all other kinds of poetry and even prose into itself as "the only one that is more than a kind, that is, as it were, poetry itself." As an ideal, Novalis's Germanness is "still in the state of becoming," just like the Russianness and Russian literature that is marked above all by its promise. As Friedrich Schlegel wrote in *Athenaeum Fragment* 26, "Germany is probably such a favorite subject for the general essayist because the less finished a nation is, the more it is a subject for criticism and not for history."[81]

No matter how great her admiration for the Germans, however, as a non-German herself Staël may also have been a little reluctant to assume her readers' equation of what is best in themselves with the "German," and she more overtly justifies her use of "us" in a way that would also gloss over the whole matter of imitation, simply by defining Romanticism more broadly as Christian. As Bestuzhev would later paraphrase her, "according to spirit and essence there exist only two literatures: literature before Christianity and literature from the time of Christianity."[82] In this sense Romantic literature is native to France as to Germany, and to be "inspired" by Germany in *De l'Allemagne* is but to clear out the clutter of Neo-Classicism to recover a past that is actually already one's own.

Still, it is not entirely clear that even with this move Staël has quite made German Romantic poetry universal without even a hint of imitation. At the very least, as Lynch argues, there is something problematic in the notion that modern literature "would recover its originality" only through "commemoration."[83] Staël's "inspiration" also still more closely approximates "imitation" in the preface to her novel *Delphine* (1802), in which she attacks contemporary French literature above all for its isolation. The ancients wrote no novels, Staël says, and accordingly for models we must turn above all to the English and the Germans. Unfortunately the French, she writes, tend to focus on their own literature alone to the point of sterility and monotony. "[S]tudy of the perfect and widely known works we possess does indeed teach us what we must avoid," Staël proclaims," but it inspires nothing new." On the other hand:

> [W]hen we read the writing of a nation whose outlook and feelings are very different from the French, our mind is excited by new comparisons, our imagination is enlivened as much by the audacities it condemns as by those it approves; and we might succeed in adapting to French taste—perhaps the purest of all—original beauties that would give to the literature of the nineteenth century a character all its own.[84]

"Adapting original beauties" sounds even more like imitation, and in fact just the sort of imitation that the Russians would later practice. Nadezhdin alone among Russian Romantics objected to the notion of original imitation. All the rest took from Staël exactly what would become theirs: a Romanticism where national and universal, original and imitation prove strangely compatible.

It is finally also Staël, again in *De l'Allemagne,* who most clearly offers the Russians a connection between their critical tendencies and their national aspirations. In Russia the whole discussion of nationality in the apparent absence of the real thing elides easily into criticism of the tendency to write endlessly about Russian literature in the absence of actual texts. For Staël as for Friedrich Schlegel, however, criticism in the absence of literature and/or nation is not a flaw, but a sign of future promise. In *Athenaeum Fragment* 26 Friedrich Schlegel himself suggests the value of criticism for a developing sense of German nationality. In *De l'Allemagne* Staël discerns its parallel effect on German literature already. She writes:

> German literature is perhaps the only one that began with criticism; everywhere else criticism arrived after the masterpieces; but in Germany it produced them. The epoch when letters had the greatest splendor is the cause of this difference. Different nations have been illustrious in the art of writing already for many centuries, but the Germans arrived after all the others, and they feared that they would have nothing to do but follow the route already traced out; it was necessary that the criticism first clarify in order that imitation give way to originality.[85]

Staël's vindication of Friedrich Schlegel's notion of a Romantic criticism that always precedes the poetry still in the process of becoming turns into the Russian Romantics' justification of their own late arrival on the literary and thus national scene.[86] Where Bestuzhev complains that already "in childhood we have become peevish old men!" Belinskii begins his "Literary Reveries" with the cry "We have no literature!" only to end by explaining that he does so "with ecstasy, with enjoyment, for in this truth I see the pledge of our future successes."[87] For the Russian Romantics only more obviously and at times perhaps even more desperately, criticism can clear the way to an origin not so much lost as apparently entirely nonexistent.

Just as Staël, despite her visit to Russia, hardly suspected the inspiration her words might serve for yet another nation new to the "art of writing," one still further East, so readers of Russian literature in turn have tended to read the Russian Romantics' redeployment of imitation as dictated by uniquely Russian circumstances, as indeed in many respects it was.[88] At the same time, however, the twists and turns of efforts to establish a Russian literary and so national identity also neatly echo a Romanticism that posits a notion of originality only to defer it. We have already seen this movement in the creation of inauthentic reader- and writer-personae who rather than reflect their "originals" in fact replace them. In similarly circular fashion, Romantic nations construct their individuality by imitating—even among the Germans, where a concept of Germanness as universal can serve only to blur the lines of national originality. Whereas the Russians are marked by a "genius of receptivity," the Germans, as Friedrich Schlegel wrote in the *Dialogue on Poetry*, "possess a genius of translation which is their own."[89] From West to East and back again, Romanticism suggests an original, national space whose borders, like those of its writer- and reader-inhabitants, are always in flux, made ever-expanding by a concomitant urge to universality and also porous by a deep-seated principle of imitation. Despite the pervasiveness of the term "Romantic nationalism," this space does not really resemble a nation. It looks instead a great deal more like an empire, and like the Russian Empire in particular.

Russia and Romanticism

In its instability, inauthenticity, and dependence on imitation while yet professing a principle of originality, Russian space as expressed above all in Russian literature and literary criticism represents the Romantic nation in perhaps its most extreme form. This extreme form might be described as an empty vessel, a nation with no nationality of its own inside. We might also take the opposite tack and understand this Romantic nation not as nowhere but as everywhere, as that apparent paradox, "the most imperial of nations, comprising more peoples than any other." If the two are ultimately the same, still the Russian context of actual empire might tend us toward the latter approach, as Russian Romanticism in all its belatedness serves finally to make clear one last tendency that existed in Romanticism from the start.

As Isbell carefully sorts the implications of Staël's choice of the word *Allemagne* in her *De l'Allemagne*, he notes the extent to which the Holy Roman Empire, finally dissolved in 1806, hovers behind notions of the German self. In German philosophy at the time, Isbell points out, the ideal state was generally described as a federation. Still Isbell argues that this notion of federation reflects more the natively German experience of empire than the foreign examples of the Swiss, Dutch, or American republics, and he suggests in particular that when "Staël and Herder consider the place for minority cultures within a larger state, the Empire might be borne in mind."[90] As Monika Greenleaf and Stephen Moeller-Sally argue, empire cannot but be borne in mind in the works of Russian Romanticism, and especially in what I have argued to be in turn its most extreme manifestation, the *Library for Reading*. It is certainly the case that with the *Library for Reading* Senkovskii achieved a critical empire in the literal sense entirely lacking in Friedrich Schlegel's aspirations for critical dominance. It is also true that empire alone could enable the play of periphery and center that so dramatically characterized Senkovskii's life and also Romanticism more generally.

Empire is in fact most often defined precisely in terms of center and periphery. As Alexander J. Motyl carefully suggests: "Let us begin the conceptual analysis of empire by unpacking what may be its two least unacceptable defining characteristics. Most scholars would probably agree that every empire consists of something called a core and something called a periphery. And most might agree that both core and periphery, whatever they are, are situated in geographically bounded spaces inhabited by culturally differentiated elites and populations."[91] For Senkovskii and Bulgarin the core was St. Petersburg and the periphery Poland, while for Scott, the *Blackwood's* people, and Maginn the opposition lay between London and either Scotland or Ireland. In the complicated case of Staël, the core was Paris, and the periphery was ten years of exile aimed in part at raising up the ghost of another empire to oppose Napoleon's. It is empire that provides for Romantic expatriates and exiles their "multilingual" and "cross-linguistic" field of play, and also empire that, as Isbell suggests, makes room for a particularly Romantic oscillation between major and minor.

The tenets of Romantic nationalism would then seem to derive from a notion of empire while also ever recurring to it, perhaps most strikingly in the persons of Staël and also Scott. If Staël and Scott as denizens of empires both based their careers on the particular charm Romanticism lent to the notion of indigenous cultures, both also blurred the edges of national specificity in various, sometimes troubling ways: Staël advocated an originality that could obtain only through imitation, while Scott offered only an ersatz Scotland, a "fantasy surrogate" that served only "to anaesthetize Scotland against real nationalism."[92] Senkovskii finally also demonstrates the Romantic eternal return to empire simply by participating in a Russian debate on *narodnost'*, which by virtue of its own anxieties lays the contradictions of Romantic nationality entirely bare.

Russian Romantics deliberately cast their national originality in terms of their unique receptivity to other cultures, imagining a Russian genius of appropriation and assimilation that expands along with the borders of the Russian Empire and even beyond to incorporate the achievements of Western Europe. If national originality can be characterized as one's receptivity to foreign borrowings, however, then neither "national" nor "originality" are left with much meaning. It becomes evident instead that what Romanticism intended was not national originality, but only ever its simulation. It is that stark clarity that Russian Romanticism brings to its Western European counterparts, although admittedly not without some loss. As Russian Romantics find that Western European theories fit their own historical and geographical considerations to an astonishing degree, they seem to miss something fundamental: Romantic irony. Russian writers almost to a man instead debate with feverish intensity a question of Russian identity that adheres perhaps a little too closely to the actual boundaries of the Russian state. Free literary play is gone; the ugly realities of Nicholas's "prison-house of nations" would seem to have replaced it.

In fairness to the Russians, it is certainly the case that simulation, if much relished by the Schlegels, is not a practice universally enjoyed. I have already offered up Wordsworth and Rousseau as particularly humorless types, and I would note also the post-Structuralist example of Baudrillard, who, for all the effort he has devoted to delineating the workings of the simulacrum, seems always horrified anew by the monster his writing has once more disclosed. Even among the literal-minded Russians, however, the pleasures of Romantic irony are not lost on Pushkin, who as late as 1836 still creates his own identity emerging as if from a palimpsest, and who also makes a point of erecting his monument of poetry just a little higher than Nicholas's monument to the power of the Russian state. Nor are they lost on that writer whom I persist in seeing as Pushkin's dark shadow: Senkovskii, although the irony in both his 1847 lecture and his representation of "Tver" perhaps more resembles open mockery.

In characterizing Romanticism by its Russian variant that is in turn characterized by the *Library for Reading*, I am not arguing just that the Russians with their enthusiasm for the world of ideas have taken their imitation of Western Europe to its extreme conclusion. That argument has already been made more than once, especially with regard to later political movements. What I am more emphatically suggesting is that the Russian experience turned back on Western Europe makes especially clear the point that in the Romantic context there is only ever imitation, if imitation that always claims to be original. If this contention is to be valid then Russian Romanticism can only exist on the edges of Europe, for Romanticism then has no real center, only a play of marginalities. Still just for a moment, if only for the sake of those for whom marginality is necessarily a deficiency, let periphery and center instead change places and let Russia represent the essentially Romantic.

For Blanchot Romanticism is a movement that "formulates the ambition of a total book, a sort of perpetually growing Bible that will not represent, but rather replace, the real," and it is Russian Romantics who most successfully fit the contours of Romantic nationalism to what we take to be their own reality.[93] For Lacoue-Labarthe and Nancy, Romanticism is literature as "its own infinite questioning and as the perpetual positing of its own question."[94] No one asks that question, in both literary and also political terms, with such strange energy as the Russians, and nowhere are the contradictions of a literary movement that both begins and ends in criticism so evident as in Senkovskii's *Library for Reading*.

Reference Matter

Notes

Introduction: Romanticism and the Library for Reading

1. Nikolai Gogol, *Dead Souls*, trans. Bernard Guilbert Guerney, ed. Susanne Fusso (New Haven, CT: Yale Univ. Press, 1996), 248.

2. Ibid., 1. On negativity in Gogol, see especially Sven Spieker (ed.), *Gogol, Exploring Absence* (Bloomington, IN: Slavica, 1999).

3. The details of Senkovskii's life can be found in the two fine monographs devoted to his work: V. Kaverin, *Baron Brambeus* (Moscow: Nauka, 1966) and Louis Pedrotti, *Józef-Julian Sękowski: Genesis of a Literary Alien* (Berkeley: Univ. of California Press, 1965). Also useful is the account of Senkovskii's contemporary and friend, P. Savel'ev, in his introduction to O. I. Senkovskii, *Sobranie sochinenii Senkovskogo (Barona Brambeusa)*, ed. P. Savel'ev, 9 vols. (St. Petersburg: V tipografii Bezobrazova i ko., 1858–59), 1: xi–cxii.

4. Important for me here especially are the scholars in and around Deconstruction, including Derrida, especially on Rousseau in *Of Grammatology* (1974), de Man, Baudrillard, Deleuze, Guattari, and above all Lacoue-Labarthe and Nancy in *The Literary Absolute* (1988). See Jacques Derrida, *Of Grammatology* (Baltimore: Johns Hopkins Univ. Press, 1976); Philippe Lacoue-Labarthe and Jean-Luc Nancy, *The Literary Absolute*, trans. Philip Bernard and Cheryl Lester (Albany: SUNY Press, 1988). The affinities between a post-Structuralist approach and Romanticism are clear, and I am also influenced by other scholars of Romanticism who operate in more or less loosely post-Structuralist terms. In the British context, for example, I would note Peter Murphy, "Impersonation and Romantic Authorship in Britain," *English Literary History* 59:3 (Fall 1992), 625–49 and Susan Eilenberg, "'Michael,' 'Christabel,' and the Poetry of Possession," *Criticism* 30:2 (Spring 1988), 205–21; in the French context, Martha Noel Evans, "*Adolphe*'s Appeal to the Reader," *Romantic Review* 83:3 (May 1982), 302–13; and in the Russian context,

Monika Greenleaf, *Pushkin and Romantic Fashion: Fragment, Elegy, Orient, Irony* (Stanford, CA: Stanford Univ. Press, 1995).

5. Peter Conrad, *Shandyism: The Character of Romantic Irony* (Oxford: Basil Blackwell, 1978), 43.

6. Gary Handwerk, *Irony and Ethics in Narrative* (New Haven, CT: Yale Univ. Press, 1985), viii, 42–43. I owe my discovery of Handwerk to Greenleaf's *Pushkin and Romantic Fashion* (1995), which is also informed by his work.

7. Handwerk, *Irony and Ethics*, 9.

8. In Handwerk's definition, we are in the presence of the Romantic ironic when a subject is "aware of and enacting its status of inadequacy in regard to an Absolute whose presence it can conjure only through engagement in a dialectic of intersubjectivity" (ibid., 36).

9. I use the word *simulation* in the sense Jean Baudrillard gives it in his essay "Simulacra and Simulations"; see Jean Baudrillard, *Selected Writings*, ed. Mark Poster (Stanford, CA: Stanford Univ. Press, 1988), 166–84.

10. Maurice Blanchot, "The Athenaeum," *Studies in Romanticism* 22:2 (Summer 1983), 171.

11. With regard to the two British journals mentioned, I would note the important exception in Mark Parker's *Literary Magazines and British Romanticism*. Parker's intention as he puts it forthrightly in his introduction is "to demonstrate that literary magazines should be an object of study in their own right, to argue that they are the preeminent literary form of the 1820s and 1830s in Britain, and to explore the ways in which literary magazines begin to frame a discussion of Romanticism." See Mark Parker, *Library Magazines and British Romanticism* (Cambridge: Cambridge Univ. Press, 2000), 1. While my focus on reader- and writer-personae has taken me in a different direction, still my ideas were very much influenced by Parker's fine study, especially his third chapter, "The Burial of Romanticism: The First Twenty Installments of '*Noctes Ambrosianae.*'"

12. Philippe Lacoue-Labarthe and Jean-Luc Nancy, *The Literary Absolute*, trans. Philip Bernard and Cheryl Lester (Albany: SUNY Press, 1988), 7.

13. Again Handwerk writes, now with particular reference to Lacan:

> Ironic utterances are . . . partial utterances requiring completion, which make evident the partialness of the utterer as subject. Unable to play all the parts at once, the ironic subject is forced to proceed to an enactment that must be an interaction as well. . . . These utterances are thus appeals for a response that would implicate the other in the dialogue, rather than a response that might directly envisage and reveal the subject. The dependence of the ironic subject on the other is fundamental, for by virtue of his replay the subject comes to be defined or distinguished (*Irony and Ethics*, 134).

14. Friedrich Schlegel, *Philosophical Fragments*, trans. Peter Firchow (Minneapolis: Univ. of Minnesota Press, 1991), 31.

15. Ibid. We might wonder what the place of "wit" is in philosophy, a question that *Athenaeum Fragment* 116 on its own does not answer. In the *Critical Fragments* published by Schlegel a few years prior, however, he defines the slippery concept of "Witz" as "absolute social feeling, or fragmentary genius" (ibid., 2).

16. Greenleaf, *Pushkin and Romantic Fashion*, 21.

17. Carlyle's comment is taken from his 1831 essay "Characteristics," as quoted in Lee Erickson, *The Economy of Literary Form: English Literature and the Industrialization of Publishing, 1800–1850* (Baltimore: Johns Hopkins Univ. Press, 1996), 90. Belinskii's remark is in a letter to his friend V. P. Botkin on October 31, 1840. See V. G. Belinskii, *Sobranie sochinenii*, 9 vols. (Moscow: Khudozhestvennaia literatura, 1976–82), 9:411.

18. Paul de Man, *Allegories of Reading* (New Haven, CT: Yale Univ. Press, 1979), 301.

19. Blanchot, "The Athenaeum," 164.

20. Lacoue-Labarthe and Nancy, *Literary Absolute*, 12.

21. Senkovskii's critical dominance was a topic of constant and very vocal concern to his contemporaries. Grits et al. quote one of the most remarkable reflections on Senkovskii's very real power, one taken from the pages of the *Moscow Observer*, a literary journal founded specifically to combat the dominance of his own *Library for Reading*: "Messieurs journalists! We advise you to climb to the top of your minarets and cry out . . . in the all-hearing of the public: There is no Allah but Allah, and Mohammed his prophet. There is no publisher of 'The Library for Reading' but A. F. Smirdin, and there is no editor and director of it, but O. I. Senkovskii, and no one, but him." T. S. Grits, V. Trenin, and M. Nikitin, *Slovesnost' i kommertsiia: knizhnaia lavka A. F. Smirdina* (Moscow: Federatsiia, 1929), 235.

22. It is a measure of the nearly legendary status of this line that Belinskii repeats it in his wonderful incarnation in part one, "Voyage," of Tom Stoppard's recent trilogy, *The Coast of Utopia* (New York: Grove Press, 2003).

23. Blanchot, "The Athenaeum," 167.

Chapter 1: Romanticism and the Literary Marketplace

1. We find that a similar problem arises with another popular distinction, one still relatively new in the early nineteenth century, between "functional" and "nonfunctional," or "imaginative" literature. The distinction clearly has value, but once again it does not quite hold up, for the *Library for Reading* as an "encyclopedic" journal was famously a purveyor both of Romantic literature and also of writings of a more practical sort, combining together in one issue everything from Pushkin's poetry to articles on the dyeing of thread and the curing of tuberculosis.

2. T. S. Grits, V. Trenin, and M. Nikitin, *Slovesnost' i kommertsiia: knizhnaia lavka A. F. Smirdina* (Moscow: Federatsiia, 1929), 237.

3. See Jon Klancher, *The Making of English Reading Audiences, 1790–1832* (Madison: Univ. of Wisconsin Press, 1987); John Brewer, "Reconstructing the Reader: Prescriptions, Texts, and Strategies in Anna Larpent's Reading," in *The Practice and Representation of Reading in England,* ed. James Raven, Helen Small, and Naomi Tadmor (Cambridge: Cambridge Univ. Press, 1996); and Robert Darnton, "Readers Respond to Rousseau: The Fabrication of Romantic Sensitivity" (last chapter), *The Great Cat Massacre and Other Episodes in French Cultural History* (New York: Basic Books, 1983).

4. See Rolf Engelsing, *Der Bürger als Leser. Lesegeschichte in Deutschland 1500– 1800* (Stuttgart: Metzler, 1974).

5. Joost Kloek, "Reconsidering the Reading Revolution: The Thesis of the 'Reading Revolution' and a Dutch Bookseller's Clientele Around 1800." *Poetics* 26:5–6 (August 1999), 290.

6. Klancher, *The Making of English Reading Audiences,* 3, 23.

7. Jeffrey Brooks, *When Russia Learned to Read: Literacy and Popular Culture, 1861–1917* (Princeton, NJ: Princeton Univ. Press, 1985), 4.

8. I. M. Bogdanov, *Gramotnost' i obrazovanie v dorevoliutsionnoi Rossii i v SSSR* (Moscow: Statistika, 1964), 21.

9. While Miranda Beaven Remnek is now involved in interesting explorations of the reading culture of the merchant class in early nineteenth-century Russia, still in *Books in Russia and the Soviet Union* we read only the parenthetical note: "There were few readers outside the gentry; as yet this class was the only one able to afford books." See Miranda Beaven Remnek (ed.), *Books in Russia and the Soviet Union* (Wiesbaden: Otto Harrassowitz, 1991), 31.

10. Gessen points out that while a year's subscription to *The Moscow Telegraph* cost 35 rubles and a two- or three-volume collected works cost approximately the same, the salary for a midlevel bureaucrat in the 1820s and 1830s was only 60–80 rubles per month, and even the well-known and well-respected censor A. V. Nikitenko until 1836 earned at the university only 1,300 rubles per year. Gessen goes on to note the high prices for any kind of luxury, including theater shows, and concludes: "We recall also that in 1831 Pushkin paid 2,500 rubles a year for his apartment in Galernaia Street and, in 1836, 4,300 rubles for the apartment in the Moika . . . , this while receiving at the same time a salary of 5,000 rubles a year." See S. Ia. Gessen, *Knigoizdatel' Aleksandr Pushkin: literaturnye dokhody Pushkina* (Leningrad: Akademia, 1930), 20.

11. M. N. Kufaev, *Istoriia russkoi knigi v XIX veke* (Leningrad: Nachatki znanii, 1927), 91. Examples of works dealing with the Decembrists' reading habits in particular would include E. N. Dunaeva, *Dekabristy i kniga* (Moscow: Kniga, 1967)

and three works by P. I. Tsuprik: "O roli knig v zhizni i deiatel'nosti dekabristov v usloviiakh zabajkal'skoi ssylki," in *Dekabristy i Sibir'*, ed. A. N. Kopylov (Novosibirsk: Nauka, Sib. Otd., 1977), 121–32; "Kniga v zhizni Dekabristov na katorge," in *Pamiati Dekabristov*, ed. F. A. Kudriavtsev (Irkutsk: Irkutskii gos. uni. im. Zdanova, 1975), 64–83; and "M. S. Lunin—chitatel'," ibid., 100–21.

12. See William Mills Todd III, *Fiction and Society in the Age of Pushkin* (Cambridge, MA: Harvard Univ. Press, 1986).

13. Remnek, *Books in Russia*, 31.

14. André Meynieux, *Pouchkine: Homme de letters, et la littérature professionelle en Russie* (Paris: Librairie de cinq continents, 1966), 471.

15. Nik. Smirnov-Sokol'skii, *Knizhnaia lavka A. F. Smirdina* (Moscow: izd. Vsesoiuznoi knizhnoi palatki, 1957), 27–28.

16. Grits et al., *Slovesnost' i kommertsiia*, 331.

17. While Miranda Beaven Remnek has not yet published her new work on merchant readers in early nineteenth-century Russia, she has posted some of her preliminary data at http://www.library.uiuc.edu/spx/rusread/index.html.

18. Grits et al., *Slovesnost' i kommertsiia*, 256.

19. Meynieux, *Pouchkine*, 471.

20. Peter Murphy, "Impersonation and Romantic Authorship in Britain," *English Literary History* 59:3 (Fall 1992), 644.

21. Lockhart is quoted in David Daiches, *Sir Walter Scott and His World* (New York: Viking, 1971), 71.

22. Matthew Josephson, *Victor Hugo: A Realistic Biography of the Great Romantic* (New York: Doubleday, 1942), 249.

23. Martha Woodmansee, *Author, Art and the Market: Rereading the History of Aesthetics* (New York: Columbia Univ. Press, 1994), 32.

24. Carla Hesse, *Publishing and Cultural Politics in Revolutionary Paris, 1789–1810* (Berkeley: Univ. of California Press, 1991), 120, 231.

25. Meynieux makes the argument for associating Pushkin with the 1828 law; S. Pereselenkov credits Pushkin, and more specifically Pushkin's widow, for the 1857 extension of copyright protection to fifty years.

26. Grits et al., *Slovesnost' i kommertsiia*, 265.

27. Todd, *Fiction and Society*, 84.

28. By comparison, when Senkovskii was earning 15,000 rubles/year for his editorial work on the *Library for Reading*, Belinskii was earning only 5,000 rubles/year for his work on *Notes of the Fatherland*, and included in that fee were honoraria for the articles and reviews he published there (nearly fifty printer's sheets per year) as well as his direction of the Criticism and Bibliography sections of the journal (nearly one hundred printer's sheets per year). See M. P. Kim (ed.), *400 let russkogo knigopechataniia, 1564–1964* (Moscow: Nauka, 1964), 274.

29. Gessen, *Knigoizdatel' Aleksandr Pushkin,* 40, 50.

30. Ibid., 51, 54, 66.

31. Ibid., 45, 46, 48.

32. Ibid., 49.

33. S. Pereselenkov, "Pushkin v istorii zakonopolozheniii ob avtorskom prave v Rossii," in *Pushkin i ego sovremenniki, materialy i issledovaniia* vyp. XI (St. Petersburg: Tip. Akademii nauk, 1909; The Hague: Mouton, 1970), 52–53.

34. Grits et al., *Slovesnost' i kommertsiia,* 46, 47.

35. Bulgarin received a ring from the Empress in 1829 for his novel *Ivan Vyzhigin* and then another from the Emperor in 1830 for the sequel, *Petr Ivanovich Vyzhigin.* See A. V. Zapadova (ed.), *Istoriia russkoi zhurnalistiki XVIII–XIX vekov* (Moscow: Vysshaia shkola, 1973), 175.

36. These figures come from T. J. Binyon, *Pushkin* (New York: Knopf, 2002), 356, 546, 615.

37. In 1843 Gogol received 1,000 rubles from the Empress, in 1844 Zhukovskii arranged to repay a 4,000-ruble debt to Gogol rather than to the Tsarevich, and in 1844 Gogol's friend Smirnova-Rosset wrote him that he should in the future borrow money only from her since the Emperor had given her money for that purpose. See Donald Fanger, *The Creation of Nikolai Gogol* (Cambridge, MA: Harvard Univ. Press, 1979), 282 n. 4.

38. Grits et al., *Slovesnost' i kommertsiia,* 152.

39. Even Victor Hugo, who later in life earned enormous amounts of money from his work and was active in the establishment of international copyright, made sure to finagle a royal pension quite early in his career. Josephson, *Victor Hugo,* 81.

40. Trollope was also involved with the Fund and sat on the Committee for the last twenty years of his life. In his *An Autobiography* (1883) he explicitly drew on this experience to advise any young aspirants against "enter[ing] boldly on a literary career in search of bread," noting with reference to his own difficult start: "Of course there have been many who have done better than I,—many whose powers have been infinitely greater. But then, too, I have seen the failure of many who were greater." Anthony Trollope, *An Autobiography* (Oxford: Oxford Univ. Press, 1980), 214.

41. Nigel Cross, *The Common Writer: Life in Nineteenth-Century Grub Street* (New York: Cambridge Univ. Press, 1985), 5.

42. *Books in Russia* refers to "culturally-motivated" publishers (Remnek, 27), and Grits et al. speak of "a new purely commercial type" (*Slovesnost' i kommertsiia,* 90); "*kulturträgers*" and "booksellers" are opposed in M. V. Muratov and N. N. Nakoriakov (ed.), *Knizhnaia torgovlia: posobie dlia rabotnikov knizhnogo dela* (Moscow: Gos. Izd., 1925), 99; while I. E. Barenbaum and T. E. Davydova refer to "publisher-Maecenases" and "publisher-merchants" in *Istoriia knigi* (Moscow:

Sovetskaia Rossiia, 1960), 79. W. Gareth Jones notes that this problematic distinction is also developed with regard to the great publisher of the eighteenth century, N. I. Novikov; see his "N. I. Novikov and the Business of Books in Late Eighteenth-Century Russia," *New England Slavonic Journal* (1986), 1–19.

43. *Kratkii obzor knizhnoi torgovli i izdatel'skoi deiatel'nosti Glazunovykh za sto let 1782–1882* (St. Petersburg: tip. Glazunova, 1903), 54–55.

44. Plavil'shchikov is another of these figures who occupies an ambiguous position between culture and commerce. He was a highly successful merchant and also, according to Smirnov-Sokol'skii in *Knizhnaia lavka A. F. Smirdina,* "one of the most enlightened public figures of his time" (p. 17), "gifted by nature with a love for the fine [arts]" (p. 18). Although the reading library was actually attached to the bookstore, Smirnov-Sokol'skii makes no connection between the two, claiming that Plavil'shchikov collected books first to complete his own inadequate education and then simply to share them with others.

45. Beaven Remnek notes that "sources differ" as to the exact amount, but not by a great deal. See Miranda Beaven, "Aleksandr Smirdin and Publishing in St. Petersburg, 1830–1840," *Canadian Slavonic Papers* 27:1 (March 1985), 17 n. 9.

46. Grits et al., *Slovesnost' i kommertsiia,* 267.

47. Ibid., 243, 235–36.

48. S. P. Shevyrev, "Slovesnost' i torgovlia," *Moskovskii nabliudatel'* 1 (March 1835), 7.

49. As he wrote in frustration to his friend Sobolevskii: "Here in Petersburg they give me (à la lettre) 10 rubles a line—but in Moscow you want to force me to work exclusively for your journal for free. What's more, they say: he's rich, he has the devil of a lot of money. Let's say that that's so, but I'm rich because of my trade in verse, not because of my ancestors' patrimony that remains in the hands of Sergei L'vovich" (Gessen, *Knigoizdatel' Aleksandr Pushkin,* 80).

50. *Kratkii obzor . . . Glazunovykh,* 55–56.

51. See Remnek, *Books in Russia,* 36.

52. Grits et al., *Slovesnost' i kommertsiia,* 344.

53. Kim, *400 let,* 474.

54. M. N. Kufaev, *Istoriia russkoi knigi v XIX veke* (Leningrad: Nachatki znanii, 1927), 19; Beaven, "Aleksandr Smirdin," 27.

55. Smirnov-Sokol'skii, *Knizhnaia lavka A. F. Smirdina,* 38, 25.

56. N. V. Gogol', *Polnoe sobranie sochinenii,* ed. L. N. Meshcheriakov, 14 vols. (Leningrad: Nauka, 1937–1952), 8:157.

57. Smirnov-Sokol'skii, *Knizhnaia lavka A. F. Smirdina,* 38.

58. Erickson, *The Economy of Literary Form,* 19.

59. Albert Joseph George, *The Development of French Romanticism* (Syracuse, NY: Syracuse Univ. Press, 1955), 20.

60. Ibid., 20–21.

61. Kim, *400 let*, 267.

62. Remnek, *Books in Russia*, 35.

63. The *Athenaeum*'s run was very brief and seems to have been accompanied by constant struggles with publishers—at one point a would-be publisher would not take on the project even when Friedrich offered to cut the honoraria by one-third. See Ernst Behler, *Die Zeitschriften der Brüder Schlegel* (Darmstadt: Wissenschaftliche Buchgesellschaft, 1983), 25. Tieck was the most successful of the group at earning his living by writing, but even his income was supplemented by grants, loans, and subsidized housing provided by various friends, including his longtime mistress, and also by his eventual position as the Dresden "Dramaturg"; in the early 1820s he also tried and failed to gain a position at the University of Berlin. See Roger Paulin, *Ludwig Tieck: A Literary Biography* (New York: Oxford Univ. Press, 1985).

64. Eichner notes that when "Schlegel applied for a professorship at Würzburg, Schelling was his sole supporter in the faculty." Hans Eichner, *Friedrich Schlegel* (New York: Twayne, 1970), 102.

65. Schlegel, *Philosophical Fragments*, 26.

66. Novalis, *Schriften*, ed. Paul Kluckhohn and Richard Samuel, 3 vols. (Stuttgart: Kohlhammer, 1960), 2:664.

67. Schlegel, *Philosophical Fragments*, 75.

68. Ibid., 4.

69. In his 1836 article, "A Few Words About the 'Contemporary.'" See V. G. Belinskii, *Sobranie sochinenii v trekh tomakh* (Moscow: Khudozhestvennaia literatura, 1948), 1:280. Herzen would later make the same point, noting in his 1846 article "One Mind Is Good But Two Are Better" that "the border between Senkovskii and Brambeus was drawn . . . with such sharpness, that the identity of these two names called forth the surprise of contemporaries." See Kaverin, *Baron Brambeus*, 420.

Chapter 2: Romantic Writers

1. Significant parts of this chapter are reprinted from *Russian Literature*, 56, no. 4, Melissa Frazier, "Personae and Personality in O. I. Senkovskij," pp. 343–62, Copyright (2004), and *Russian Literature*, 47, no. 1, Melissa Frazier, "Erasing the Borders of Criticism: Senkovskij, Readers and Writers," pp. 15–32, Copyright (2000), both with permission from Elsevier.

2. Monika Greenleaf, *Pushkin and Romantic Fashion: Fragment, Elegy, Orient, Irony* (Stanford, CA: Stanford Univ. Press, 1995), 38. Greenleaf herself disagrees, writing, "Byron and Pushkin, it seems to me, never give up their right not to coincide with themselves, to create a sincere new identity with every utterance—a series of 'stills' of a subjectivity in constant motion" (p. 46).

3. While the title page of the *Tales* as first published in 1831 identified them as "published by A. P.," by the second publication in 1834 they became "published by Alexander Pushkin."

4. I take the notion of the writer as "editor" or "collector" from Kevin McLaughlin, *Writing in Parts: Imitation and Exchange in Nineteenth-Century Literature* (Stanford, CA: Stanford Univ. Press, 1995); more on McLaughlin below.

5. In his fascinating multileveled analysis of an unfinished work purportedly also by Belkin, "The History of the Village Goriukhino" (1830), David Glenn Kropf argues that "Belkin's history presents four different types of writers who relate to the works they produce in distinct ways: the plagiarist, the forger/copyist, the imitator, and the 'original' writer." My argument is only that these four different types ultimately collapse into one. See David Glenn Kropf, *Authorship as Alchemy: Subversive Writing in Pushkin, Scott, Hoffmann* (Stanford, CA: Stanford Univ. Press, 1994), 87.

6. Peter Murphy, "Impersonation and Romantic Authorship in Britain," *English Literary History* 59:3 (Fall 1992), 626.

7. O. I. Senkovskii, "O dramakh: *Rossiia i Batory, Barona Rozena, Torkvato Tasso, N. Kukol'nika . . . ,*" *Biblioteka dlia chteniia* 1, otd. 5 (1834), 37, 38.

8. O. I. Senkovskii, "Est' li u nas literatura? . . . *Mazepa*, roman Bulgarina," *Biblioteka dlia chteniia* 2, otd. 5 (1834), 1.

9. Ibid., 5, 6.

10. Ibid., 10, 13.

11. William Mills Todd III, *Fiction and Society in the Age of Pushkin* (Cambridge, MA: Harvard Univ. Press, 1986), 98.

12. Jean Baudrillard, *Selected Writings*, ed. Mark Poster (Stanford, CA: Stanford Univ. Press, 1988), 167.

13. Ibid., 171. While Baudrillard is seeking to account for a phenomenon of the late twentieth century, his description of the four stages of the image that ends with "it bears no relation to any reality whatever: it is its own pure simulacrum" (p. 170), is a strikingly exact description of Romantic literary criticism, especially Russian, which finally bears no relation to literature at all but is instead entirely self-sufficient.

14. These "friends" actually refer largely to Belinskii, who in "Literary Reveries" accused Senkovskii of only pretending to condemn the new French writing while actually imitating it.

15. O. I. Senkovskii, "Brambeus i Iunaia slovesnost'," *Biblioteka dlia chteniia* 3, otd. 1 (1834), 35.

16. Senkovskii, "Iunaia," 35, 38.

17. Both Rudyi Pan'ko and Irinei Modestovich Gomozeiko speak in their own voices and so are not only more present to their texts than the shadowy Belkin

but also have been more closely associated with the writers whose masks they are. Pan'ko, like Gogol, is from Ukraine, and his name can be seen to refer to Gogol as well, as according to one scholar "Rudyi" points to Gogol's reddish coloring, while "Pan'ko" derives by way of Ukrainian peasant tradition from the first name of Gogol's grandfather, Panasa. Gomozeiko might have been even more closely associated with his creator, as Odoevskii's own mother read the *Motley Tales* and wrote to her son, "Best of all I like that man sitting in the corner and saying, 'leave me in peace' . . . it really resembles you." See M. A. Tur'ian, *Strannaia moia sud'ba: O zhizni Vladimira Fëdorovicha Odoevskogo* (Moscow: Kniga, 1991), 213.

18. On the issue of Scott's shaky authority and the distinction between history and fiction that he both deliberately draws and equally deliberately obscures, see Robert Mayer, "The Internal Machinery Displayed: *The Heart of Midlothian* and Scott's Apparatus for the Waverley Novels," *CLIO* 17:1 (1987), 1–20.

19. Critics have long argued that Jedediah Cleishbotham was the model specifically for Gogol's Rudyi Pan'ko; see, for example, V. V. Vinogradov, *Gogol i natural'naia shkola* (Leningrad: Obrazovanie, 1925); V. V. Vinogradov, *Etiudy o stile Gogolia* (Leningrad: Akademiia, 1926); and S. B. Davis, "From Scotland to Russia via France: Scott, Defauconpret and Gogol," *Scottish Slavonic Review* 17 (Autumn 1991), 21–36. Pushkin also borrowed elements of plot together with their intertexts from *The Heart of Midlothian*; see Melissa Frazier, "*Kapitanskaia dochka* and the Creativity of Borrowing," *Slavic and East European Journal* 37:4 (1993), 472–89.

20. Sir Walter Scott, *The Heart of Midlothian* (Oxford: Oxford Univ. Press, 1999), 10, 11. Murphy argues that Cleishbotham's maneuver here as elsewhere gives the reader fair warning of what will be Scott's repeated tendency to set up dramatic tensions in the novel only to defuse them: "The baffling cleverness of Scott's method is that he inevitably finds a latent and passive third term, like Jedediah's Quaker ancestor, which he produces triumphantly, even though this sort of resolution never presents a triumph." In Murphy's view, "Jedediah Cleishbotham personifies the antifictional Scott, and his materialistic and ultimately trivializing introduction expresses perfectly the forces that take the heart out of *The Heart of Midlothian*. We cannot complain that Scott failed to tell us what he was up to." Peter Murphy, "Scott's Disappointments: Reading *The Heart of Midlothian*," *Modern Philology* 92:2 (1994), 196–97, 195.

21. While all of Senkovskii's criticism is based on the truth of an openly apocryphal life experience, the most obvious parallel he offers to Cleishbotham's claim of his Quaker ancestor is in Tiutiun'dzhiu-Oglu's dependence on his status as an "actual Turkish philosopher" in the scholarly "Letter" that, as noted earlier, actually predates the *Library for Reading*.

22. Jean Jacques Rousseau, *Julie, or the New Heloise*, vol. 6, in *The Collected Writings of Rousseau* (Hanover, NH: Univ. Press of New England, 1997), 19.

23. Robert Darnton, "Readers Respond to Rousseau: The Fabrication of Romantic Sensitivity" (last chapter), *The Great Cat Massacre and Other Episodes in French Cultural History* (New York: Basic Books, 1983), 234.

24. Ibid.

25. Martha Noel Evans, "*Adolphe*'s Appeal to the Reader," *Romantic Review* 83:3 (May 1982), 302.

26. *Adolphe* was of course very well known in Russia, and many explicit parallels have been noted between Lermontov's work and Constant's; see, for example, John Mersereau Jr., *Mikhail Lermontov* (Carbondale: Southern Illinois Univ. Press, 1977), 146.

27. On irony and unreliable narrators in *A Hero of Our Time,* see Marie Gilroy, *Lermontov's Ironic Vision* (Birmingham, UK: Univ. of Birmingham, 1989), esp. 15–17 (on the frame narrator's unreliability), 22–26 (on Pechorin's unreliability as narrator), and Chapter Five, "The Language Game."

28. M. Yu. Lermontov, *A Hero of Our Time*, trans. Paul Foote (Harmondsworth, Middlesex: Penguin, 1966), 75.

29. Ossian is certainly equally famous, but I'm not sure that James Macpherson's relationship to the renowned Scottish bard exactly counts as plagiarism; see, for example, Fiona J. Stafford, *Sublime Savage: A Study of James MacPherson and the Poems of Ossian* (Edinburgh: Edinburgh Univ. Press, 1988).

30. De Quincey exposed four instances of Coleridge's plagiarism, including the now well-known borrowings from Schelling in *Biographia Literaria* in "Samuel Taylor Coleridge: by the English Opium Eater," an article he published in *Tait's Edinburgh Magazine* in September 1834. For more on De Quincey as himself a plagiarist, see Albert Goldman, *The Mine and the Mint* (Carbondale: Southern Illinois Univ. Press, 1965).

31. See Norman Fruman, *Coleridge, the Damaged Archangel* (New York: Braziller, 1971), 142.

32. On the case of Sterne see Thomas Mallon, *Stolen Words: Forays into the Origins and Ravages of Plagiarism* (New York: Ticknor & Fields, 1989), 1–24.

33. Michael Gamer, *Romanticism and the Gothic* (Cambridge: Cambridge Univ. Press, 2000), 117.

34. William Wordsworth, *Lyrical Ballads, and Other Poems, 1797–1800*, eds. James Butler and Karen Green (Ithaca, NY: Cornell Univ. Press, 1992), 29. "Christabel," still unfinished, did not appear in print until 1816, although it had already circulated in manuscript and gained many admirers and even imitators, including Scott. Apparently anxious that the delay in publication would suggest to a larger readership that it was in fact "Christabel" that was the imitation, Coleridge published it with a note that, in his words, would serve "the exclusive purpose of excluding charges of plagiarism or servile imitation from myself." As Eilenberg

notes, however, the preface reads as "[t]he words . . . of a guilty man we know to be innocent." Susan Eilenberg, "'Michael,' 'Christabel,' and the Poetry of Possession," *Criticism* 30:2 (Spring 1988), 215.

35. Wordsworth, *Lyrical Ballads*, 30.

36. Eilenberg, "'Michael,' 'Christabel,' and the Poetry of Possession," 220, 221.

37. Senkovskii notably published an excerpt from the last of the *Noctes Ambrosianae* LXXI. See O. I. Senkovskii, "Ambroziianskiie nochi," *Biblioteka dlia chteniia* 10, otd. II (1834), 121–37.

38. Murphy, "Impersonation," 626.

39. Ambrose's Tavern in *Noctes Ambrosianae* referred to two real locations, the tavern run by the Yorkshireman William Ambrose at 1 Gabriel's Road, and from No. 29 (November 1826), his "superior establishment," Ambrose's North British Hotel, Tavern, and Coffee-House at 15 Picardy Place; see J. H. Alexander, *The Tavern Sages* (Aberdeen: Association for Scottish Literary Studies, 1992), vii. In summer, Alexander notes, the Ambrosians often met at the fictional Buchanan Lodge outside Edinburgh overlooking the Firth of Forth, while other approximately fictional locations also appear, including an unnamed inn in Pisa where Odoherty encounters Lord Byron, and the King's Yacht when the Ambrosians met during the real King's visit to Edinburgh in 1822.

40. Over time and in *Fraser's* as well as *Blackwood's*, Maginn spelled his pseudonym in various ways, including Odoherty, O'Doherty, and Odocherty.

41. Murphy, "Impersonation," 639.

42. O. I. Senkovskii, "O zhizni sira V. Skotta," *Biblioteka dlia chteniia* 9, otd. 6 (1835), 26–27.

43. J. H. Alexander, "*Blackwood's*: Magazine as Romantic Form," *The Wordsworth Circle* 15:2 (1984), 64.

44. Cited in Murphy, "Impersonation," 638. *Blackwood's* famously initiated the criticism of Keats that Keats's supporters later claimed killed him.

45. Alexander, "*Blackwood's*," 64.

46. See Louis Pedrotti, *Józef-Julian Sękowski: Genesis of a Literary Alien* (Berkeley: Univ. of California Press, 1965), 144–48.

47. Murphy, "Impersonation," 644.

48. Baudrillard, *Selected Writings*, 179.

49. My shifting of Baudrillard's notion of the simulacrum from the post-Modern to the Romantic age may or may not be doing a violence to Baudrillard's original theory. As Mark Poster points out, part of Baudrillard's (Marxist-inspired) intent was to show that "[t]he structuralist concept of the sign naturalizes or universalizes what is in fact . . . a historically based semiological formation." Mark Poster, "Technology and Culture in Habermas and Baudrillard," *Contemporary Literature* 22:4 (1981), 471; on the other hand, as Poster also points out, Baudrillard is not entirely consistent as

to when this "historically based semiological formation" becomes significant, arguing, for example, both that the critical moment comes at the shift to fully developed capitalism and also that, in Poster's words, "the sign and the commodity arose together at the beginning of the process of the birth of capitalism" (p. 473).

50. S. P. Shevyrev, "O kritike voobshche i u nas v Rossii," *Moskovskii nabliudatel'* bk. 1 (April 1835), 524, 510.

51. Shevyrev, "Slovesnost'," 7, 8.

52. Wordsworth, *Lyrical Ballads*, 22.

53. Scott, *The Heart of Midlothian*, 10.

54. Richard Waswo, "Story as Historiography in the Waverley Novels," *English Literary History* 47:2 (1980), 308.

55. Scott, *The Heart of Midlothian*, 9. In his article, Waswo argues that the sort of "mutual conferral of identity" that this quote suggests whereby Scott in his critical apparata recognizes his audience for recognizing him is central to Scott's view of history as deriving from the social nexus, from the meanings that people attribute to events.

56. I don't mean to suggest that *Dead Souls* is anything other than anticommercialist but that there is considerable ambiguity about the material nature of words raised by the very idea of Chichikov's con.

57. McLaughlin, *Writing in Parts*, 12.

58. Ibid., 12, 15.

59. J. Thomas Shaw, "The Problem of the *Persona* in Journalism: Puškin's Feofilakt Kosičkin," *American Contributions to the Fifth International Conference of Slavists* (The Hague: Mouton, 1963), 301–26.

60. See A. I. Reitblat (ed.), *Vidok Figliarin: Pis'ma I agenturnye zapiski F. V. Bulgarina v III otdelenie* (Moscow: Novoe literaturnoe obozrenie, 1998).

61. The epigram was published in February 1831 only with some subterfuge; see V. V. Gippius's account in "Pushkin v bor'be s Bulgarinym v 1830–1831 gg.," *Pushkin: Vremennik Pushkinskoi komissii* 6 (1941), 235–55.

62. Feofilakt Kosichkin, "Torzhestvo druzhby, ili opravdannyi Aleksandr Anfimovich Orlov," *Teleskop* 13, ch. 4 (1831), 137.

63. Ibid., 138.

64. Ibid., 139.

65. Feofilakt Kosichkin, "Neskol'ko slov o mizintse g. Bulgarina i o prochem," *Teleskop* 15, ch. 4 (1831), 417–18.

66. N. N. Nadezhdin, "Biblioteka dlia chteniia," *Molva* 10 (1834), 156.

67. N. N. Nadezhdin, "Zdravyi smysl i Baron Brambeus," *Teleskop* 21 (1834), 140.

68. N. N. Nadezhdin,"Eshche pretensiia na familiiu Barona Brambeusa," *Molva* 20 (1834), 306.

69. Baudrillard, *Selected Writings,* 171.

70. Eilenberg, "'Michael,' 'Christabel,' and the Poetry of Possession," 221.

71. O. I. Senkovskii, "Pervoe pis'mo trekh tverskikh pomeshchikov k baronu Brambeusu," *Biblioteka dlia chteniia* 22, otd. 1 (1837), 70, 72.

72. Ibid., 65.

73. Jacques Derrida, "Plato's Pharmacy," *Disseminations,* trans. Barbara Johnson (Chicago: Univ. of Chicago Press, 1981), 109.

74. Ibid., 133.

75. Schlegel, *Philosophical Fragments,* 31, 10, 11.

76. Friedrich Schlegel, *Dialogue on Poetry and Literary Aphorisms,* trans. Ernst Behler and Roman Struc (University Park: Pennsylvania State Univ. Press, 1968), 103.

77. Ibid., 41.

78. Other "dialogues" published in the *Athenaeum* include A. W. Schlegel, "A Dialogue on Klopstock's Grammatical Dialogues" and A. W. and Caroline Schlegel, "The Paintings. A Dialogue." On a more implicit level, we could include other pieces, for example, Friedrich's purported letter to Dorothea, "On Philosophy. To Dorothea." See *Athenäum,* ed. August Wilhelm Schlegel and Friedrich Schlegel, 3 vols. (1798–1800; Stuttgart: J. G. Cotta'sche Buchhandlung, 1960).

79. According to Hans Eichner, some three hundred of the *Fragments* are by Friedrich and not quite half that number contributed by his brother, Novalis, and Schleiermacher. See Eichner, *Friedrich Schlegel,* 46.

80. Friedrich Schlegel, *Kritische Schriften,* ed. Wolfdietrich Rasch (Munich: Carl Hanser Verlag, 1964), 400.

81. Walter Benjamin, "The Concept of Criticism in German Romanticism," *Selected Writings: Vol. 1, 1913–1926,* ed. Marcus Bullock and Michael W. Jennings (Cambridge, MA: Belknap Press of Harvard Univ. Press, 1996), 151.

82. When the work is the Subject-Work producing its own readings of itself, the criticisms I have described as coming from without and from within the work are conflated into one, and it is in this sense that Novalis writes that "Many books need no review, only an announcement; they already contain their own review" (Benjamin, "The Concept of Criticism in German Romanticism," 150).

83. Philippe Lacoue-Labarthe and Jean-Luc Nancy, *The Literary Absolute,* trans. Philip Bernard and Cheryl Lester (Albany: SUNY Press, 1988), 115.

84. This contradiction is caught in Friedrich's pseudomathematical formula, "The poetic idea = 1/0 square root of FSM/0 (1/0 = God)"; Eichner explains that F is for "fantastic," S for "sentimental," and M for "mimic," although I think he underplays the importance of the latter (see Eichner, *Friedrich Schlegel,* 65–69).

85. Lacoue-Labarthe and Nancy, *Literary Absolute,* 111–12.

86. Baudrillard, *Selected Writings,* 170.

Chapter 3: Romantic Readers

1. Michel Foucault, "What Is an Author?" in *The Foucault Reader*, ed. Paul Rabinowitz (New York: Pantheon Books, 1984), 119, 120.

2. Ibid., 119.

3. Ibid., 108, 108–9.

4. Tilotamma Rajan, *The Supplement of Reading* (Ithaca, NY: Cornell Univ. Press, 1990), 3–4.

5. In his own reading of readers, Garrett Stewart faces the same problem, and he, like Rajan, tries to steer a more or less middle course between what he calls "socio-historical studies of the popular audience, on the one hand, and so-called reader-response criticism, on the other" or "between approaches to a readership at purchasing or processing ends of the fictional contract." Garrett Stewart, *Dear Reader: The Conscripted Audience in Nineteenth-Century British Fiction* (Baltimore: Johns Hopkins Univ. Press, 1996), 8. Where Stewart carefully picks his way between two apparently opposing scholarly approaches, however, I hope instead to show how the two, once more in Eilenberg's phrase, "take mutual possession of one another."

6. Rajan, *The Supplement of Reading*, 166.

7. V. Kaverin, *Baron Brambeus* (Moscow: Nauka, 1966), 53.

8. Parts of the following are again reprinted from *Russian Literature*, 47, no. 1, Melissa Frazier, "Erasing the Borders of Criticism: Senkovskij, Readers and Writers," pp. 15–32, Copyright (2000), with permission from Elsevier. I am also grateful to Charles Schlacks Publishers for permission to reprint in this chapter material that originally appeared in Melissa Frazier, "Romantic Relationships: Senkovskii and Romantic Literary Criticism," *Romantic Russia* 3–5 (2001), 25–44.

9. O. I. Senkovskii, "Pervoe pis'mo trekh tverskikh pomeshchikov k baronu Brambeusu," *Biblioteka dlia chteniia* 22, otd. 1 (1837), 69, 84.

10. Ibid., 66.

11. O. I. Senkovskii, "Brambeus i Iunaia slovesnost," *Biblioteka dlia chteniia* 3, otd. 1 (1834), 50.

12. Ibid., 51.

13. Ibid., 55, 58–59.

14. See also "O zhizni sira V. Skotta," which appears a mere six issues after Brambeus's adventure with the first Baronessa.

15. O. I. Senkovskii, "Literaturnaia letopis' ianvar' 1838 goda," *Biblioteka dlia chteniia* 26, otd. 5 (1838), 35, 36.

16. See Guinevere L. Griest, *Mudie's Circulating Library and the Victorian Novel* (Bloomington: Indiana Univ. Press, 1970).

17. Paul Delbouille, *Genèse, Structure et Destin d'*Adolphe (Paris: Société d'Edition "Les Belles Lettres," 1971), 386–87. Martha Noel Evans starts with the

fact of these startlingly different responses in "*Adolphe*'s Appeal to the Reader," *Romantic Review* 83:3 (May 1982), 302–13.

18. Philippe Lacoue-Labarthe and Jean-Luc Nancy, *The Literary Absolute*, trans. Philip Bernard and Cheryl Lester (Albany: SUNY Press, 1988), 89.

19. Friedrich Schlegel, *Dialogue on Poetry and Literary Aphorisms*, trans. Ernst Behler and Roman Struc (University Park: Pennsylvania State Univ. Press, 1968), 9. Note that Tieck's biographer Roger Paulin does not mention this particular quote, and in fact paints quite a different picture of an atmosphere that, in his words, "could vary from Platonic dialogue to Bedlam." Roger Paulin, *Ludwig Tieck: A Literary Biography* (New York: Oxford Univ. Press, 1985), 102. As I argue below, despite its reputation, the *Athenaeum*'s signs of friendship do not point to reality in any straightforward way.

20. Rajan, *The Supplement of Reading*, 115–16.

21. See, for example, V. Sh. Krivonos, *Problema chitatelia v tvorchestve Gogolia* (Voronezh: Izd. Voronezhskogo universiteta, 1981).

22. Pushkin's engagement with his reading public is evident also on other levels; see, for example, Monika Greenleaf's concise updating of our understanding of Pushkin's relationship to his readers in light of more recent scholarship on Byron, Martin's included, in "Pushkin's Byronic Apprenticeship: A Problem in Cultural Syncretism," *Russian Review* 53:3 (July 1994), 382–98.

23. David M. Bethea and Sergei Davydov, "Pushkin's Saturnine Cupid: The Poetics of Parody in *The Tales of Belkin*," *Periodicals of the Modern Language Association* 96:1 (Jan. 1981), 18.

24. E. S. Afanas'ev, "'Povesti Belkina' A. S. Pushkina: Ironicheskaia proza," *Russkaia literatura* (2000), 184.

25. Krivonos, *Problema chitatelia*, 21.

26. Bulgarin had edited the biweekly *Northern Archive* since 1822, and Grech the weekly *Son of the Fatherland* since 1816. In 1825 Grech invited Bulgarin to join him on the then struggling *Son of the Fatherland* as a co-editor, and Bulgarin returned the favor with *Northern Archive*. As the two journals began to look very much alike, Grech and Bulgarin then worried that one of them would end up without any subscribers at all, and they decided instead to publish one periodical jointly. See A. V. Zapadova (ed.), *Istoriia russkoi zhurnalistiki XVIII–XIX vekov* (Moscow: Vysshaia shkola, 1973), 156–57.

27. "Smes'," *Syn otechestva i severnyi arkhiv*, ch. 2 (1828), 253. The idea of the "box" seems to be a borrowing from the British periodical tradition. When Joseph Addison took over editorship of the *Guardian* from Richard Steele in 1714, he had a carved and gilt wooden lion's head affixed to the west side of Button's Coffee House in 1714, and any letters to the editor of the *Guardian* submitted through the lion's jaws were then published in the journal weekly as the "Roaring of the

Lion." Before John Scott then perished for impugning the honor of the *Blackwood's* people in 1821, he rendered Addison's lion's head mailbox in more abstract terms by gathering together notes to correspondents of and contributors to the *London Magazine* in a regular column called "The Lion's Head."

28. In 1828 the editor of the *Herald of Europe*, M. T. Kachenovskii, met the young Nadezhdin and, impressed with his erudition, both introduced him into university circles and invited him to contribute to the magazine. Until its demise in 1831, in addition to his feuilletons as Nadoumko, Nadezhdin also contributed to the *Herald* longer and more serious pieces under his own name. See Zapadova, *Istoriia russkoi zhurnalistiki,* 199–201.

29. *Ne*doumko rather than *Na*doumko suggests something like "Not up to thinking."

30. N. N. Nadezhdin, "O zakrytii Tipograficheskogo iashchika, sostoiavshego pri Syne Otechestva i Severnom Arkhive, i o prochem," *Vestnik Evropy* 9 (May 1829), 58–59.

31. For the story of Maginn's move to *Fraser's* and relatively rapid decline into scandal, debts, and drinking, see Patrick Leary, "Fraser's Magazine and the Literary Life," *Victorian Periodicals Review* 27:2 (Summer 1994), 111.

32. Ibid., 112.

33. Leary describes the author of the account, James Grant, as "himself a versatile literary journalist" (p. 111).

34. *Fraser's Magazine for Town and Country* 1:3 (April 1830), n.p. (inside front cover).

35. Ibid., 1:4 (May 1830), 496, 497.

36. Ibid., 507.

37. Ibid., 1:6 (July 1830), 756–57. The Fraserians referred to *Fraser's* more familiarly as Regina, an allusion to its headquarters on Regent St.

38. Ibid., 2:10 (November 1830), 489.

39. Jonathan Culler, "Prolegomena to a Theory of Reading," in *The Reader in the Text,* ed. Susan Suleiman and Inge Crosman (Princeton, NJ: Princeton Univ. Press, 1980), 48–49.

40. Jonathan Culler, *On Deconstruction* (Ithaca, NY: Cornell Univ. Press, 1982), 37.

41. Culler, "Prolegomena," 52.

42. Stanley Fish, *Is There a Text in This Class?* (Cambridge, MA: Harvard Univ. Press, 1980), 368.

43. M. M. Bakhtin, *The Dialogic Imagination,* ed. Michael Holquist, trans. Caryl Emerson and Michael Holquist (Austin: Univ. of Texas Press, 1981), 280. Note that in Bakhtin's argument it is the novel or "roman" that best exploits that feature of language; on Bakhtin's borrowing from Romantic aesthetic theory see

Tzvetan Todorov, *Mikhail Bakhtin: The Dialogic Principle*, trans. Wlad Godzich (Minneapolis: Univ. of Minnesota Press, 1984).

44. This quote is taken from her paper given at the MLA conference in Toronto, "From Public Sphere to Virtual Marketplace: Romantic Satire and the Periodical Press" (December 1997). I remain deeply indebted to Ms. Leaver for her talk that introduced me to *Fraser's* and *Blackwood's* and for sending me a copy of her text.

45. Peter Murphy, "Impersonation and Romantic Authorship in Britain," *English Literary History* 59:3 (Fall 1992), 644.

46. It nonetheless seems evident that the various speeches often recorded in the "Protocols" sometimes did reach a larger audience, including even the very targets of the Arzamassians' criticism; see M. S. Borovkovoi-Maikovoi (ed.), *Arzamas i Arzamasskie protokoly* (Leningrad: Izd. pisatelei, 1933), 53. There were also plans for an associated journal under way in 1816 (see p. 254). On the reflection of salon culture in Russian literature of the 1820s and 1830s, see William Mills Todd III, *Fiction and Society in the Age of Pushkin* (Cambridge, MA: Harvard Univ. Press, 1986).

47. Walter Benjamin, "The Concept of Criticism in German Romanticism," *Selected Writings: Vol. 1, 1913–1926*, ed. Marcus Bullock and Michael W. Jennings (Cambridge, MA: Belknap Press of Harvard Univ. Press, 1996), 151.

48. Friedrich Schlegel, *Philosophical Fragments*, trans. Peter Firchow (Minneapolis: Univ. of Minnesota Press, 1991), 12.

49. Consider, for example, *Critical Fragment* 98 and *Athenaeum Fragment* 342. See Schlegel, *Philosophical Fragments*, 12, 69–70.

50. Schlegel, *Philosophical Fragments*, 2; Schlegel, *Dialogue*, 55.

51. Schlegel, *Dialogue*, 94.

52. Schlegel, *Philosophical Fragments*, 14.

53. Sara Friedrichsmeyer, *The Androgyne in Early German Romanticism* (Bern: Peter Lang, 1983), 90.

54. While Schlegel vacillates between androgyny and marriage in his fully fledged Romantic writing, he also moves from the former to the latter as these ideas and various real-life relationships develop and his friendships with men and his fascination with his brother's fiancée give way to his affair with Dorothea. See ibid., 109–29.

55. Friedrich Schlegel, "Über Philosophie. An Dorothea," *Athenäum*, ed. August Wilhelm Schlegel and Friedrich Schlegel, 3 vols. (1778–1800; Stuttgart: J. G. Cotta'sche Buchhandlung, 1960), 2:7, 9.

56. Ibid., 3–4.

57. Ibid., 30–31.

58. Ibid., 31, 33, 36–37.

59. Ibid., 37.

60. Ibid., 37–38.

61. Ibid., 37.

62. Ibid., 33.

63. Monika Greenleaf, *Pushkin and Romantic Fashion: Fragment, Elegy, Orient, Irony* (Stanford, CA: Stanford Univ. Press, 1995), 24.

64. Jean Jacques Rousseau, *Julie, or the New Heloise,* vol. 6 in *The Collected Writings of Rousseau* (Hanover, NH: Univ. Press of New England, 1997), 3–4.

65. Jonathan Culler, *Pursuit of Signs* (Ithaca, NY: Cornell Univ. Press, 1981), 135, 146.

Chapter 4: The Romantic Library

1. Lacoue-Labarthe and Nancy define Romanticism as "a place (Jena) and a journal (the *Athenaeum*)." Philippe Lacoue-Labarte and Jean-Luc Nancy, *The Literary Absolute*, trans. Philip Bernard and Cheryl Lester (Albany: SUNY Press, 1988), 7.

2. The Boston Athenaeum opened in 1807. Its members conceived of the library on the model of the Liverpool Lyceum and Athenaeum.

3. The February 2004 issue of *Praxis*, "Romantic Libraries," explores the more intimate aspects of this form of library while always returning to the issues of materiality and finally of nation-building that I discuss here; see especially Ina Ferris, "Bibliographic Romance: Bibliophilia and the Book-Object" and Deidre Lynch, "'Wedded to Books': Bibliomania and the Romantic Essayists," both at http://www.rc.umd.edu/praxis/libraries.

4. Peter Conrad, *Shandyism: The Character of Romantic Irony* (Oxford: Basil Blackwell, 1978), 27.

5. Edward Said, *Orientalism* (New York: Vintage, 1979), 88.

6. Friedrich Schlegel, *Philosophical Fragments*, trans. Peter Firchow (Minneapolis: Univ. of Minnesota Press, 1991), 31–32.

7. John Neubauer, *Novalis* (New York: Twayne Publishers, 1980), 126.

8. Novalis, *Schriften*, ed. Paul Kluckhohn and Richard Samuel, 3 vols. (Stuttgart: Kohlhammer, 1960), 2:664.

9. Maurice Blanchot, "The Athenaeum," *Studies in Romanticism* 22:2 (Summer 1983), 164.

10. Gary Handwerk, *Irony and Ethics in Narrative* (New Haven, CT: Yale Univ. Press, 1985), 9.

11. Alexander, "*Blackwood's*," 65. Striking is the use of the word "classical" exactly in the Schlegelian sense. As Greenleaf explains, Schlegel reinterpreted Herder's claim "If we do not become Greeks, we will remain barbarians" to mean: "The Greeks were the Germans of their time in their youth and vitality. To become 'classical,' one must first be 'modern.'" Monika Greenleaf, *Pushkin and Romantic Fashion: Fragment, Elegy, Orient, Irony* (Stanford, CA: Stanford Univ. Press, 1995), 30.

12. Alexander, "*Blackwood's*," 65.

13. Ibid., 63.

14. Lacoue-Labarthe and Nancy, *Literary Absolute*, 54.

15. Grits et al. make another Romantic connection, commenting: "It is possible that in such a way this motliness had the same artistic intent as the combination of styles in Heine's *Travel Notes*." T. S. Grits, V. Trenin, and M. Nikitin, *Slovesnost' i kommertsiia: knizhnaia lavka A. F. Smirdina* (Moscow: Federatsiia, 1929), 301.

16. Most of them promptly and even indignantly withdrew their names, and the list did not appear in the second issue.

17. V. G. Belinskii, "Nichto o nichem," *Sobranie sochinenii v trekh tomakh*, 1, 193–94.

18. Grits et al., *Slovesnost' i kommertsiia*, 298.

19. A. A. Zaitseva, "'Kabinety dlia chteniia' v Sankt-Peterburge kontsa XVIII-nachala XIX veka," *Russkie biblioteka i chastnye knizhnye sobraniia XVI–XIX vekov, sbornik nauchnykh trudov* (Leningrad: Biblioteka akademii nauk, 1979), 29.

20. Ts. I. Grin and A. M. Tret'iak, *Publichnaia biblioteka glazami sovremennikov (1795–1917)* (St. Petersburg: Izd. rossiiskoi natsional'noi biblioteki, 1998), 68; the quote comes from an account published in *Russkii invalid* in 1817. I want to thank Mikhail Afanas'ev of the Historical Library, Moscow, and Susan Smith-Peters of the College of Staten Island/CUNY for suggesting this source and also for considerably complicating my picture of public libraries in Russia throughout the nineteenth century.

21. Miranda Beaven Remnek (ed.), *Books in Russia and the Soviet Union* (Wiesbaden: Otto Harrassowitz, 1991), 109.

22. John Lough, *Writer and Public in France* (Oxford: Clarendon Press, 1978), 133, 248–49.

23. Guinevere L. Griest, *Mudie's Circulating Library and the Victorian Novel* (Bloomington: Indiana Univ. Press, 1970), 8.

24. Ibid., 21.

25. Harry Earl Whitmore, "Readers, Writers, and Literary Taste in the Early 1830s: The *Cabinet de lecture* as Focal Point," *Journal of Library History* 13:2 (1978), 120.

26. Harry Earl Whitmore, "The *Cabinet de Lecture* in France, 1800–1850," *Library Quarterly* 48:1 (1978), 32.

27. Griest, *Mudie's Circulating Library*, 50.

28. Nik. Smirnov-Sokol'skii, *Knizhnaia lavka A. F. Smirdina* (Moscow: izd. Vsesoiuznoi knizhnoi palatki, 1957), 51.

29. Miranda Beaven, "Aleksandr Smirdin and Publishing in St. Petersburg, 1830–1840," *Canadian Slavonic Papers* 27:1 (March 1985), 17 n. 8.

30. The phrase comes from Grits et al., *Slovesnost' i kommertsiia*, 56.

31. See Smirnov-Sokol'skii, *Knizhnaia lavka A. F. Smirdina*, 31, 33.

32. The phrase "literary club" is found in Beaven, "Aleksandr Smirdin," 18. Both versions of Pushkin's verse can be found in G. Nazarova, "Kol' ty k Smirdinu voidesh'," *Neva* 6 (June 1984), 187.

33. This phrase is found in Remnek, *Books in Russia*, 110.

34. Conrad, *Shandyism*, 27.

35. Czesław Miłosz, *The History of Polish Literature* (Berkeley: Univ. of California Press, 1969), 209.

36. For all these pieces and more, see P. Savel'ev's bibliography of Senkovskii's works at the end of his introduction to O. I. Senkovskii, *Sobranie sochinenii Senkovskogo (Barona Brambeusa)*, ed. P. Savel'ev, 9 vols. (St. Petersburg: V tipografii Bezobrazova i ko., 1858–59) 1:cxiii–cxxxviii.

37. Mr. Spectator's name, of course, makes his intended lack of personality clear, but Ketcham argues that the same is true for all of Addison and Steele's personae, as he writes, "the periodical's persona is Horatian. In each of his various manifestations (as Isaac Bickerstaff, as Mr. Spectator, as Mr. Censor, as Hercules Vinegar, as Mr. Rambler) the essays' persona is a keen observer of the world, but one who is not involved in it." Michael G. Ketcham, *Transparent Designs: Reading, Performance, and Form in the Spectator Papers.* (Athens: Univ. of Georgia Press, 1985), 161.

38. Conrad, *Shandyism*, 43.

39. Lacoue-Labarthe and Nancy, *Literary Absolute*, 89.

40. Conrad, *Shandyism*, 46, 49.

41. Schlegel, *Philosophical Fragments*, 100.

42. "Ironic enactment" is Handwerk's very evocative phrase; see *Irony and Ethics*, 35–36, 42–43, 50.

43. In *The Antiquary* (1816) Scott describes the antiquarian Oldbuck as "being in correspondence with most of the virtuosi of his time, who, like him, measured decayed entrenchments, made plans of ruined castles, read illegible inscriptions, and wrote essays upon medals in proportion of twelve pages to each letter of the legend." Sir Walter Scott, *The Antiquary* (Edinburgh: Univ. of Edinburgh Press, 1995), 15.

44. See Paul A. Karpuk, "Gogol's Research on Ukrainian Customs for the *Dikan'ka* Tales," *The Russian Review* 56 (April 1997), 209–32.

45. Philippa Levine, *The Amateur and the Professional* (Cambridge: Cambridge Univ. Press, 1986), 71.

46. John Sutherland, *The Life of Sir Walter Scott: A Critical Biography* (Oxford: Blackwell, 1995), 46.

47. Ibid., 76, 47–48.

48. Conrad, *Shandyism*, 28. Conrad is quoting from Scott's *Lives of the Novelists* (1821–1824); see Sir Walter Scott, *The Lives of the Novelists* (London: J. M. Dent; New York: Dutton, 1910).

49. Sutherland, *The Life of Sir Walter Scott*, 156–57.

50. Levine, *The Amateur and the Professional*, 15.

51. Lee also notes to great effect the ironies of Scott's collection of the relics of war in the trip to Waterloo that he recounts in his *Paul's Letters to his Kinfolk* (1815). See Yoon Sun Lee, "A Divided Inheritance: Scott's Antiquarian Novel and the British Nation," *English Literary History* 64:2 (Summer 1997), 537–67.

52. Scott, *The Antiquary*, 23, 24–25, 23–24.

53. Aleksandr Sergeevich Pushkin, *Pushkin-kritik* (Moscow: Khudozhestvennaia literatura, 1950), 54.

54. Edward Said, *Orientalism* (New York: Vintage, 1979), 51.

55. Ibid., 98, 7–8.

56. Ibid., 128, 125.

57. Scholars of Russian literature have noted Said's glossing over of the Russian experience, starting with Monika Greenleaf who writes very straightforwardly: "Edward Said considers France and Britain, the principal nineteenth-century colonial powers, to be the primary elaborators and practitioners of Orientalist discourse; 'less so Germany and Russia.' In the case of Russia he is incorrect." Greenleaf, *Pushkin and Romantic Fashion*, 108.

58. See V. Kaverin, *Baron Brambeus* (Moscow: Nauka, 1966), 11.

59. As Savel'ev points out, the still very young St. Petersburg University had suffered just before Senkovskii's arrival a complete reorganization after a great number of the faculty were accused of too strong a bent toward mysticism and a corresponding failure to teach in a fully Christian manner. Among the professors fired were the two Frenchmen who taught Turkish and Arabic, conveniently leaving an opening that the young Senkovskii was uniquely qualified to fill.

60. Louis Pedrotti, *Józef-Julian Sękowski: Genesis of a Literary Alien* (Berkeley: Univ. of California Press, 1965), 49.

61. Senkovskii's move is typical. As Monika Greenleaf points out, "Oriental travel was preeminently a system of citation from other textual authorities [as] a typical traveler collated his own experiences with those of his predecessors." Greenleaf, *Pushkin and Romantic Fashion*, 146. Said addresses this tendency as well and associates it with the increasing professionalization of the discipline of Orientalism; note that his examples all considerably antedate Senkovskii. See Said, *Orientalism*, 151.

62. O. I. Senkovskii, *Sobranie*, 1:20.

63. Ibid., 14–15.

64. Ibid., 123.

65. Ibid., 122–23, 13.

66. Ibid., 192.

67. Ibid., 206.

68. Baron Domique Vivant Denon, *Travels in Upper and Lower Egypt, 2 vols.* (New York: Arno Press, 1973), 2:46.

69. Senkovskii, *Sobranie*, 2:207.

70. Ibid., 14–15.

71. Said, *Orientalism*, 175.

72. Kaverin, *Baron Brambeus*, 36.

73. O. I. Senkovskii, "Pis'mo Tiutiun'dzhiu-Oglu-Mustafy-Agi, nastoiashchego Turetskogo filosofa, k odnomu iz izdatelei Severnoi pchely," *Severnaia pchela* 129 (1827). The letter was published sequentially in parts in issues 129–33; for lack of page numbers in *Severnaia pchela*, all citations refer to issue alone.

74. Ibid., 130.

75. Ibid., 130, 130, 131, 132.

76. Ibid., 133. The chief such "Ulem," of course, is Friedrich Schlegel himself.

77. Ibid., 129, 133, 129.

78. Savel'ev assumes that Tiutiun'dzhiu-Oglu is the author of "O dramakh: Rossiia i Batori, barona Rozena, Torkvato Tasso, N. Kukol'nika, i Torkvato-Tasso (M. Kireeva)," *Biblioteka dlia chteniia* 1, otd. 1 (1834), 1–41; and "Panorama Peter-burga," *Biblioteka dlia chteniia* 2, otd. 1 (1834), 77–100, both of which are signed "T.-O."

79. Shevyrev, "O kritike," 508, 509.

80. Senkovskii, *Sobranie*, 2:461.

Chapter 5: Romantic Empire

1. Brambeus, that is, as the three landowners from Tver who are in turn quoting the Marquis of Londonderry.

2. See Monika Greenleaf and Stephen Moeller-Sally, "Introduction," *Russian Subjects: Empire, Nation and the Culture of the Golden Age*, ed. Monika Greenleaf and Stephen Moeller-Sally (Evanston, IL: Northwestern Univ. Press, 1998), 6.

3. V. Kaverin, *Baron Brambeus* (Moscow: Nauka, 1966), 190.

4. Ibid., 191.

5. The importance of empire to the Russian Romantic project is a point of increasing interest to scholars and I would note not just *Russian Subjects* but also the work by Katya Hokanson and Harsha Ram, both in *Russian Subjects* and else-where. In his reconceptualization of the Decembrists' literary and political aims in *The Imperial Sublime* (2003), Ram writes: "Since the Decembrist uprising has been primarily understood in terms of its opposition to autocracy and its role in the Russian romantic discovery of the *narod*, considerably less attention has been

paid to the role of empire in shaping Decembrist politics and poetics." His own work effectively fills that gap. Harsha Ram, *The Imperial Sublime: A Russian Poetics of Empire* (Madison: Univ. of Wisconsin Press, 2003), 127.

6. Benedict Anderson argues the conflation of "official nationalism" and empire, although his focus is a little later than Romanticism; note also the interesting exception he makes of Scotland. See Benedict Anderson, *Imagined Communities* (London: Verso, 1991), 83–111.

7. Katya Hokanson, "Pushkin's Captive Crimea" in Greenleaf and Moeller-Sally, *Russian Subjects*, 133.

8. Andreas Kappeler, *The Russian Empire*, trans. Alfred Clayton (Harlow: Longman, 2001), 86.

9. Frank W. Thackeray, *Antecedents of Revolution: Alexander I and the Polish Kingdom, 1815–1825* (Boulder, CO: East European Monographs, 1980), 56.

10. Ibid., 35.

11. W. H. Zawadzki, *A Man of Honour: Adam Czartoyrski as a Statesman of Russia and Poland* (Oxford: Clarendon Press, 1993), 203.

12. Ram notes the contradictory tendencies at work here, explaining that "Pushkin's poems of 1831 were welcomed by Emperor Nicholas but marked only a momentary rapprochement between poet and tsar"; he also offers the example of F. I. Tiutchev's very similar response in his 1831 poem "As [Agamemnon] led his own daughter to her death." *Imperial Sublime*, 214, 218.

13. A. S. Pushkin, *Sochineniia v trekh tomakh* (Moscow: Khudozhestvennaia literatura, 1958), 1:313.

14. This point is actually still under some debate in some circles. V. S. Listov argues that Pushkin, far from sharing any anti-Polish or pan-Slavist tendencies, simply saw in the Polish rebellion the end of any chance for reform in Russia under Nicholas; see his "Pushkin i pol'skoe vosstanie, 1830–31 gg.," *Moskovskii pushkinist* 6 (1999), 285–91. A. S. Pushkarev takes a more extreme tack, arguing that Pushkin's attitude was entirely appropriate in its own historical context, that it is not for us to judge geniuses anyway, and finally that the ideal of a greater Russia remains valid. See his "'Vy grozny na slovakh—poprobuite na dele!': A. S. Pushkin kak vyrazitel' russkogo obshchestvennogo mneniia o pol'skom vosstanii 1830–1831 gg.," *Nash Sovremennik* 6 (2001), 246–53.

15. Largely under the influence of Alexander's friend and close adviser, the Polish exile Prince Adam Czartoryski, first hostage for his family's estates in the wake of the Kościuszko rebellion, then member of Alexander's Unofficial Committee (1795–1803), then member of various Russian government ministries, and finally, in 1830, initially reluctant but nonetheless committed participant in the Polish uprising. After the Polish defeat, Czartoryski made the Hotel Lambert the gathering point for the Polish emigration in France.

16. Angela T. Pienkos, *The Imperfect Autocrat: Grand Duke Constantine Pavlovich and the Polish Congress Kingdom* (Boulder, CO: East European Monographs, 1987), 12.

17. The increase in suicides is noted in both Pienkos (ibid., 47) and Zawadzki (*A Man of Honour*, 265). According to Pienkos, while the situation improved after 1825, in Constantine's first four years as commander-in-chief at least forty-nine such acts occurred.

18. Pienkos, *The Imperfect Autocrat*, 112.

19. Pushkin, *Sochineniia*, 1:314.

20. As the well-respected government censor A. V. Nikitenko wrote in his diary: "Our worthy men of letters are enraged that Smirdin is paying Senkovskii 15 thousand rubles a year. Every one of them would like to wring Senkovskii's neck, and I'm already hearing the cries: 'How is that possible? They've allowed a Pole to direct the spirit of society—And he's a revolutionary! Wasn't it almost him together with Lelewel who brought about the Polish rebellion!'" T. S. Grits, V. Trenin, and M. Nikitin, *Slovesnost' i kommertsiia: knizhnaia lavka A. F. Smirdina (Moscow: Federatsiia, 1929)*, 326. Kaverin works his way through the most common accusations thrown at Senkovskii, including various of his writings often deemed anti-Polish; while most of the accusations Kaverin is able to easily dismiss, the affair of the Belorussian school remains for him the most problematic. See Kaverin, *Baron Brambeus*, 24–36.

21. Kaverin, *Baron Brambeus*, 27, 27, 29. The protest in the second quote comes in an angry letter from D. P. Runich to then Minister of the People's Education, Admiral A. S. Shishkov. Runich had originally been intended to head up the inspection, but had delayed his departure due to his involvement in the investigation following the Decembrist revolt. With that affair wound up, Runich was ready to head off to Belorussia when the University Council changed its mind and decided to send Senkovskii instead, prompting Runich to send a stinging letter of criticism to Shishkov. Runich was also indirectly responsible for Senkovskii's job at the university, since it was his actions as a member of the central school board and administrator of the St. Petersburg region in 1821 that led to the dismissal of a number of professors at St. Petersburg University.

22. Ibid., 33.

23. David Bethea and Serge Davydov also note the aspersions Pushkin casts on Bulgarin in his second, unfinished work purportedly by Belkin, "The History of the Village Goriukhino" (1830). In an encounter in a café in St. Petersburg, a man marked only by his pea-green coat takes from beneath the journal Belkin is reading a copy of the *Hamburg Gazette*. Belkin then overhears something about the "writer B." and goes after the man in the pea-green coat, convinced that he is the celebrated author. The "writer B.," Bethea and Davydov argue, can only be

Bulgarin, especially because Bulgarin was well known for plagiarizing articles from the *Hamburg Gazette* for his journal at the time, the *Emulator of Enlightenment*. See David M. Bethea and Serge Davydov, "The History of the Village Gojuxino: In Praise of Puškin's Folly," *Slavic and East European Journal* 38:3 (Autumn 1984), 291–309. As David Glenn Kropf then adds, Bulgarin "emulates the Enlightenment of Western Europe by taking it as his own creation." David Glenn Kropf, *Authorship as Alchemy: Subversive Writing in Pushkin, Scott, Hoffmann* (Stanford, CA: Stanford Univ. Press, 1994), 88.

24. Frank Mocha, "Tadeusz Bułharyn (Faddej V. Bulgarin) 1789–1859: A Study in Literary Maneuver" (Ph.D. diss., Columbia University, 1970, 1973), 125–26. Mocha repeatedly notes Bulgarin's tendency to befriend other foreigners, singling out as particularly important Count Fersen and Col. Frederick Maximilian von Klinger, a German émigré and inspector at the Cadet Corps, and also his later ties to Maksimilian Iakovlevich von Fok, director of the Special Chancellory of the Ministry of Internal Affairs.

25. A. I. Reitblat (ed.), *Vidok Figliarin: Pis'ma i agenturnye zapiski F. V. Bulgarina v III otdelenie* (Moscow: Novoe literaturnoe obozrenie, 1998), 6.

26. J. H. Alexander (ed.), *The Tavern Sages: Selections from the Noctes Ambrosianae (Aberdeen: The Association for Scottish Literary Studies, 1992)*, 36. Odoherty continues, "It took Marsham of Serampore seven years. Would your lordship wish to hear a Sanscrit ode I wrote to A. W. Schlegel?"

27. Yoon Sun Lee, "A Divided Inheritance: Scott's Antiquarian Novel and the British Nation," *English Literary History* 64:2 (Summer 1997), 562–63.

28. John Sutherland, *The Life of Sir Walter Scott: A Critical Biography* (Oxford: Blackwell, 1995), 258.

29. Alexander, *Tavern Sages*, 59.

30. Cairns Craig is paraphrasing Tom Nairn on Scott; Craig also notes the irony of Scott taking the King to *Rob Roy*, see his "Scott's Staging of the Nation," in *Studies in Romanticism* 40:1 (Spring 2001), 16, 15.

31. Kropf, *Authorship as Alchemy*, 5. Kropf takes the notion of "milieu" and more fundamentally "hecceity" or "this-ness," identity as "the specificity of a constellation of adjustments that are subject to change" from Gilles Deleuze and Felix Guattari, *A Thousand Plateaus: Capitalism and Schizophrenia* (Minneapolis: Univ. of Minnesota Press, 1987), 29.

32. Only apparent, however, as Kropf claims: "with each becoming Don Juan *is* Don Juan. Each milieu is unique, and Don Juan always becomes anew, hence he is always sincere." Kropf, *Authorship as Alchemy*, 16. Although Kropf's argument in many respects anticipates my own, one difference is that while Kropf opposes this new kind of unstable identity that he calls, again after Deleuze and Guattari, "hecceity" or "this-ness," to subjectivity, I would see "hecceity" instead as an alternate,

more ironic form of (inter-) subjectivity that is nonetheless deeply dependent on a more stable, traditional, and singular form.

33. George Steiner, "Extraterrestrial," *Triquarterly* 17 (1970), 119, 123.

34. Given especially the examples of both Pushkin and Lermontov, the paradoxical centrality of involuntary exile to Russian Romanticism has long been noted, and I would note in particular Stephanie Sandler's *Distant Pleasures: Alexander Pushkin and the Writing of Exile* (Stanford, CA: Stanford Univ. Press, 1989) and Harsha Ram's *The Imperial Sublime*. Especially interesting is Ram's claim that "[t]he hero's Byronic flight from European civilization, it seems, is not inimical to the civilizing mission of the Russian imperial state: on the contrary, one might argue that the pervasive Russian romantic paradigm of exile (*izgnanie*), whether in Pushkin or Lermontov, functions as a deeply alienated biographical correlative to imperial expansion." Ram, *Imperial Sublime*, 195. My own argument draws on this insight, although to focus on expatriation rather than exile, European rather than Russian Romanticism, and a different kind of "deeply alienated biographical correlative."

35. In both the 1805 and 1850 versions of Book Fifth, "Books." See William Wordsworth, *The Prelude* (New York: Norton, 1979), 180, 181.

36. Gilles Deleuze and Felix Guattari, *Kafka: Toward a Minor Literature*, trans. Dana Polan (Minneapolis: Univ. of Minnesota Press, 1986), 17.

37. O. I. Senkovskii, "Pervoe pis'mo trekh tverskikh pomeshchikov k baronu Brambeusu," *Biblioteka dlia chteniia* 22, otd. 1 (1837), 72.

38. Ibid., 67.

39. See George Gutsche, "Puškin and Belinskij: The Role of the 'Offended Provincial,'" in *New Perspectives on Russian Nineteenth Century Prose*, ed. George J. Gutsche and Lauren G. Leighton (Columbus, Ohio: Slavica Publishers, 1982), 41–59.

40. Richard Wortman, *Scenarios of Power: Myth and Ceremony in Russian Monarchy*, 2 vols. (Princeton, NJ: Princeton Univ. Press, 1995), 1:406, 6.

41. Ibid., 86, 407.

42. Ibid., 275.

43. According to Riasanovsky, the term was initiated by Prof. A. Pypin in his 1890 work *Kharakteristiki literaturnykh mnenii ot dvadtsatykh do piatidesiatykh godov* and was quickly adopted by other historians. See Nicholas V. Riasanovsky, *Nicholas I and Official Nationality* (Berkeley: Univ. of California Press, 1959), 73 n. 2.

44. Riasanovsky, *Nicholas I*, 124.

45. Wortman, *Scenarios of Power*, 299.

46. Ibid., 136.

47. Ibid., 53.

48. Ibid., 384.

49. Ibid., 385.

50. Katya Hokanson, "Literary Imperialism, Narodnost' and Pushkin's Invention of the Caucasus," *Russian Review* 53:3 (1994), 338.

51. Zhukovskii was the founder and spiritual center of the literary group Arzamas in 1815, and a mentor to poets younger than himself, including a sometimes unappreciative Pushkin. After the ascension of Nicholas I to the throne in 1825, Zhukovskii also took on the position of tutor to Nicholas's son, the future Alexander II. Batiushkov was less of a literary and political player, not least because he saw active duty in the Napoleonic wars and then gained a long-sought diplomatic appointment to Naples in 1821, only to suffer a nervous breakdown while in Italy; mental illness would continue to trouble Batiushkov for the rest of his life. For a fascinating and highly Schlegelian look at the poetic identity of the latter, see Monika Greenleaf, "Found in Translation: The Subject of Batiushkov's Poetry," in Greenleaf and Moeller-Sally, *Russian Subjects*, 51–79.

52. Both remarks quoted in Iu. Tynianov, "Arkhaisty i Pushkin," *Arkhaisty i novatory* (Leningrad: Priboi, 1929; Ann Arbor, MI: Ardis, 1985), 111.

53. V. K. Kiukhel'beker, "O napravlenii nashei poezii, osobenno liricheskoi, v poslednee desiatiletie," in *Russkie esteticheskie traktaty pervoi treti XIX veka, ed. Z. A. Kamenskii,* 2 vols. (Moscow: Iskusstvo, 1974), 2:572, 573.

54. As Greenleaf defends Batiushkov: "The boundary between exact and 'free' translation, between translation and 'imitation,' between 'imitation' and 'poetry in the spirit of the ancients' in this period was still very fluid." Greenleaf, "Found in Translation," 51.

55. A. A. Akhmatova, "'Adol'f' Benzhamena Konstana v tvorchestve Pushkina," *Sochineniia v dvukh tomakh* (Moscow: Khudozhestvennaia literatura, 1986), 2, 51. Another poet, E. A. Baratynskii (1800–1844), put the matter even more clearly. In a letter to Viazemskii (ibid., 51), Baratynskii wrote:

> I sense how difficult it is to translate the fashionable *Adolphe* into a language that no one speaks in the fashionable world, but one must keep in mind that it one day will be spoken and that the expressions, that now seem to us recherché sooner or later will be ordinary. It seems to me that one shouldn't be frightened by as-yet unused expressions. With time they will be accepted and will enter into daily language.
> We should remember that those of them who speak Russian speak the languages of Pushkin, of Zhukovskii, and of you, the language of poets, and accordingly it follows that it is not the public that teaches us, but for us to teach the public.

56. A. A. Bestuzhev-Marlinskii, *Sochineniia v dvukh tomakh* (Moscow: Khudozhestvennaia literatura, 1958), 2:541.

57. B. V. Tomashevskii, *Pushkin,* 2 vols. (Moscow: Akademiia nauk, 1956–61), 2:121.

58. Ibid., 129.

59. P. A. Viazemskii, *Sochineniia*, 2 vols. (Moscow: Khudozhestvennaia literatura, 1982), 2:96–97.

60. Lauren G. Leighton, *Russian Romanticism: Two Essays* (Mouton: The Hague, 1975), 82.

61. Bestuzhev-Marlinskii, *Sochineniia*, 547.

62. Largely, but not entirely, and I would note an important alternative strategy in the Decembrist concept of the sublime. Ram argues that for the Decembrists it is the sublime that bridges the gap between the two, and he writes of a particular passage from an 1831 work by Kiukhel'beker: "In this immensely suggestive exchange the sublime is presented as culturally universal, and hence capable of rhetorically mediating between the romantic premise of national specificity and the political context of imperial appropriation." Ram, *Imperial Sublime*, 150.

63. O. I. Somov, "O romanticheskoi poezii," *Russkie esteticheskie traktaty* 2, 556.

64. Harsha Ram, "Russian Poetry and the Imperial Sublime," in Greenleaf and Moeller-Sally, *Russian Subjects*, 21. While Ram does not actually use it as an example of the imperial sublime either here or in his later book, Somov's critical stance clearly fits the model.

65. Viazemskii, *Sochineniia*, 46, 112.

66. I. Kireevskii, *Kritika i estetika* (Moscow: Iskusstvo, 1979), 45, 46, 53.

67. N. V. Gogol, *Sobranie sochinenii*, 6 vols. (Moscow: Khudozhestvennaia literatura, 1959), 6:170.

68. Hokanson, "Literary Imperialism," 342.

69. Ibid., 343.

70. Pushkin, *Sochineniia*, 1:389.

71. According to Kappeler, Rus' included "a considerable portion of tribes who spoke Finnish as well as Baltic languages, a small number of Turkic-speaking soldiers, and in the early period, Scandinavian Varangians" (Kappeler, *The Russian Empire*, 14).

72. Pushkin, *Sochineniia*, 1:388.

73. Ram, "Russian Poetry," 48. Again, while Ram does not draw on this example in either this article or his later book, my reading of this most famous of Pushkin's claims is indebted to his argument.

74. Leighton, *Russian Romanticism*, 84.

75. On earlier German conflations of nationality and universality, see especially Friedrich Meinecke's *Cosmopolitanism and the Nation State*, trans. Robert B. Kimber (Princeton, NJ: Princeton Univ. Press, 1970). I feel obliged to pass over Fichte for fear of rendering my argument too cumbersome. Still I would note that his distinction between the living (because original) German language and the borrowed (and so-dead) "neo-Latin" languages strikingly underlies Russian discussions

of their own national originality. When Kiukhel'beker, for example, writes: "Of course, primitive [*pervobytnye*] languages as, for example, our Slavo-Russian, enjoy a great number of advantages over languages that are made up of the fragments of others" (Tynianov, "Arkhaisty i Pushkin," 92–93), he has only substituted "Slavo-Russian" for Fichte's "German."

76. John Clairborne Isbell credits Staël with bringing "the modern term *Romantic* to France and England alike, while Deidre Shauna Lynch claims that John Murray's 1813 translation of *De l'Allemagne* marked also the first appearance in English of the word "nationality." See John Clairborne Isbell, *The Birth of European Romanticism: Truth and Propaganda in Staël's 'De l'Allemagne'* (Cambridge: Cambridge Univ. Press, 1994), 90; Deidre Shauna Lynch "The (Dis)locations of Romantic Nationalism: Shelley, Staël, and the Home-Schooling of Monsters," *The Literary Channel*, ed. Margaret Cohen and Carolyn Dever (Princeton, NJ: Princeton Univ. Press, 2002), 20.

77. Lynch, "(Dis)locations of Romantic Nationalism," 197, 194. Isbell makes the same point and indeed is Lynch's inspiration.

78. Lynch, "(Dis)locations of Romantic Nationalism," 202.

79. Germaine de Staël, *De l'Allemagne*, 2 vols. (Paris: Garnier-Flammarion, 1968), 1: 213.

80. The letter to A. W. Schlegel is quoted in Meinecke, *Cosmopolitanism and the Nation State*, 55. While *Athenaeum Fragment* 291 was published anonymously, it is usually credited to Novalis. My quotation nonetheless derives from Friedrich Schlegel, *Philosophical Fragments*, trans. Peter Firchow (Minneapolis: Univ. of Minnesota Press, 1991), 58.

81. Schlegel, *Philosophical Fragments*, 21.

82. Bestuzhev-Marlinskii, *Sochineniia*, 564.

83. Lynch, "(Dis)locations of Romantic Nationalism," 199.

84. Germaine de Staël, *Delphine*, trans. Avriel H. Goldberger (De Kalb: Northern Illinois Univ. Press, 1995), 6. On another level, "adapting original beauties" is exactly what Staël practiced in *De l'Allemagne*, as the main argument of Isbell's book is the extent to which Staël deliberately mistranslated and misrepresented German literature for her own anti-Napoleonic ends. Isbell in fact describes Staël's methods with reference to the contemporary taste for "found" books whereby "authors make someone else responsible for their remarks" and argues that "Staël adds a novel twist to this method by using real writers not imaginary ones as the mouthpieces for her political allegory." Isbell, *Birth of European Romanticism*, 91.

85. Staël, *De l'Allemagne*, 1: 183.

86. I make the point of Staël's vindication of Friedrich Schlegel despite the fact

that Friedrich seems to have been very disappointed with *De l'Allemagne*. In *Birth of European Romanticism*, Isbell notes:

> Friedrich Schlegel wrote to his brother in January 1813, "I cannot leaf through that book without a certain antipathy. For the deliberate manner in which I in particular have been pushed into the background was not something I had expected; I had not attributed this degree of ingratitude to her." Friedrich had some cause: his first stay at Coppet, in October 1804, included unrecorded talks on recent German philosophy; in 1806–7, soon before his conversion, he gave Staël a private lecture on metaphysics [p. 56].

87. Belinskii, *Sobranie sochinenii v trekh tomakh*, 1:101.

88. Of the Slavs Staël writes, "one sees among them up until to the present time imitation rather than originality: what they have of the European is French; what they have of the Asiatic is too little developed for their writers to be able yet to manifest the true character which would be natural for them." (*De l'Allemagne*, 1:46); note that the Russians are not even original in claiming their lack of originality.

89. Friedrich Schlegel, *Dialogue on Poetry and Literary Aphorisms*, trans. Ernst Behler and Roman Struc (University Park: Pennsylvania State Univ. Press, 1968), 86–87. Meinecke also quotes Friedrich Schlegel in his pre-*Athenaeum History of the Poetry of the Greeks and Romans* (1798) as including one last element needed for the construction of national character: "the striving for universality and completeness of culture in a cosmopolitan sense that does not scorn the acceptance of something foreign that might transform oneself" (*Cosmopolitanism and the Nation State*, 62).

90. Isbell, *Birth of European Romanticism*, 21. Meinecke also notes the extent to which empire comes to dominate Friedrich Schlegel's thought, for example, in his 1804–6 *Lectures* in which he argued that "The demands for both division and union between nations will be satisfied by an empire with an all-inclusive feudal system and a hierarch" (p. 69).

91. Alexander J. Motyl, "Thinking About Empire," in *After Empire: Multiethnic Societies and Nation-Building: The Soviet Union and the Russian, Ottoman and Habsburg Empires*, ed. Karen Barkey and Mark von Hagen (Boulder, CO: Westview Press, 1997), 21.

92. Benedict Anderson articulates the problematic aspects attending both Staël and Scott's careers when he describes the later nineteenth-century "willed merger of nation and dynastic empire" as "an anticipatory strategy adopted by dominant groups which are threatened with marginalization or exclusion from an emerging nationally-imagined community." Anderson, *Imagined Communities*, 86, 101.

93. Maurice Blanchot, "The Athenaeum," *Studies in Romanticism* 22:2 (Summer 1983), 171.

94. Philippe Lacoue-Labarthe and Jean-Luc Nancy, *The Literary Absolute*, trans. Philip Bernard and Cheryl Lester (Albany: SUNY Press, 1988), 83.

Index

Thon, K. A., 186–87
Three landowners from Tver. *See* Senkovskii, O. I.
Tieck, Ludwig, 41, 98, 214n63
Tiutchev, F. I., 230n12
Tiutiun'dzhiu-Oglu. *See* Senkovskii, O. I.
Todd, William Mills III, 17, 22, 26–27, 52
Todorov, Tzvetan, 223–24n43
Tomashevskii, B. V., 188
Trolloppe, Anthony, 32, 212n40
Trubetskoi, Sergei, 170
Tsuprik, P. I., 211n11
Tur'ian, M. A., 216n17
Tver. *See* Senkovskii, O. I.
Tynianov, Iu., 189

Uvarov S. S., 168, 185, 187

Venevitinov, D. M., 192
Viazemskii, Prince P. A., 27, 28–29, 132–33, 190, 191–92, 193–94, 197, 198
Vidocq, Eugène François, 76, 77

Vinogradov, V. V., 216n19
Voltaire, François Marie Arouet de, 140–41

Waswo, Richard, 72–73
Whitmore, Harry Earl, 135
Williams, Raymond, 111
Wilson, John. See *Blackwood's*
Witz. See Schlegel, Friedrich
Woodmansee, Martha, 25–26
Wordsworth, Dorothy, 64, 89
Wordsworth, William, 19, 47–48, 89, 107, 121, 130, 180, 203; and copyright, 25–26, 42; "Michael," 63–65, 72. See also *Lyrical Ballads*
Wortman, Richard, 184–87, 188

Yorke, Oliver. *See* Maginn, William

Zaitseva, A. A., 136
Zapadova, A. V., 222n26
Zawadzki, W. H., 230n11
Zhukovskii, V. A., 28, 189–90, 195